The Baby Bust

The Baby Bust

Who Will Do the Work? Who Will Pay the Taxes?

Edited by

Fred R. Harris

A Milton S. Eisenhower Foundation Book

ROWMAN & LITTLEFIELD PUBLISHERS, INC.
Lanham • Boulder • New York • Toronto • Oxford

ROWMAN & LITTLEFIELD PUBLISHERS, INC.

Published in the United States of America
by Rowman & Littlefield Publishers, Inc.
A wholly owned subsidary of The Rowman & Littlefield Publishing Group, Inc.
4501 Forbes Boulevard, Suite 200, Lanham, Maryland 20706
www.rowmanlittlefield.com

P.O. Box 317, Oxford OX2 9RU, UK

British Library Cataloguing in Publication Information Available

Library of Congress Cataloguing-in-Publication Data

The baby bust : who will do the work? who will pay the taxes? / edited by Fred R. Harris.
 p. cm.
 Includes bibliographical references and index.
 ISBN 0-7425-3854-0 (cloth : alk. paper) — ISBN 0-7425-3855-9 (pbk. : alk. paper)
 1. Age distribution (Demography) —United States. 2. Age distribution
(Demography)—Europe. 3. Age distribution (Demography) —Japan.
 4. Demographic transition—United States. 5. Demographic transition—Europe.
 6. Demographic transition—Japan. 7. Immigrants—Government policy—United
States. 8. United States—Social policy. I. Harris, Fred R., 1930–
HB1545.B33 2006
304.6′2—dc22

                                                          2005022039

Printed in the United States of America

∞™ The paper used in this publication meets the minimum requirements of
American National Standard for Information Sciences—Permanence of Paper for Printed
Library Materials, ANSI/NISO Z39.48–1992.

To Owen López, Norty Kaufman, and
Alan Curtis—with thanks

Contents

Foreword

Alan Curtis

President Lyndon B. Johnson appointed a blue-ribbon citizens' commission—the President's National Advisory Commission on Civil Disorders, the Kerner Commission—following the terrible riots that broke out in the African American sections of so many of America's cities during the summer of 1967. The Kerner Report, which Fred R. Harris, as a member of the commission, helped to write, recommended "compassionate, massive, and sustained" federal efforts to combat the nation's intertwined problems of racism and poverty that, the commission found, had most harshly impacted the nation's inner cities and that were the root causes of the urban disorders.

After the 1968 assassinations of Dr. Martin Luther King Jr. and Senator Robert F. Kennedy, President Johnson appointed another citizens' body, the National Commission on the Causes and Prevention of Violence, headed by Milton S. Eisenhower. Its December 1969 report, which I, as a member of the commission's staff, helped to write, declared: "The greatness and durability of most civilizations has been finally determined by how they responded to the challenges from within. Ours is no exception."

For a time following those reports, America made considerable progress in solving the problems that the reports addressed. But, now, poverty is again growing in our country, and the divide between the rich and poor is widening. The challenges from within are becoming more formidable.

The Milton S. Eisenhower Foundation is the private-sector continuation of the Kerner and Eisenhower Commissions—the "keeper of the flame." It is a non-endowed and nonprofit foundation and a national intermediary organization. The foundation replicates and evaluates multiple-solution, successful programs for children, youth, and families in the inner cities. And it communicates what works to citizens, the media, and decision-makers.

The foundation also, very importantly, fosters research and policy analysis concerning the serious economic and social problems that continue to plague our country—and we work to disseminate widely the findings and results of such research and analysis. Examples include our book *Locked in the Poorhouse: Cities, Race, and Poverty in the United States*, which updated the Kerner Report, and more recently, our book *Patriotism, Democracy, and Common Sense: Restoring America's Promise at Home and Abroad.*

The present groundbreaking book—*The Baby Bust: Who Will Do the Work? Who Will Pay the Taxes?*—grew out of a seminar sponsored by the Milton S. Eisenhower Foundation in Washington, D.C., on March 11, 2005.

As President of the Eisenhower Foundation, I want to express appreciation to Fred R. Harris, who directed and organized the seminar and served as the editor of this book. Our special thanks go, too, to the distinguished presenters at the seminar whose papers are collected here, to the McCune Charitable Foundation for their generous contribution, which helped to underwrite the costs of the seminar, and to Rowman & Littlefield Publishers for making this important book a reality.

Introduction

Fred R. Harris

In my senior year at Walters High School in Oklahoma in 1948, I won the Future Farmers of America statewide oratorical contest. (I had no intention of becoming a farmer, but the required school alternative to taking that course was "shop," and I couldn't saw a board straight.) My winning FFA speech was entitled "Can Our Earth Feed Its People?"

I expressed alarm in that speech about the world population explosion then occurring and seemingly in view at the same rate forever. I quoted Malthus a lot. I then concluded with the assertion that our only hope was to learn to farm better, to produce more food, since there obviously was no way that the world's burgeoning population growth could be slowed, much less reversed.

Wrong. (But Robert Retherford, co-author of chapter 1 in this book, has told me that I should not feel bad; he says that demographers did not, themselves, foresee the decline in total fertility rate that is presently in evidence all over the world.) I did not realize, back when I gave that FFA speech in 1948, that following a period of unusual birthrate suppression during the Great Depression and World War II, the United States (and many other countries) had already entered upon a new period of birthrate increase that would come to be called the Baby Boom. And I did not know, of course, that the U.S. Baby Boom itself was an aberration, a temporary blip upward on the already existing, and soon to reappear, downward trend-line in the U.S. native-born, non-Hispanic white fertility rate.

While the world's population presently continues to grow, particularly because of the great numbers of people already born, the total fertility rate (number of children of childbearing-age women) is dropping below replacement (2.1 children per woman) in so many of the world's developed countries and in many of its developing countries as well. The resultant drop in

1

worker–nonworker ratios in the affected countries puts greater pressures on social security systems, increases the need to improve worker productivity, and enhances the importance of establishing acceptable levels of legal immigration.

In part I of this book, we first look at the global Baby Bust, concentrating in detail on two foreign case studies.

In chapter 1, Robert D. Retherford and Naohiro Ogawa focus our attention on Japan's Baby Bust—and the causes, implications, and policy responses to it there. Japan's population is rapidly aging, and the country's total population will begin to decline in the year 2006.

In chapter 2, Hans-Peter Kohler, Francesco C. Billari, and José Antonio Ortega deal with low fertility in Europe—causes, implications, and policy options. In the process, they make some comparisons between the situation in Europe and the different, less problematic one that exists in the United States.

In part II, we turn our attention to the Baby Bust in the United States. In chapter 3, Herbert S. Klein puts the U.S. Baby Bust in historical perspective, showing that, except for the Baby Boom, it is part of a long-time U.S. trend. He points out, however, that while the fertility rate in this country for native-born, non-Hispanic whites is below replacement level, more like that of Europe, the overall U.S. fertility rate is at replacement level, and he shows how this is at least in part due to the presence here of large numbers of minority and immigrant families.

In chapter 4, Robert G. Lynch first debunks false assertions that the U.S. Social Security system is in "crisis" or is going to go "bankrupt" or "bust." He shows that the system's actuarial soundness can be assured through relatively simple adjustments. Lynch then goes on to make an overwhelming case for greater government investment in early childhood development, particularly for poor children—investment that, among other things, would increase productivity and, thus, federal tax collections for Social Security.

In chapter 5, Rodolfo O. de la Garza refutes false nativist claims by Samuel P. Huntington and others that the presence of so many Mexicans in the United States is a threat to our "Anglo Protestant" culture. He shows that Mexicans and their offspring actually assimilate surprisingly well here, adapting themselves relatively quickly to the English language and to U.S. values.

In chapter 6, Peter Edelman makes an unassailable case that we must end the present waste of so much of our human resources, generally, and invest more in underutilized members of our potential workforce (including poor people and minority and immigrant families).

Part I

THE GLOBAL BABY BUST

1

Japan's Baby Bust: Causes, Implications, and Policy Responses

Robert D. Retherford and Naohiro Ogawa

This chapter describes the trend in fertility in Japan, analyzes the causes and implications of the Baby Bust after 1973, and discusses the Japanese government's efforts to raise fertility, which by 2003 had fallen to 1.29 children (i.e., births) per woman, as indicated by the total fertility rate (TFR). Also addressed are the questions of why the government's efforts to raise fertility have not been effective and what additional steps the government might take.

First, a couple of definitions. The TFR is the measure of fertility most frequently used in this chapter. The TFR for a particular calendar year is defined as the number of births that a woman would have by age 50 if, hypothetically, she lived through her reproductive years experiencing the age-specific fertility rates that prevailed in the population in the particular calendar year.

An age-specific fertility rate (ASFR) in a particular calendar year is calculated as the number of births that occurred during the year to women at a given age, divided by the midyear number of women at that same age. An ASFR has units of births per woman per year. The TFR is calculated by summing the ASFRs (births per woman per year at each age) between the ages of 15 and 50.

THE TREND IN FERTILITY IN JAPAN

It is convenient to divide the trend in fertility in Japan since World War II into three time periods: first, 1947–1957, during which fertility declined by more than half; second, 1957–1973, during which fertility leveled off; and third, 1973 to the present, during which fertility resumed its decline. The decline after 1973 is what is referred to in this chapter as the Japanese Baby Bust.

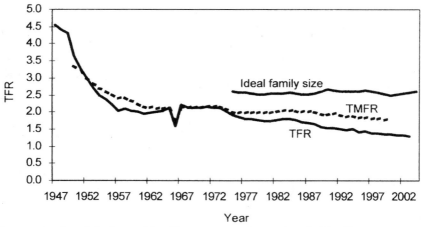

Figure 1.1. Trends in the total fertility rate (TFR), the total marital fertility rate (TMFR), and ideal family size (number of children), Japan, 1947–2004.
Sources: TFRs up to 2003 are from Ministry of Health and Welfare, *Vital Statistics,* various years. TMFRs are calculated from period parity progression ratios (see text and figure 1.4). Values of ideal family size are from various rounds of the National Survey on Family Planning and the 2004 round of the National Survey on Population, Families, and Generations, conducted by the Mainichi Newspapers of Japan.

Figure 1.1 provides a more detailed picture of the trend in the TFR. Following a brief Baby Boom after World War II when soldiers returned home, the TFR declined sharply from 4.54 children per woman in 1947 to 2.04 in 1957. During this period postwar devastation and reconstruction posed hardships that motivated families to have fewer children. The decline in fertility was facilitated by the legalization of abortion in 1948, which led to a steep rise in the number of abortions.

After 1957, fertility leveled off at the replacement level of about two children per woman and remained there until 1973, albeit with some fluctuation. The period 1957–1973 was a period of unprecedented prosperity during which per capita real income increased by about 10 percent per year. This prosperity facilitated marriage and childbearing and temporarily halted Japan's fertility decline. The unusual downward spike in the TFR in 1966, followed by recovery the next year, occurred because 1966 was the Year of the Fire Horse. According to Japanese superstition, girls born in that year are believed to be unlucky in life, with the result that many couples avoided having a birth in 1966.

The 1973 oil shock abruptly terminated the period of rapid economic growth. The steep increase in the price of oil implemented by the Organization of the Petroleum Exporting Countries (OPEC) affected Japan more than most countries, because Japan imports virtually all of its oil. The oil shock plunged Japan into a recession that was followed by a rebound three years later to a much lower economic growth rate of about 3–4 percent per year. The recession was accompanied by rapid inflation, amounting to 53 percent over three years. Unions reacted by negotiating large wage increases for regular full-time workers, after which struggling companies started hiring large numbers of non-union part-time workers at much lower wages. Part-time workers not only cost less but also could be laid off as needed, giving firms more flexibility during future economic downturns. Most part-time workers were women, many of whom previously did piece-work at home but now worked in production work outside the home. As a consequence of these and other developments, age at marriage started rising again, and the TFR started falling again. The TFR gradually fell from 2.14 children per woman in 1973 to 1.29 in 2003.

Figure 1.1 also shows that after 1973 the TFR fell faster than the total marital fertility rate, or TMFR. (The TFR pertains to all women, regardless of marital status, whereas the TMFR pertains only to ever-married women.) This occurred because the TFR is affected not only by fertility within marriage but also by age at marriage and the proportion who never marry, both of which started to rise after 1973. The effect of age at marriage and the proportion never marrying on fertility is especially important in Japan because only about 2 percent of births occur out of wedlock. Indeed, as we shall see shortly, later marriage and less marriage account for about half of the decline in the TFR since 1973.

Figure 1.1 also shows the trend in ideal family size, which remained almost constant at approximately 2.5 children per woman between 1974 and 2003. Because the TFR fell over this same period, the gap between the TFR and ideal family size increased from 0.69 to 1.30 children, indicating that fertility values, as measured by ideal number of children, have increasingly lagged behind the trend in actual fertility. Because ideal family size has been higher than the TFR and has changed little over time, it has been a poor predictor of fertility in Japan during the past three decades.

Figure 1.2 shows the trend in the singulate mean age at marriage or SMAM—so-called because it is calculated from age-specific proportions still single (that is, never married) in a census or survey. It is what the mean age at marriage would be if, hypothetically, women (or men) lived through their reproductive years experiencing the age-specific proportions still single, calculated from the census or survey (Shryock and Siegel 1971). SMAM rose between 1950 and 1960 but then leveled off for men and declined slightly for women between 1960 and 1973 due to the economic boom during that period (Retherford et al. 2001). After the 1973 oil shock, SMAM began to climb steeply for both men and women. Between 1975 and 2000, SMAM increased from 27.6 to 30.8 years for men and from 24.5 to 28.8 years for women. (In figure 1.2, 1975 is shown instead of 1973 because SMAM is calculated for census years.)

Figure 1.3 shows that the synthetic lifetime celibacy rate, S_{50} (the proportion who have never married by age 50), also began to rise steeply after 1975. S_{50}

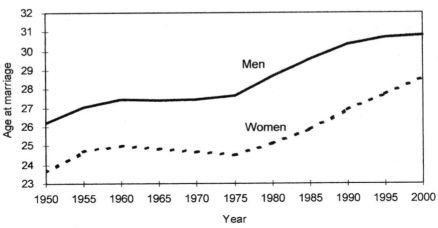

Figure 1.2.   Trend in the singulate mean age at marriage (SMAM) by sex, Japan, 1950–2000.
Source: Base data for calculating SMAM are from Statistics Bureau, *Population Census of Japan*, various years.

for a particular calendar year is calculated as what the proportion still single at age 50 would be if, hypothetically, single persons (women or men) lived until age 50 experiencing the age-specific first-marriage rates that prevailed in the particular calendar year. Remarkably, between 1970 and 2000, S_{50} increased from 2 percent to 25 percent for men and from 3 percent to 19 percent for women, indicating that Japan has moved far from the "universal marriage

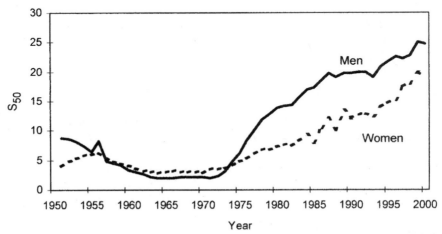

Figure 1.3.   Trend in the synthetic lifetime celibacy rate (S_{50}), by sex, Japan, 1950–2000.
Source: Calculated from data on period parity progression ratios pertaining to the transition from a woman's own birth to her own first marriage.

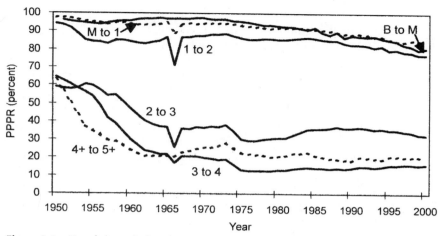

Figure 1.4. Trends in period parity progression ratios (PPPRs), Japanese women, 1950–2000.

Sources: Ogawa and Retherford (1993), updated with more recent data. PPPRs were calculated from published vital registration and census data using methodology described by Feeney and Saito (1985) and Feeney (1986).

society" that it was only three decades earlier. (It should be noted that the actual proportions still single at age 50 in a particular calendar year are much lower than the synthetic proportions, because the actual proportions reflect age-specific first-marriage rates that prevailed two to three decades earlier. The actual proportions still single at age 50 in 2000 were 13 percent for men and 6 percent for women. The synthetic proportions provide a rough indication of where the actual proportions are headed.)

The components of fertility change are clarified further by trends in period parity progression ratios (PPPRs), which are shown in figure 1.4. A woman's parity is defined as the number of children that she has ever borne. A parity progression ratio is simply the fraction of women at any given parity who go on to have another child (that is, progress to the next parity). A period parity progression ratio (PPPR) pertains to a particular time period, usually a single calendar year. A PPPR is a synthetic measure that indicates what the parity progression ratio would be if, hypothetically, women of a given parity lived through their remaining reproductive years experiencing the birthrates specified by parity and duration in parity (that is, by time elapsed since the last birth) that prevailed in the particular calendar year. PPPR(B–M) is the fraction of women who eventually progress from their own birth to their first marriage, that is, who eventually get married. In this case, the concept of parity is extended to include the state, M, of being in a first marriage but still without children. The synthetic lifetime celibacy rate, S_{50}, is calculated as 1–PPPR(B–M).

Figure 1.4 shows that most of the fertility decline between 1947 and 1973 occurred because of declines in PPPR(2–3) and higher-order PPPRs. By contrast, after 1973 most of the fertility decline occurred because of declines in PPPR(B–M), PPPR(M–1), and PPPR(1–2). Decomposition of the change in the TFR between 1973 and 2000 into components indicates that 52 percent of the change in the TFR is accounted for by change in PPPR(B–M), 23 percent by change in PPPR(M–1), 18 percent by change in PPPR(1–2), and 7 percent by changes in higher-order PPPRs (results based on calculation of the TFR from PPPRs instead of age-specific fertility rates).

The fall of PPPR(B–M), PPPR(M–1), and PPPR(1–2) after 1973 occurred in part because of large-scale movement of young women into the paid labor force after 1973, which contributed to later marriage and a lengthening of the interval between marriage and first birth (Retherford et al. 1996). PPPR(1–2) rose slightly after 1975, then resumed declining after 1985 when the economy started to heat up. Skyrocketing housing prices between 1985 and 1990 (one aspect of the bubble economy that emerged in the late 1980s) may partially explain this trend, as many young couples initially living with parents wanted to move into their own housing before having a second child but found it increasingly difficult to do so. PPPR(2–3) rose sharply after 1975 but did not turn downward until the bubble economy burst in 1990. A possible reason for the later downturn of PPPR(2–3) may be that many or most young parents with two children already had their own housing. Higher-order PPPRs did not change much after 1975, perhaps because couples with three or more children tended to be older, more economically secure, and therefore less affected by the bubble economy and the recession that followed it (Ogawa 2003).

The PPPRs for 2000, were they to remain constant in the future, imply that 19 percent of women would never marry, 12 percent would marry but remain childless, 16 percent would have only one child, 36 percent would have two children, 15 percent would have three children, and 3 percent would have four or more children (Ogawa 2003). Fully 31 percent of women would have no children at all, and 47 percent would have either no children or only one child.

CAUSES OF THE BABY BUST AFTER 1973

The previous section on the demographics of the Baby Bust has already mentioned some of the macroeconomic trends that help explain the Baby Bust. Another socioeconomic trend affecting the Baby Bust has been rapidly rising levels of educational attainment. Empirically it has been found in many earlier studies that education is one of the most important socioeconomic determinants of fertility. Figure 1.5 shows trends in the proportions of 23–29-year-old men and women who have completed junior college or university. The figure

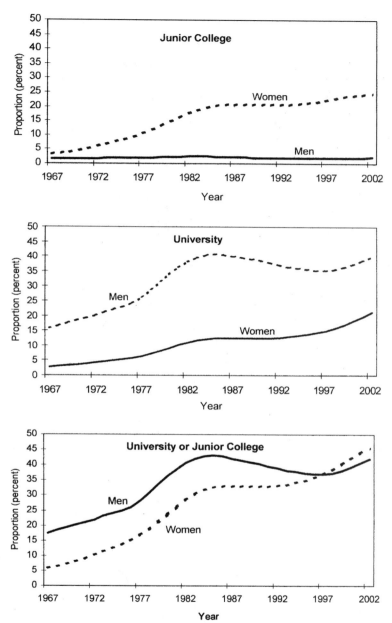

Figure 1.5.   Trends in the proportion of persons age 23–29 who completed junior college, university, and junior college or university, Japan, 1967–2002.
Source: Calculated from census data by age and sex (using estimated population for intercensal years) and annual numbers of junior college and university graduates by sex obtained from Ministry of Education, *School Basic Survey* (various years).
Note: The calculation involved following particular age-sex cohorts over time. Numerators and denominators of proportions were initially calculated for single years of age and time and then aggregated over ages 23–29 before dividing to obtain the proportions for each calendar year. The figure shows three-year moving averages of these proportions.

shows huge gains in educational attainment for both men and women, but especially for women. Initially women went mainly to junior college and men went mainly to university, but in recent years women's enrollment gains have been concentrated at the university level, where women are catching up with men. The dip in university enrollment between 1975 and 1990, which was concentrated among men, was a result of enrollment caps following student unrest in the late 1960s and early 1970s. The caps were applied more stringently to men because of ongoing efforts to ease discrimination against women in universities, and because of rapidly rising numbers of women applicants to universities, which occurred in large part because of rising economic returns to education (wage gain per additional year of education), which in recent years have been higher for women than for men (Ogawa and Clark 1995; Ogawa 2000). When one considers junior college and university together, women's average educational attainment at ages 23–29 surpassed that of men in 1996.

Figure 1.6 shows how the TFR varies by education in Japan. The figure shows that women with more education have lower fertility, conforming to the typical pattern observed in other countries. But it also shows that fertility has fallen in all education groups, implying that compositional shifts in the population by educational attainment cannot explain all of the fertility decline that has occurred. (If compositional shifts were the sole explanation, fertility at each level of education would remain constant over time.) Moreover, the pattern of differential fertility by education has changed somewhat over time. In 1966–1970, the fertility of women with a junior high education was considerably

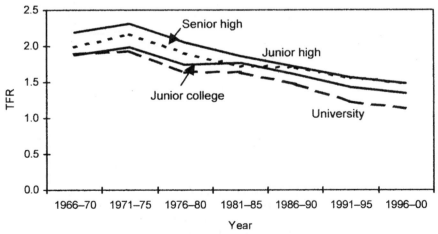

Figure 1.6.   Trend in the total fertility rate (TFR) by education, Japan, 1966–1970 to 1996–2000.
Source: Retherford et al. (2004).

higher than the fertility of women in the other three educational attainment groups, whereas in 1996–2000, junior high fertility and senior high fertility were about the same, and university fertility was well below the fertility of the other three groups. The downward divergence of university fertility began in 1986–1990, roughly coinciding with the passage of the Equal Opportunity Act of 1986, which aimed at ending job discrimination against women. The rapid increase in university-level educational qualifications of women after 1985, combined with greater opportunity for university-educated women to move into higher-level career jobs, may explain much of the widening fertility gap between university-educated women and women with less education, as shown in figure 1.6.

Because later marriage and less marriage account for about half of the Baby Bust since 1973, a deeper explanation of the Baby Bust must go beyond an examination of total fertility rates and look separately at factors affecting marriage and factors affecting fertility within marriage. This is done in the next two sections.

CAUSES OF LATER MARRIAGE AND LESS MARRIAGE AFTER 1973

The main causes of later marriage and less marriage after 1973 can be summarized as follows:

- Educational gains by women.
- Increases in the proportion of single women who work.
- Changing values about marriage:
    Decline in the proportion of marriages that are arranged.
    Decline in the proportion of newly married couples who reside with parents.
    Increases in premarital sex.
    Emergence of the "new single concept" (it is okay to enjoy single life without pressure to get married).
    Increasing desire of women for more help from husbands and a more egalitarian marital relationship.

Table 1.1 shows how education affects SMAM and the lifetime celibacy rate. In this case, for reasons of data availability, we examine the actual lifetime celibacy rate (LCR) rather than the synthetic lifetime celibacy rate (S_{50}). Values of SMAM and LCR by education are shown for both women and men in 1990 and 2000. In both 1990 and 2000, SMAM rises steeply with education for women but not for men. One important reason for this pattern is that

Table 1.1. Singulate Mean Age at Marriage (SMAM) and Actual Lifetime Celibacy Rate (LCR) by Sex and Education, Japan, 1990 and 2000

	SMAM		LCR	
Characteristic and census year	*Women*	*Men*	*Women*	*Men*
1990				
Junior high school or less	24.6	30.3	4	8
Senior high school	25.9	29.9	4	4
Junior college	27.4	30.3	6	4
University	28.1	30.7	9	3
2000				
Junior high school or less	26.6	29.6	6	21
Senior high school	27.3	30.4	5	12
Junior college	28.8	30.9	7	10
University	30.1	31.4	9	8

Source: Base data are from the 1990 and 2000 censuses of Japan. A specified level of education, such as senior high, means that persons classified at that level graduated that level.

the opportunity cost of getting married increases with education much more for women than for men, because women often quit working when they get married whereas men do not, and because wages foregone due to quitting rise with education. It is also noteworthy that between 1990 and 2000, SMAM increased substantially in every education group for women but not for men. A likely reason for this pattern is that labor market attachment increased within every education group for women but not for men.

The lifetime celibacy rates by education in table 1.1 show a somewhat different pattern. The LCR tends to rise with education for women but fall with education for men. The reason is that men tend to prefer women with less education than they have, and women tend to prefer men with more education than they have. The result is that women with high education and men with low education find it especially difficult to find spouses. Between 1990 and 2000, the pattern of LCRs by education did not change much for women, but it changed considerably for men. LCRs increased considerably in all education groups for men, especially less-educated men. A likely reason is an increasing education-related marriage squeeze on men as a result of narrowing educational differences between women and men. Rising educational qualifications of women have made it increasingly difficult for men with less education to find women willing to marry them (Retherford et al. 2001).

Figure 1.7 shows trends relating to the labor force participation of single women, based on survey questions to married women regarding work before marriage. The figure shows trends in the proportion who worked before marriage and the proportion who worked for pay before marriage, where the trend

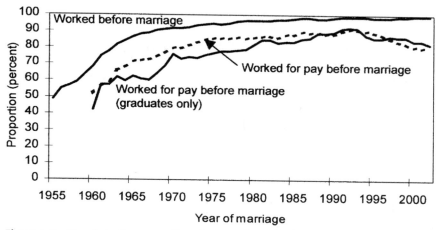

Figure 1.7. Trends in the proportion of currently married women who worked before marriage and who worked for pay before marriage, and trend in the proportion of currently married women who graduated from junior college or university who worked for pay before marriage, Japan, 1955–2002.
Source: Three-year moving averages, based on pooled data for currently married women age 15–49 from various rounds of the National Survey on Family Planning between 1986 and 2000 and the 2004 round of the National Survey on Population, Families, and Generations, conducted by the Mainichi Newspapers of Japan.

in the latter proportion is plotted both for all women and for those women who graduated junior college or university. The proportion who worked before marriage increased from 49 percent in 1955 to almost 100 percent in 2000. The trend in the proportion who worked for pay before marriage, which is about 10–15 percentage points lower, rose until the bursting of the bubble economy in 1990 and then gradually dropped off after 1993 by about 10 percentage points during Japan's long economic recession (commonly referred to as Japan's lost decade) that began in the early 1990s and continued until 2002, the latest year shown in the figure. Until 1990, the difference between the two curves (worked before marriage and worked for pay before marriage) shrank somewhat over time because of declines in the proportion of women engaged in unpaid work on farms and in other family enterprises. The trend in the proportion of junior college and university graduates who worked for pay is somewhat lower than the trend in the proportion of all woman who worked for pay, but only in earlier years. By 1989, the two curves approximately coincided, and after 1997, the proportion of junior college and university graduates who worked for pay surpassed slightly the proportion of all women who worked for pay, apparently because more educated women were increasingly being drawn into the job market and were perhaps more successful at finding or keeping jobs during the long recession.

The overall rise in the proportion of young single women who work for pay has meant that the vast majority of single women do not have any compelling financial need to get married. This financial independence has also contributed to the rise in the mean age at marriage and the proportion never marrying. The impact of women's work on the mean age at marriage and the proportion never marrying is even greater than suggested by figure 1.7, because the figure does not include women who never married, almost all of whom work.

Figure 1.7 also suggests that the proportion working for pay would have continued to increase after 1993, had it not been for the bursting of the bubble economy in 1990 and the long recession that followed. If so, women's attachment to the labor market may have continued to increase after 1993. This inference is supported by figure 1.8, which shows, among women who have had at least one child and who worked before marriage, trends in, first, the proportion who quit working when they got married; second, the proportion who quit working when they had their first child; and third, the proportion who quit working either when they got married or when they had their first child. The proportion who quit when they got married declined from 80 to 24 percent between 1965 and 2002. The proportion who quit at first birth rose from 5 to 40 percent between 1965 and 2001, with most of the rise occurring after 1993

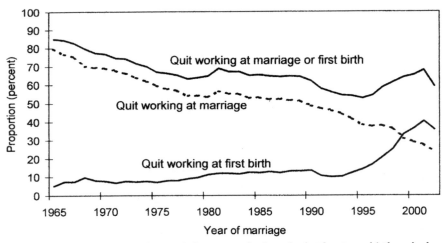

Figure 1.8. Among currently married women who have had at least one birth and who worked before marriage, trends in the proportion who quit when they got married, who quit when they had a first birth, and who quit either when they got married or when they had a first birth, Japan, 1965–2002.
Source: Three-year moving averages, based on pooled data for currently married women age 15–49 from various rounds of the National Survey on Family Planning between 1986 and 2000 and the 2004 round of the National Survey on Population, Families, and Generations, conducted by the Mainichi Newspapers of Japan.

when unemployment rose during Japan's lost decade, and then fell off slightly to 36 percent in 2002. The falloff may have occurred because of more generous compensation during child-care leave, as mandated by the 2001 revision of the Child Care and Family Care Leave Act, which will be discussed later. Overall, the figure shows a shift from quitting at first marriage to quitting at first birth and, until a few years into Japan's lost decade when unemployment rose, a decline in the proportion quitting at either marriage or first birth.

Of course, women who worked before marriage did not necessarily work continuously between completion of their education and getting married. In 2004, according to the National Survey on Population, Families, and Generations conducted by the Mainichi Newspapers of Japan, 52 percent of single women worked in regular full-time jobs, 21 percent worked part-time, 7 percent were full-time temporary contract workers, 2 percent were self-employed, and less than 1 percent were unpaid family workers.

Figure 1.9 shows trends in the proportion of marriages that were arranged and the proportion of newly married couples who co-resided with parents at the time of marriage. The steep decline in arranged marriage has contributed to later marriage and less marriage because the decline in arranged marriage has not been compensated by the emergence of a well-developed marriage market (Fukutake 1989). In contemporary Japan, contact with potential spouses tends

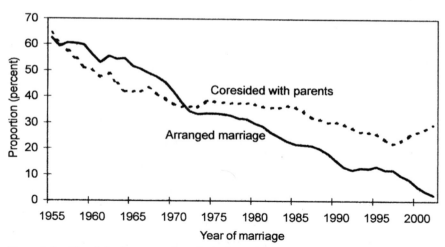

Figure 1.9. Trends in the proportion of marriages that were arranged and the proportion of newly married couples who resided with parents at the time of marriage, Japan, 1955–2002.
Source: Three-year moving averages, based on pooled data for currently married women age 15–49 from various rounds of the National Survey on Family Planning between 1986 and 2000 and the 2004 round of the National Survey on Population, Families, and Generations, conducted by the Mainichi Newspapers of Japan.

to be limited to a small circle of colleagues at work and former schoolmates, so it is difficult to meet and get to know potential spouses. Among single women age 20 and over, the proportion saying they have no male friend (neither a boyfriend nor any other male friend) was 34 percent in the 1990 round of the National Survey on Family Planning (also conducted by the Mainichi Newspapers), 38 percent in the 1994 round, 41 percent in both the 1996 and 1998 rounds, and 39 percent in the 2004 Survey of Population, Families, and Generations.

The decline of co-residence of newly married couples with parents (usually the husband's parents) at the time of marriage has also contributed to later marriage and less marriage, because in the absence of co-residence, the newly married couple must bear all or most of the substantial cost of setting up a new household. Figure 1.9 shows that the trend in the proportion of newly married couples who resided with parents at the time of marriage has been mostly downward; the proportion declined from 64 to 23 percent between 1955 and 1998, then rose to 29 percent in 2002.

The trends in figure 1.9 show fluctuations, and up until 1998 the nature of these fluctuations was that the proportion arranged and the proportion co-residing both tended to decline during economic good times and to decline less steeply or not at all or even to increase during economic hard times. This occurred because love marriages, but not arranged marriages, entail large costs of setting up an independent household, so that love matches are more likely than arranged marriages to be postponed during economic hard times. This pattern is observed in the figure, although not consistently so. For example, the proportion arranged rose in 1962 and did not start declining again until 1965, following the economic downturn during 1961–1964 (which occurred at high rates of economic growth, but was still a downturn). The proportion co-residing also rose in 1962, but, unlike the proportion arranged, it started falling again the next year. Somewhat later, following the oil shock of 1973, the proportion arranged and the proportion co-residing both rose slightly and then leveled off for several years during the subsequent restructuring of the economy. More economic restructuring commenced in 1993, after which the proportion arranged rose and the proportion co-residing leveled off until 1998.

A major change of pattern occurred in 1998, which saw another major economic downturn following a brief recovery that was aborted because of an ill-timed increase in the national sales tax (that is, consumption tax). As shown in figure 1.9, during this downturn the proportion co-residing increased, as expected, but the proportion arranged fell steeply, which was not expected at all. The unexpected fall in the proportion arranged was probably a consequence of the long recession, which by 1998 was in its eighth year, well into Japan's lost decade. During this decade, mean age at marriage rose to very high levels, as seen earlier. The sharp economic downturn in 1998 appears to have caused many couples to give up on waiting for the return of economic good times and to finally get married. Because these marriages were delayed love marriages, their occurrence drove down the proportion of marriages that were arranged. And because times were hard and jobs increasingly insecure, many of these newly married couples moved in with parents, driving up the proportion co-residing. They co-resided also because wives were reluctant to give up hard-to-get jobs, and because the couples were getting older and wanted to start having children. Co-residence allowed women to stay on the job after having their first birth, since the husband's or (increasingly) the woman's mother could help with child care. This may also be the reason why the proportion who quit working after first birth stopped rising and turned downward after 2001, as seen earlier in figure 1.8. (One expects this downturn to occur around 2001, because the delayed love marriages that finally occurred as a result of the economic downturn in 1998 would result in first births roughly two to three years after the economic downturn.) Given the changes in values and attitudes that have also occurred—especially new values of individualism among young wives who increasingly do not want to live with their mother-in-law—most young couples probably do not view these co-residence arrangements as ideal. If so, when Japan's economy revives as it appears to be doing at the present time, the proportion co-residing may resume its long-term decline.

If the above explanation of the trends in proportions arranged and co-residing is correct, an implication is that the rise in age at marriage that began in 1975 will slow down and may be coming to an end. In that case, there might be a temporary upturn in the TFR in the near future, because births that would otherwise occur later would instead occur sooner (Bongaarts and Feeney 1998). This potential upturn may be more than offset, however, by other forces that continue to push fertility downward, such as the continuing movement of women into higher-level career jobs, and increasing job insecurity as the restructuring of Japan's economy continues in response to the competitive pressures of economic globalization.

Another factor contributing to the sustained rise in age at marriage in Japan after 1973 has been the increasing social acceptability and prevalence of premarital sex, which means that sexual gratification can be obtained without getting married. As reported in the National Survey on Sexual Behavior of Youth, the proportion of junior college and university students who reported having had sexual intercourse increased from 23 to 63 percent among men and from 11 to 51 percent among women between 1974 and 1999 (Retherford et al. 1996; Japanese Association of Sex Education 2001). Also, as calculated from the 1990 and 2000 rounds of the National Survey on Family Planning, the proportion of single women age 16 and over who reported that they were currently using contraception rose from 39 to 57 percent between 1990 and 2000 (Retherford et al. 2001). (Despite the current high level of premarital sex, only about 2 percent of births in Japan occur out of wedlock, as mentioned earlier. Contraception—mainly by means of condoms, since the contraceptive pill was legalized only in 1999—is backed up by abortion, which is both legal and socially acceptable, so that pregnancies that are not followed quickly by marriage are almost always aborted.)

The rise of a new single lifestyle, dubbed by the news media in the late 1980s as the "new single concept," has also contributed to later marriage in Japan. The new single concept refers to enjoying single life without pressure to get married. Previously there was considerable pressure, especially on women. As already shown earlier, almost all young single women in Japan (and men too) work for a while before getting married. At the same time they mostly live with parents without contributing much to household expenses, thereby enabling a rather carefree lifestyle dubbed by the news media as "parasite single." Surveys have shown that the proportion of single persons favoring the new single concept was already fairly high by 1988, suggesting that considerable value change had already occurred before the new single concept surfaced in the news media. Surveys in 1988 and 1993 indicated that the proportion favoring the new single concept was 78 percent in 1988 and 76 percent in 1993 among young single women, and 59 percent in 1988 and 62 percent in 1993 among young single men (Retherford et al. 1996).

Rising education and paid employment among young women have also resulted in a rise in women's expectations of a more egalitarian marital relationship. Men's attitudes, however, have lagged somewhat behind women's attitudes in this regard, and this makes marriage less attractive to women, thereby also contributing to later marriage and less marriage (Tsuya and Bumpass 2004). Exacerbating this problem is that men's working hours continue to be long in Japan. According to background information included in the government's latest "Angel Plan" (discussed in more detail later), men in their 30s with a child less than five years old spend an average of 48 minutes a day on childrearing and household chores. Moreover, 23 percent of husbands in their 30s work more than four hours of overtime per day, resulting in a total workweek of more than 60 hours.

REASONS FOR THE DECLINE IN MARITAL
FERTILITY AFTER 1973

As seen earlier in figure 1.4, the decline in marital fertility after 1973 has been confined mainly to declines in PPPR(M–1) and PPPR(1–2), that is, in the proportion progressing from marriage to first birth and the proportion progressing from first to second birth. The main reasons for declines in these progression ratios can be summarized as follows:

- The direct costs of children have risen, involving a substitution of quality for quantity of children (Becker 1960).
- The opportunity costs of children, in terms of lost income for women, have risen.
- Preferences have shifted away from children toward "other goods," involving a decline in the "consumption utility" of children.
- In many respects families are less secure, so that the wife's job has come to play a more important role in family finances.

Rising higher-education enrollment ratios have been a major contributor to the rising direct cost of children. It has been estimated that the average undiscounted direct economic cost of raising and educating a child in Japan through four years of university is 28,600,000 yen (about $286,000 at current exchange rates), assuming the least expensive option of enrollment in government schools only. The calculation of this cost uses several sources of data and pertains approximately to the year 2000. The cost of the most expensive option, involving education entirely in private schools through medical school, is 63,010,000 yen ($630,100) (AIU Insurance Company 2001). Neither of these options includes expenses for *juku*, which are expensive, privately run cram schools whose main purpose is to prepare children for entrance examinations for elite junior high schools, high schools, and universities. Also not included are rising child-care costs (that is, day-care costs) for working women as a result of declining co-residence with parents.

The average undiscounted opportunity cost of children for women, in terms of lost income as a result of quitting a job, is even higher than the direct cost of children. It has risen because the proportion of married women who work for pay outside the home has risen and because their pay has risen. Among married Japanese women age 20–54, the proportion working for pay outside the home increased from 13 to 48 percent between 1963 and 2000 (Shimada and Higuchi 1985; Ogawa and Ermisch 1996; Statistics Bureau 2001).

A recent government White Paper (Cabinet Office 2003) has estimated the average opportunity cost of children for women university graduates in terms of income lost as a result of temporarily dropping out of the labor market for six years to have children. The calculation assumes that a woman starts working at age 22, works for six years at a regular full-time job, quits for six years to have children, then comes back to the labor force at age 34 in another regular full-time job. In this scenario, the undiscounted lifetime income lost by the time the woman retires at age 60 is 84,770,000 yen ($847,700). In a second scenario in which the woman returns to a part-time job instead of a full-time job, the lost income is considerably greater, amounting to 237,930,000 yen ($2,379,300). These estimates would be even higher had they taken into account reductions in social security pensions after age 60 as a consequence of lost social security contributions resulting from lost income. In the second scenario, the main reason why the opportunity cost is so large is that part-timers are so poorly paid in Japan, the typical annual earnings being in the neighborhood of 1,000,000 yen ($10,000).

The decline of co-residence of young couples with parents has also contributed to the rise in the average opportunity cost of children, because the lack of grandparents or other relatives in the household who can help with child care makes it more likely that a woman will drop out of the labor force when she has a child.

The average opportunity cost of children is likely to keep on increasing, because married women's propensity to work full-time is likely to keep on increasing. This will occur partly because women's educational attainment will continue to rise. The propensity to work full-time will receive an additional boost by private-sector firms' ongoing elimination of nonworking spouse benefits as part of salary, and by a revision to the tax system in 2004 that abolished tax breaks to wives earning less than about 1 million yen ($10,000) a year. Partly because of these tax breaks, many women have chosen in the past to work part-time instead of full-time. Without the tax breaks, more will choose to work full-time, especially the more educated wives of higher-income husbands, for whom the tax break was larger. Another boost to women's labor force participation may come when Japan's Baby Boomers start retiring at age 60 in 2007. Japan's labor force already started declining in 1998, and the decline will accelerate starting in 2007 when the Boomers start retiring, thereby drawing more women into full-time jobs when the economy finally recovers from prolonged recession.

The continuing rise in divorce rates will also boost women's full-time work participation. Japan's crude divorce rate (divorces per 1,000 population) rose from 0.74 in 1960 to 2.25 in 2003 (the rate was 1.9 for France and 2.4 for Germany in 2000) (Ministry of Health, Labour, and Welfare 2005). Divorce rates in Japan may continue to rise, one reason being that, starting in 2007, a divorced woman will have the right to as much as half of her husband's pension. Another reason the divorce rate may continue to rise is the continuing rise in women's paid employment and income, which makes divorce more financially feasible for women. On the other hand, a major reason why divorce increased during Japan's lost decade was increasing instability of husbands' earnings (Ogawa and Ermisch 1994). If the economy recovers to the extent that this income instability declines, the divorce rate could fall. The increasing likelihood that a marriage will end in divorce has meant that women increasingly have had to hedge their bets by getting a good education and a good full-time job.

The "consumption utility" of children—a term coined by economist Harvey Leibenstein (1957)—may be thought of simply as the joys of children. It has been declining for a number of reasons. Some of these reasons are demographic. People increasingly grow up with only one sibling who is close in age, or with no siblings. As a consequence, teenagers and young adults rarely interact with young children and are not socialized to enjoy them. The trend toward later marriage magnifies this effect, because young single adults have more time to settle into a lifestyle without children. Another reason is the rise of new individualistic values of "finding oneself," "realizing one's potential," and (in the case of women) pursuing a career, especially among persons with more education who grew up in higher-income households. According to van de Kaa (1987, 1997, 2001) and Lesthaeghe (1995), these new values among young adults have resulted in "post-modern fertility preferences" that are the main driving force of the "second demographic transition" to very low fertility. As Aries (1980, quoted in Caldwell and Schindlmayr 2003) put it, "His [the child's] existence is related to plans for a future in which he is no longer the essential variable . . . his role is changing today. . . . It is diminishing." The decline in the consumption utility of children has no doubt contributed to the decline of marital fertility in Japan since 1973, but it is difficult to quantify the size of this contribution.

The decline in consumption utility of children in Japan could be described as the "new marriage concept," meaning that it is all right for a woman to pursue a career and enjoy married life without pressure to have children. (The term "new marriage concept" has not been used either by academics or by the news media in Japan, however.) Evidence of this new marriage concept is that the proportion of women age 20–59 who agree or strongly agree with the statement "The husband should be the breadwinner and the wife should stay at home" declined from 71 to 46 percent between 1982 and 1997, and the proportion of single women age 20 and over who agree or strongly agree with the statement "Marriage does not mean that one must have children" increased from 52 to 63 percent between 1992 and 1997 (Tokyo Metropolitan Government 1992; Prime Minister's Office 1997; Retherford et al. 2001). Indeed, it appears that the "new single concept" has led rather quickly to the "new marriage concept."

In some important respects, economic and social changes in Japan since 1973 have led to less security for families, and this has also contributed to later childbearing and fewer children. (See Hobcraft and Kiernan 1995 and Hobcraft 2004 for discussions of the importance of this factor in Europe's recent fertility declines.) For example, the decline of the co-resident extended family has contributed to economic insecurity because parents and other relatives are less available to help with child care and housing expenses during hard times. Rising divorce rates have additionally contributed to rising insecurity, especially for wives. The rise of divorce reduces a wife's motivation to have children because she increasingly has to hedge her bets by getting a good education and a good job, especially because she is the one who is likely to have custody of children in the event of a divorce. Holding down a good job usually conflicts with childbearing and childrearing to some extent. The increasing likelihood of divorce also reduces the motivation of husbands to have children, because in the event of a divorce, husbands are likely to have to continue paying for children without receiving many of the benefits of children, again because the wife usually retains custody.

Another change leading to less security for families is that ongoing market reforms aimed at maintaining Japan's competitive edge in the global economy have resulted in less job security for both husbands and wives, thereby increasing the couple's uncertainty about their future income stream, as well as other disruptions entailed in moving from job to job, such as changes of residence. Figures 1.10 and 1.11 present evidence of less job security since 1993, when major restructuring of Japan's economy commenced in response to the recession that followed the bursting of the bubble economy in 1990. Figure 1.10 shows trends in the proportion of firms of different sizes that report that they follow the lifetime employment system. Between 1993 and 2002, this proportion fell by more than half in all firm size categories. Figure 1.11 shows trends in the proportion of firms that report that their promotion system is primarily merit based rather than seniority based. This proportion increased substantially since 1993 in all firm size categories.

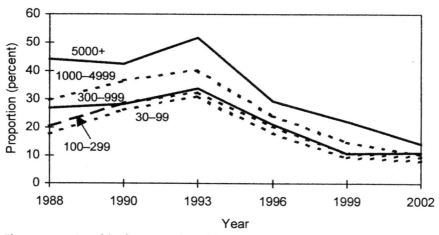

Figure 1.10. Trend in the proportion of firms reporting that they follow the lifetime employment system, by firm size (number of employees), Japan, 1988–2002.
Source: Ministry of Health, Labour, and Welfare, *Survey on Employment Management* (various rounds).

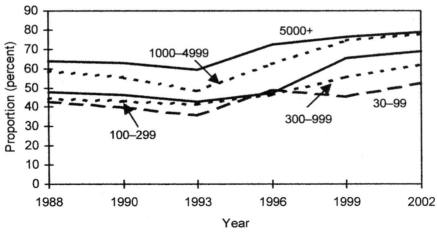

Figure 1.11. Trend in the proportion of firms reporting that they are moving toward a merit-based promotion system, by firm size (number of employees), Japan, 1988–2002. *Source:* Ministry of Health, Labour, and Welfare, *Survey on Employment Management* (various rounds).

Another aspect of insecurity relates to Japan's social security system, covering both pension and medical benefits. This system has been characterized by universal coverage since 1961 (Ogawa and Retherford 1997). The downsizing of pension and medical benefits and the huge growth of government debt after the bursting of the bubble economy (Japan currently has by far the highest debt-to-GDP ratio of any economically advanced country) have resulted in substantial increases in the proportions of the population who view social security pension benefits and medical benefits as inadequate. The increases in these proportions are shown in figure 1.12. The figure shows that between 1993 and 2000, the proportion viewing pension benefits as adequate fell from 34 to 16 percent, and the proportion viewing medical benefits as adequate fell from 51 to 31 percent. A possible demographic response would be to have more children who could help parents financially in their old age. But survey data on what parents expect from their children show no sign of this response. Instead, the proportion expecting to rely on children in their old age has continued to fall, from 18 percent in 1990 to 11 percent in 2004, according to the 1990 round of the National Survey on Family Planning and the 2004 Survey on Population, Families, and Generations, both conducted by the Mainichi Newspapers of Japan.

All of these aspects of rising economic insecurity of families indicate that couples increasingly consider that two incomes are necessary in order to guard against the possibility of having to sell the couple's home or other assets in the event that the main breadwinner loses his or her job and is unemployed

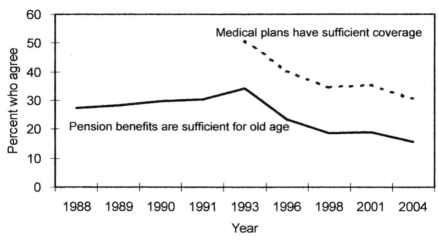

Figure 1.12.   Proportion of persons age 18–69 who feel that the social security system's pension and medical benefits are adequate, Japan, 1988–2004.
Source: Japan Institute of Life Insurance, *Survey on Life Security* (various rounds).

for a while. The result is that the wife's job becomes more precious, thereby contributing to delayed childbearing and fewer children because of the difficulties of managing both work and childrearing.

WHY THE JAPANESE GOVERNMENT IS CONCERNED ABOUT BELOW-REPLACEMENT FERTILITY

The Japanese government is increasingly concerned about Japan's very low fertility. One reason is that low fertility is an important cause of rapid population aging (typically measured by the proportion of the population age 65 and over). This worries the government because population aging is causing difficulties in funding Japan's social security system. Another reason is that Japan's population is projected to start declining in 2006, which could cause an economic slowdown because of possible labor shortages and declining demand for goods and services.

Figure 1.13 illustrates the concern about rapid population aging. The figure shows Japan's age–sex distribution in 1950, 1965, 2000, and 2050. The distribution for 2050 is based on the medium variant of the 2002 revision of the United Nations population projections for countries of the world (United Nations 2003a,b). Normally an age–sex distribution has a pyramidal shape that is broad at the young ages and tapers off at the old ages, as in the case of 1950 in the figure. Hence, the term "age pyramid" for this type of graph. By

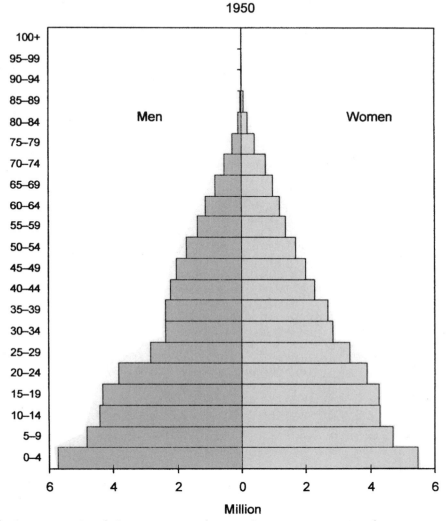

Figure 1.13.   Population age structure for Japan in 1950, 1965, 2000, and 2050.
Source: United Nations (2003a,b).

2050, however, this pyramidal shape is projected to be inverted at ages below 80 years, with the largest five-year age group being the 75–79 age group. The overall distribution in 2050, as shown in the figure, is "coffin-shaped," broad at the shoulders and tapering off at the head and feet. The reason for the inverted shape up to age 75–79 is that the absolute number of births in Japan has been declining or is projected to decline almost every year between 1974 and 2050.

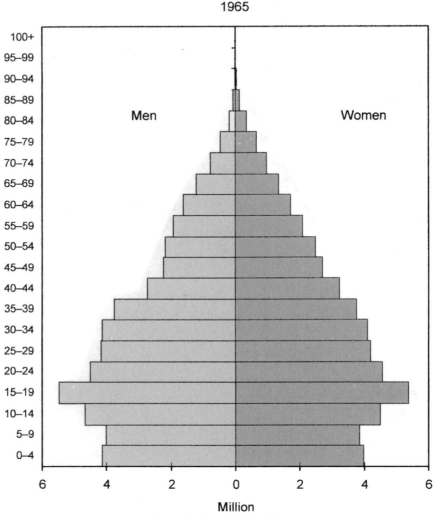

Figure 1.13.   (*Continued*)

The tendency of mortality to thin out the population as age increases is more than offset by the annual decline in the number of births in previous years, with the result that in 2050, the number of persons in each age group usually increases rather than decreases with age up to age 75–79. With some justification, the pyramid for 2050 in figure 1.13 could be described as a social security administrator's worst nightmare, because it means that a relatively small population of working age will have to pay for pensions and medical services for a relatively large elderly population.

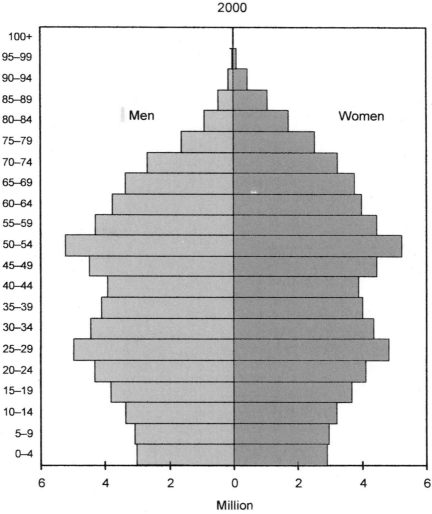

2000

Men

Women

Million

Figure 1.13. (*Continued*)

Table 1.2 provides additional detail, in terms of the changes that are projected to occur between 2000 and 2050 in the relative size of three broad age groups, <15, 15–64, and 65+. The age group 15–64 is meant to approximate the working ages, and the age group below 15 and the age group 65+ are meant to approximate young-age and old-age dependents whom those in the working ages must support. The table shows that the proportion of population at the working ages will decline by 36 percent, and the proportion at the retirement ages will increase by 83 percent. The table also shows that the old-age

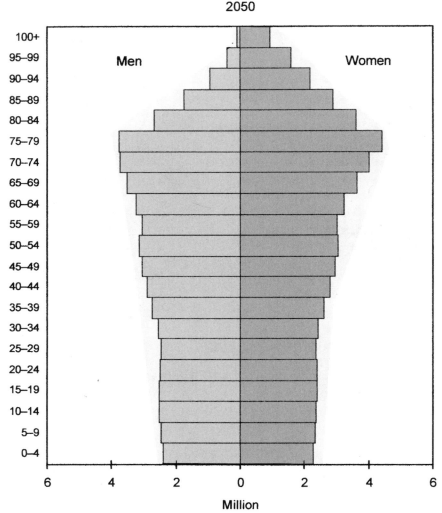

Figure 1.13. (*Continued*)

dependency ratio will almost triple and the total dependency ratio will more than double, while the young-age dependency ratio will increase only slightly. These trends imply huge increases in government social security expenditures (both pension and medical), and this is occurring in a situation where, at the present time, the Japanese government is already reeling from a huge and rapidly growing government debt.

Table 1.2 also shows that total population is projected to decline by 14 percent between 2000 and 2050. The decline would be much larger were it not

Table 1.2. Japan's Population in 2000 and 2050 (in millions)

	2000	2050	Percent change in population
Total	127	110	−14
<15	19	14	−23
15–64	87	55	−36
65+	22	40	+83
Young-age dependency ratio	21	26	—
Old-age dependency ratio	25	72	—
Total dependency ratio	47	98	—

Notes: The young-age dependency ratio is defined as the ratio of population <15 to population 15–64, the old-age dependency ratio as the ratio of population 65+ to population 15–64, and the total dependency ratio is defined as the sum of the young-age and old-age dependency ratios.
Source: Calculated from the medium-variant population projection for Japan in the 2002 revision of the United Nations population projections for countries of the world (United Nations 2003b).

for what demographers call "population momentum." This is the tendency for the population to keep on growing for a while even after the TFR drops to the replacement level of 2.1 children per woman. There are two sources of population momentum: first, a temporarily inflated proportion of the population in the reproductive ages, and second, a temporarily small proportion of the population in the elderly ages where age-specific mortality rates are high. These temporary distortions in the age structure of the population occur because it takes time for the age structure to adjust to rapid mortality and fertility decline.

The sources of population momentum can be better understood by considering what the age distribution looks like after the first 15 years of a fertility decline. In Japan, fertility fell steeply between 1947 and 1957, following Japan's brief postwar Baby Boom. The population pyramid for 1965 in figure 1.13 shows the age distribution a little more than 15 years after the postwar fertility decline began. The pyramid shows that by 1965 the proportion of children had fallen, resulting in a temporary bulge in the age distribution at the peak reproductive ages. The proportion who were elderly, on the other hand, remained small in 1965, because the elderly were born much earlier, when infant and child mortality rates were high. The figure also shows that by the year 2000 there were two bulges in the age distribution. Between 1965 and 2000, the first bulge moved upward in age by 35 years, and a second, smaller bulge appeared in the young reproductive ages as a result of a baby boomlet that was an echo of the first Baby Boom some 30 years earlier (30 years being the length of a generation as approximated by the mean age at childbearing). As is evident from figure 1.13, it takes the better part of a century for the temporary distortions in age structure that result from mortality and fertility decline to work themselves completely out of the age distribution.

The effects of population momentum on population growth are large. Japan's TFR dropped to replacement level in 1957, and it started falling below replacement in 1973, reaching 1.29 in 2003. Yet population continued to grow by 35 percent between the 1960 and 2000 censuses, and it is projected to start declining only in 2006. The delayed advent of population decline is perhaps the main reason why the Japanese government has thus far been concerned more about population aging than about population decline. Another reason is that, although the Japanese labor force already started declining in 1998, there has as yet been no sign of a labor shortage because of relatively high unemployment since the early 1990s. But labor shortages are another worry on the horizon once the economy recovers.

It is simple to calculate roughly the generational decline in population implied by a TFR of 1.29 children per woman that would occur in the absence of population momentum. The calculation assumes that the TFR has been constant at 1.29 for a long time, so that no distortions in the population age distribution remain. A TFR of 1.29 implies that on average a woman replaces herself by approximately $1.29/2 = 0.65$ girl. That is 0.40 girl short of the replacement level of 1.05 girl (half of 2.1). In other words, a TFR of 1.29, if continued indefinitely, implies that the population will eventually decline at a constant rate of about 38 percent $(0.40/1.05)$ per generation. A generation is approximately equal to the mean age at childbearing, which in Japan is about 30 years. Thus a constant TFR of 1.29 implies that population will decline by about 38 percent every 30 years.

PRONATALIST POLICIES AND PROGRAMS IN JAPAN

The Japanese government initiated child allowances in 1972, when fertility was still close to replacement level (see figure 1.1 and table 1.3) and the economy still booming. Initially the intent was not pronatalist, but rather to help low-income couples with at least three children. Allowances were accordingly limited to third and higher-order children. In 1986, the allowances were extended to cover the second child, and in 1992 (by then for pronatalist reasons), they were extended again to cover the first child. The cost of the child allowances is shared by the national, prefectural, and municipal governments and by employers. The amount of the allowances has been revised upward from time to time. A series of revisions since 1992 have extended the benefit period, which currently extends until the child reaches the end of third grade in school. As of 2004, employers pay most of the allowance for children below age three, and the government pays entirely for children age three and older. The allowance is 5,000 yen ($50) per month for each of the first two children and 10,000 yen ($100) per month for each additional child beyond the

Table 1.3. Major Japanese Government Actions Aimed at Raising Fertility

TFR	Year	Action
2.14	1972	Establishment of child allowances (no pronatalist intent at first)
1.54	1990	Establishment of inter-ministry committee on "Creating a Sound Environment for Bearing and Rearing Children"
1.53	1991	Enactment of Child Care Leave Act
1.50	1994	Announcement of Angel Plan for 1995–1999
1.42	1995	Enactment of Child Care and Family Care Leave Act
1.34	1999	Announcement of New Angel Plan for 2000–2004
1.33	2001	Amendment to the Employment Insurance Law, specifying 40 percent of salary to be paid to regular full-time employees during child-care leave
1.32	2002	Announcement of "plus one" plan
1.29	2003	Enactment of "next generation" law
	2003	Enactment of law on "Basic Measures to Cope with a Declining Fertility Society"
NA	2004	Announcement of New Angel Plan for 2005–2009
NA	2004	Revision of Child Care and Family Care Leave Act

NA = Not yet available.
Source: NIPSSR (2003).

second. There is a means test, however: if annual household income exceeds 4.15 million yen per year ($41,500) for a four-person household, the household is not eligible to receive child allowances. The threshold income level varies by household size and composition.

Prior to 1989, there was little public awareness that the country's fertility had fallen well below replacement level. In 1989, however, Japan's TFR reached an all-time low of 1.57 children per woman, and in 1990, when this figure was publicly released, Japan's low fertility burst into public consciousness when the news media coined the term "1.57 shock," which received wide publicity both inside and outside Japan (Ogawa and Retherford 1993). In that same year, the government initiated the first of a series of pronatalist policies and programs. Table 1.3 shows the chronology.

In 1990, the government established an inter-ministry committee on "Creating a Sound Environment for Bearing and Rearing Children." This led to enactment of the 1991 Child Care Leave Act. The intent of this law was to make it easier for working women to have children. The law provided up to one year of unpaid leave for either the mother or father to care for an infant. Coverage was restricted, however, to regular full-time employees. Temporary workers (including part-time workers) were not covered. Firms and organizations with more than 30 employees were directed to establish a child-care leave scheme for their employees by the time the law went into effect on April 1, 1992. The law did not specify penalties for noncompliance, however, and firms and organizations with 30 or fewer employees were exempt from the law until 1995. There was some noncompliance, inasmuch as some firms and organizations did not establish leave schemes according to the timetable requested by the government.

In 1994, the government announced its "Angel Plan" for 1995–1999 (officially known as the plan on "Basic Direction for Future Childrearing Support Measures"). The core of the plan was a major expansion of the number of day-care centers in the country, and the intent was to raise the fertility of working women by making it easier for them to juggle the demands of both work and childrearing. The new day-care centers were established at the local level with subsidies from the national government, funded out of the Ministry of Health and Welfare's annual budget. As a result of the Angel Plan, day-care center capacity for children age 0–2 in the country increased from 451,000 in 1994 to 564,000 in 1999 (1994 and 1999 are fiscal years ending on March 31 of 1995 and 2000). The Angel Plan also called for more after-school sports and other after-school activities, which were intended to help working women who did not return home until well after the end of normal school hours. The plan also called for the establishment of regional family support centers. For a modest fee that varied by locality, these centers provided services such as picking up children from school and taking them to a day-care center, and arranging for medical care for a sick child until one of the parents could return from work.

As in the case of child allowances, services available under the Angel Plan were means tested, which usually meant that higher-income persons had to pay more for services. Eligibility criteria varied by locality and are not well documented. It appears that day-care centers and family support centers established in localities where there was not much demand for them (mainly in rural areas) eased eligibility criteria in order to attract clients. In some urban areas where there was unsatisfied demand and long waiting lists, higher-income couples were simply turned away. Because many mothers who were eligible for leave under the 1991 Child Care Leave Act were either not eligible for services provided by the Angel Plan or had to pay too much for them because of high income, day-care services in the private sector also expanded.

It should be noted that Japan's ubiquitous *juku* (private cram schools for entrance examinations, as mentioned earlier) also serve to some extent as child care for older school-age children whose mothers work. Between 1976 and 1993, the proportion attending *juku* increased nationwide from 12 to 24 percent among elementary school students, and from 38 to 60 percent among junior high school students. These numbers are based on a survey question to women on whether each of their children attended *juku* regularly. The survey question changed in 1994. In 1994 and subsequently, mothers were asked for each child whether they spent any money on *juku*. Based on this new question, the proportion attending *juku* was 41 percent for elementary school students and 77 percent for junior high school students in 1994. Between 1994 and

2000, the proportion attending *juku* by this new definition fell slightly from 41 to 37 percent for elementary students and from 77 to 76 percent for junior high school students, perhaps because of recession-related economic hardship. Allowing for the change in the survey question in 1994, the data indicate that the proportions attending *juku* did not change much after 1993 (Cabinet Office 2001).

In 1995, the 1991 Child Care Leave Act was superceded by the 1995 Child Care and Family Care Leave Act. Under the 1995 law, it was no longer necessary for the employer to have a child-care leave scheme. Regular full-time employees were simply entitled to one year of leave for either child care or caring for another family member, with the added benefit that the employee now received 25 percent of salary while on leave, paid out of the National Employment Insurance Scheme (originally established to pay out unemployment benefits). For care of a child under one year of age, the law allowed up to one year of leave. For care of other family members (such as a sick elderly parent), it allowed up to three months of leave. Because the employee continued on the payroll during the leave, the employer continued to contribute as usual (and in the same amount) to the social security pension and medical schemes on behalf of the employee, and the employee continued to accumulate seniority at the usual rate. The government paid the employee's contributions to the schemes during the leave, and starting in 2000, the government starting paying the employer's contribution as well. Neither the employer nor the employee pays into the employment insurance scheme during the leave, because contributions to this scheme are calculated on earnings, not on benefits from the scheme. Again part-time workers were not covered, nor were full-time contract workers, even if their contracts were renewed continuously from year to year. In 2004, however, fewer than 2.5 percent of married women of reproductive age were on such contracts (percentage calculated from the 2004 Survey on Population, Family, and Generations.)

In 1999, the original Angel Plan for 1995–1999 was succeeded by the New Angel Plan for 2000–2004. The new plan called for further expansion of day-care centers, and day-care center capacity for children age 0–2 in the country subsequently increased from 564,000 in 1999 to 644,000 in 2002, the latest year for which data are available. The New Angel Plan also expanded support for after-school sports and other after-school activities. In 2003, 671,000 children were enrolled in after-school programs nationwide. The new plan also called for further expansion of family support centers, which increased in number from 82 to 286 between 2000 and 2002, and it called for improved baby-sitting services. As of 2003, 307 cities and towns had government-subsidized baby-sitting services. The new plan also called for subsidized infertility consulting services. By 2002, these latter services were available in 36 localities, and by 2004, 1.3 percent of births in the country occurred as a result of artificial insemination and other infertility treatments (figures from Ministry of Health, Labour, and Welfare website). In a few localities, these treatments, which are expensive, are partially subsidized by local governments. As in the original Angel Plan, services under the New Angel Plan for 2000–2004 were made available on a means-tested basis that varied by locality.

The proportion of pre-school children who were enrolled in day-care centers (both public and private) increased from 24 to 34 percent between 1990 and 2004 (Ogawa 2004). The proportion in 2004 is still rather low, mainly because full-time mothering is still considered very important by a majority of Japanese women. The 2004 Survey on Population, Families, and Generations asked mothers whose pre-school children were not in day-care centers why they were not using day-care services. The question allowed multiple responses. Sixty-one percent of the mothers said "because I am a full-time housewife," 45 percent said "I want to raise my children on my own," and 15 percent said "relatives or friends are helping." Only 9 percent said "too costly," only 2 percent said "no day-care center in the neighborhood," and only 1 percent said "day-care center service hours do not coincide with my work hours," indicating that the supply of day-care facilities is largely adequate to meet the demand for them. Further evidence that supply is adequate is that the majority of the more than 3,000 administrative districts in the country do not have waiting lists for their public day-care centers, and only a handful of those with waiting lists have waiting lists amounting to more than 10 percent of capacity. The 2004 Survey on Population, Families, and Generations also showed that, among mothers who did have pre-school children in day-care centers, 45 percent said that they felt uneasy about having their children in a day-care center (Ogawa 2004).

In large urban areas, where waiting lists for public day-care centers are sometimes lengthy, public day-care centers are very costly to the government. In Tokyo in 2000, for example, the average running cost of public day-care services for infants was about 500,000 yen ($5,000) per infant per month, an amount that exceeded the average male worker's monthly salary in Tokyo of 440,100 yen ($4,401) (Ogawa 2003). Charges to parents using these services come nowhere near covering this cost, which is heavily subsidized.

During the late 1980s and 1990s, the government also took steps to reduce working hours. Initially, there was no pronatalist intent, and the approach was to increase the number of national holidays and to celebrate some national holidays on a Monday if they happen to fall on a Sunday. Collectively, these changes reduced annual hours worked by about 40 hours, or five days.

Starting in 1992, there was also an effort to reduce the length of the work-week. This effort was motivated in part by pronatalist considerations, inasmuch as reductions in weekly working hours were seen as a way of improving the quality of family life so that couples would want more children. The government's five-year plan for 1992–1997, titled "Five-Year Plan for Becoming a Quality-of-Life Superpower," stated as one of its goals the reduction of annual hours worked to 1,800 hours per year (roughly equivalent to a 40-hour workweek) by 1997. In 1997, the government followed through and reduced the workweek from 48 to 40 hours. This goal was achieved immediately for assembly-line workers, because once an assembly line shuts down, workers have to go home. Between 1990 and 2002, average annual hours worked in secondary industry (manufacturing) in Japan, including overtime, declined from 2,124 to 1,954 hours (Ministry of Health, Labour, and Welfare 2004). But in the case of other workers, large numbers continued to work longer hours, usually for no additional pay. This is indicated by the fact that in 2000, the proportion of the workforce who worked more than 50 hours a week was 28 percent in Japan, 20 percent in the United States, and 1 percent in the Netherlands. The highest proportion in Europe was 6 percent for Greece (Lee 2004).

In 1997, the government also took steps to reduce the "examination hell" faced by Japanese schoolchildren and their parents. Again, the intent was partly pronatalist, to reduce pressures on families so that parents would want more children. The result was a relaxation of educational standards. As a result of directives from the Ministry of Education, considerable material was deleted from the curriculum, mathematics requirements were made simpler, the number of Chinese characters to be learned was reduced, the number of examinations was reduced, and school no longer met on Saturday. The downside was a decline in academic performance, as indicated by the performance of 15-year-old students on the 2003 Programme for International Student Assessment (PISA) tests conducted periodically by the Organization for Economic Cooperation and Development (OECD). The 2003 test was conducted in 41 countries. Japan's performance on the mathematics part of the 2003 test did not change significantly since the previous PISA test in 2000, but Japan was one of nine countries in which performance on the reading part of the test declined significantly (OECD 2005). Japan registered the largest drop in reading scores among all participating countries, and its international ranking on the reading part of the test dropped from eighth to 14th (Asahi Shimbun 2004).

In 2001, a new amendment to the Employment Insurance Law specified that an employee would henceforth receive 40 percent (up from 25 percent) of salary while on child-care or family-care leave. Coverage continued to be limited to regular full-time workers, and benefits continued to be paid out of the National Employment Insurance Scheme. Despite the fact that the government rather than the employer pays 40 percent of salary as well as social security contributions for the employee during the leave, the improved child-care leave benefits for full-time workers appear to have had a downside, because they apparently made employers less willing to hire women as regular full-time workers. Between 2000 and 2004, among currently married women below

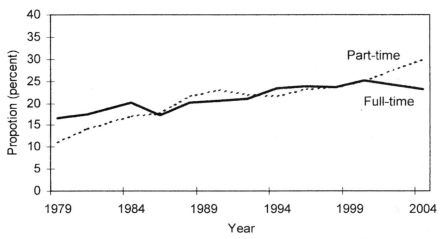

Figure 1.14.   Among currently married women below age 50, trends in the proportions working full-time and part-time.
Source: **Various rounds of the National Survey on Family Planning between 1986 and 2000 and the 2004 round of National Survey on Population, Families, and Generations, conducted by the Mainichi Newspapers of Japan.**

age 50, the proportion working full-time fell and the proportion working part-time rose, as shown in figure 1.14. This trend, if it continues, will make it more difficult for women to find regular full-time jobs in the future. In that case, the average opportunity cost of leaving the labor market for six years to have two children will increase substantially for full-time women workers, because a greater proportion of women who leave will have to come back to part-time jobs. This higher opportunity cost could cause the fertility of working women to fall, not rise. There are, however, other forces, described earlier, that will tend to increase the proportion working full-time, so it is not clear that the decline in this proportion between 2000 and 2004 will continue, especially when Japan finally pulls out of recession and unemployment falls.

The pattern shown in figure 1.14 is confirmed by a preliminary report for 2004 released recently by the Ministry of Health, Labour, and Welfare. The report indicates that during 2004, the workforce grew for the first time in seven years as the economy picked up, but only by 0.4 percent. The increase was entirely accounted for by an increase in the number of part-time workers, most of whom are women. (According to an earlier survey conducted by the Ministry of Health, Labour, and Welfare in 2001, 24 percent of part-time workers were men and 76 percent were women, as reported on the Ministry's website.) Among payroll employees who worked in the same place for more than one month, the number of full-time workers declined for the seventh straight year, by 1.1 percent during 2004, while the number of part-time workers grew by

5.5 percent. Also during 2004, the average monthly wage for all workers fell by 0.7 percent. The ministry attributes the decline in wages, which has continued for four consecutive years, to the increase in part-time workers (Japan Times 2005b). The increase in part-time workers makes a big difference in the average wage because in Japan, as already mentioned, there is a huge wage gap between full-time and part-time workers, many of whom actually work full-time or very close to it. In its recent economic survey of Japan, the Organization for Economic Cooperation and Development reported, "There are . . . important equity problems, given that the difference in productivity between regular and nonregular [mostly part-time] workers is much smaller than the wage gap. The equity concern is magnified by the lack of movement between the two segments of the workforce, trapping a significant portion of the labor force in a low-wage category from which it is difficult to escape" (Japan Times 2005a).

In 2002, the government announced a plan on "Measures to Cope with a Fewer Number of Children Plus One." The "plus one" plan argued that an important reason why fertility has continued to decline, despite the government's efforts to raise it (table 1.3), is that husbands are not doing enough to help with childrearing. The phrase "plus one" means that the effort to raise marital fertility should be strengthened, and that a greater role for husbands in childrearing should be a major component of this increased effort. The plan said that fathers should take at least a five-day leave when a child is born. It also said that, among regular full-time workers eligible for child-care leave, at least 10 percent of men and 80 percent of women should take child-care leave. The targets of 10 and 80 percent were based on a survey in which, among persons with young children, 7 percent of men and 76 percent of women said that they would take child-care leave if there were less social disapproval of child-care leave by employers and co-workers. The plan also said that there should be provisions for flex-time and shorter hours for couples with pre-school children, and it called for a target of 25 percent of eligible couples (husband or wife) working shorter hours. The plan also called for further expansion of day-care centers for pre-school children in accordance with a new "no queue" policy. The no queue provision is the real "plus one" in terms of the budgetary implications of the plan. But a no queue policy may not be needed because, as indicated earlier, long waiting lists are a problem in only a handful of administrative districts in the country. (This could change if eligibility criteria were relaxed and charges to parents reduced, but so far there is no plan to do this.)

Following the issuance of the "plus one" plan, two laws were enacted in July 2003 in order to implement the goals set forth in the plan: the Law for Measures to Support the Development of the Next Generation, and the Law for Basic Measures to Cope with a Declining Fertility Society. The Law for Measures to Support the Development of the Next Generation (the "next generation" law) became effective on April 1, 2005, and will remain in effect for 10 years. The law pertains only to firms with more than 300 workers on the payroll (including part-time workers and full-time contract workers). Within these firms, the law covers not only regular full-time employees but also all other employees who have been working continuously for more than a year, regardless of whether they are full-time or part-time and regardless of the length of their contracts. Each employer falling under the law is asked to prepare a plan to raise fertility among its employees. The plan must include targets, and it had to be submitted to the prefectural government by the time the law went into effect on April 1, 2005. There are no penalties for not coming up with a plan, but if the employer does not do so, the government can send the employer a notice urging the employer to take action. (In Japan such urging by the government is usually quite effective, although less so than previously because of less government leverage over business as a consequence of reductions in government regulation as part of the ongoing restructuring of the economy.) The submitted plan must span at least two years but no more than five years. If the plan is approved, the employer receives permission to use a special logo that the employer can display on products, advertisements, and other promotional literature. At the end of the plan, the employer has to report progress under the plan to the prefectural government. The Labor Bureau of the prefectural government evaluates the plan with guidance from the national government's Ministry of Health, Labour, and Welfare. If progress is evaluated as unsatisfactory, the firm can no longer use the logo. The logo is shown in figure 1.15.

The goals of the "next generation" law are mostly the same as those laid out in the "plus one" report a year earlier. The main targets are that, among eligible workers in eligible firms and organizations, 10 percent of men and 80 percent of women should take the child-care leave to which they are entitled. The main intent of these targets, and of the plans that had to be submitted by April 1, 2005, is to change the workplace atmosphere so that parents, and especially women, feel more comfortable about taking the child-care leave to which they are entitled. According to the 2002 round of the government's Basic Survey of Female Employment Management (firm-level reporting), among eligible workers in eligible firms, only 0.3 percent of men and 64 percent of women had taken child-care leave. The "next generation" law also sets a target that 25 percent of firms with more than 300 employees should have policies that allow women with pre-school children to work shorter hours.

In December 2004, the Child Care and Family Care Leave Act was revised to bring it into line with the "next generation" law, which specifies that all part-time workers and full-time contract employees who have worked continuously at a firm for more than a year are to be included in a firm's plan to raise fertility. The revised Child Care and Family Leave Act went into effect on April 1, 2005. Before this revision, temporary workers (including part-time workers and full-time contract workers) were not entitled to child-care leave.

Figure 1.15. Logo for government-certified child-friendly employer.
Note: In firms with more than 300 employees, the "next generation" law of 2003 asks that each employer prepare a plan to raise fertility among its employees and submit this plan to the government by the time the law goes into effect on April 1, 2005. If the plan is approved, the employer will have the right to use the logo on products, advertisements, and other promotional literature. Loosely translated, the top part of the logo says: "We support childrearing among our employees." The four zeros at the bottom are to be replaced with the year (e.g., 2005). Loosely translated, the bottom says after the zeros: "Government-certified child-friendly employer." The logo is scarlet in color.

The Law for Basic Measures to Cope with a Declining Fertility Society (the "basic measures" law), also enacted in 2003, states: "We are being strongly called upon to halt the decrease in children by creating an environment where parents can feel secure in giving birth and raising children who will be the next generation of society, and to realize a society in which children grow up equal and healthy in mind and body, and parents truly feel pride and joy" (Doteuchi 2004). This law contains general language that appears to be intended to set the stage for future government action, but the law does not indicate specific actions to be taken. The specific actions are contained in the "next generation" law that was passed at the same time in July 2003.

The government is now implementing another New Angel Plan for 2005–2009. The general goals are the same as those in the "next generation" and "basic measures" laws of 2003. A major objective is to increase husbands' involvement in child care and household chores. As mentioned earlier, according to background information included in the plan, men in their 30s with a child less than five years old spend an average of 48 minutes a day on childrearing and household chores. The plan sets a goal of raising that to two hours a day (two hours being about average for other economically advanced countries). Additional background information contained in the plan is that 23 percent of husbands in their 30s work more than four hours of overtime per day, resulting in a total workweek of more than 60 hours. The plan sets a target of reducing this percentage by half by the end of 2009. The plan also calls for a further increase in the number of family support centers from 368 in 2005 to 710 by 2010 (at that time covering almost a quarter of the more than 3,000 administrative districts in the country).

To the extent that the goal is to prevent population decline, an alternative to raising fertility is immigration from abroad. But this is not a politically feasible solution at this time, and it is not under consideration by the government. Japan is a very homogenous society without a multicultural and multi-ethnic tradition. With almost no exceptions, it bars foreigners from becoming Japanese citizens. Earlier it was noted that a TFR of 1.29, were it to continue for a long time into the future, would result in a population decline of approximately 38 percent per generation, which is approximately every 30 years. Were that gap to be filled by immigration, a large majority of Japan's population would be foreign born after only two generations, and Japan would be a very different society from what it is today. It is unlikely that the government will ever allow immigration on this scale to occur. If Japan's fertility remains at very low levels, however, it is likely that some immigration will eventually be allowed.

What can Japan do that it is not already doing to raise fertility? According to Caldwell et al. (2002):

"Nearly all the methods likely to be used to raise fertility have been implemented over the last half-century by either France or communist Eastern Europe (Bourgeois-Pichat 1974; McIntosh 1981; Hohn 1988; Heitlinger 1976; Gauthier 1991, 1993, 1996). They include bonus payments for births, family allowances, paid maternity and parental leave, leave to care for sick children, tax relief for parents, care facilities for young children or tax relief for child care, flexible working arrangements for mothers and guarantees of retained promotion rights, labour force re-entry training programs, housing benefits for families with children, and educational supplements for children."

To this list might be added measures to encourage more marriage and earlier marriage, which are quite relevant to Japan's situation, because, as seen earlier, increases in the mean age at marriage and the proportion never marrying account for about half of Japan's fertility decline since 1973. This suggests the need for policy initiatives aimed at improving the functioning of the marriage market.

One way that has been tried is dating services, which were pioneered in Japan, but so far only in the private sector. At the present time there are about 3,100 dating services in the country. As a service to their employees, some large firms contract with dating services, and these large firms sometimes cooperate with each other in providing these services. For example, the Mizuho Financial Group (formerly the Fuyou Family) contracts collectively with a dating service for their employees. The Mizuho Financial Group is a large industry group, or *keiretsu*, that includes Mizuho Bank, Hitachi, Canon, Sapporo Beer, Marubeni, NKK Steel, and a number of other major corporations. For an employee in one of the group's companies to get the services, he or she must join the Fuyou Family Club and pay an annual membership fee of 50,000 yen ($500), plus another 70,000 yen ($700) if a marriage results. These rates are subsidized by the companies and are low compared with the fees that individuals must pay if they deal directly with a dating service. The Fuyou Family Club claims 7,000 members and a 10 percent success rate in terms of matches that result in marriages (information obtained at www.omiai-web.com/hikaku/fuyou01.com). Most other large industry groups have similar outsourcing arrangements with dating services.

The Japanese government may soon get involved in matchmaking by providing government support for dating and related services. On January 24, 2005, the Ministry of Economy, Trade, and Industry held its first expert group meeting to investigate the possibility of government support of "marriage information services," including not only dating services but also "life support" services such as training to improve interpersonal communication skills (Asahi Shimbun 2005).

Most of the pronatalist measures listed by Caldwell et al. (2002), as quoted above, are costly, and Japan is implementing only some of them. In order to do more, the government must first put the economy on a steady growth path and reduce Japan's huge government debt. This would reduce unemployment and other economic pressures on couples that cause them to reduce their fertility, and it would expand the government's financial capacity to implement the costly pronatalist measures that it would like to put into effect. A discussion of what needs to be done to restore the nation's economic health is beyond the scope of this chapter. Suffice it to say that Japan was slow to restructure its economy during the 1990s and instead relied mainly on Keynesian-style pump priming (that is, deficit spending) to revive the economy. The pump priming probably helped to avoid a much worse recession than what actually occurred, but it did not pull Japan out of recession, and it has resulted in a ballooning of government debt to extraordinarily high levels. In 2000, the ratio of central government debt service to recurring revenues was about 65 percent and rising (Asher 2000). The ratio of debt at all levels of government to GDP was 69 percent in 1990, 92 percent in 1995, 139 percent in 2000, and 159 percent in 2002 (Cabinet Office 2004).

Given the imperative of restoring the health of the economy, it is important that pronatalist measures do not erode the efficiency of Japanese firms by placing too much of the burden of those policies directly on firms. Given the government's huge budget deficits, the temptation to unload the costs of pronatalist measures on firms is considerable. Some of these costs must inevitably fall directly on firms, but to the extent possible the costs should be spread over all taxpayers. Large income tax exemptions (that is, deductions from taxable income) for dependent children are an example of a pronatalist measure the cost of which is spread over all taxpayers (assuming that the government raises income tax rates to compensate for lost revenue) and which does not erode the efficiency and competitiveness of firms.

Another point concerns the impact of Japan's various pronatalist measures on differential fertility by income and education. At the present time, fertility tends to be lower among those with higher income and more education. If the goal is to raise the fertility of all income and education groups equally, then financial incentives to have more children must rise with income, since couples gauge the attractiveness of a financial incentive relative to their income. Because income and education are positively correlated, financial incentives that increase with income also increase with more education, although this is true only on average and not in every individual case.

As seen earlier in figure 1.6, women with more education have lower fertility than those with less education, and this gap has been increasing in Japan for some time, especially the gap between university-educated women, who are an increasingly large proportion of all women, and women with less education. Financial incentives that do not increase with income would likely increase this gap even further. From a population perspective, this is not desirable, because on average those with higher income and education have more to offer children and are better equipped to bring up the next generation.

Some of Japan's pronatalist measures favor more-educated women and some do not. Among the measures that favor more-educated women has been the child-care leave provision of the Child Care and Family Leave Act, because this provision until recently applied only to regular full-time employees, who tend to have higher than average educational qualifications. The "next generation" law also benefits the more-educated more than the less-educated, because employees in firms and organizations with more than 300 employees are also more educated than average. This is evident from the 2002 Employment Status Survey, which shows that among male paid employees age 15–49, the proportion working in firms with 300 or more employees is 14 percent for those with a junior high education, 42 percent for senior high, 44 percent for junior college, and 67 percent for university. Among female paid employees age 15–49, the proportions are 27 percent for junior high, 42 percent for senior high, 59 percent for junior college, and 68 percent for university. Income tax exemptions for children also tend to favor the more educated (to the extent that education is positively correlated with income), because in a progressive tax system like Japan's, where marginal tax rates rise with income, the tax saving on tax-exempt income rises with income. On the other hand, the means-tested child allowances and the means-tested services provided by the Angel Plans disproportionately benefit lower-income groups who on average are less educated. Thus the means-tested measures tend to widen negative fertility differentials by income and education.

In 2000 the government reduced the tax exemption for children age 0–15 from 480,000 yen ($4,800) to 380,000 yen ($3,800) per child, and raised the tax exemption for children age 16–22 from 630,000 yen ($6,300) to 680,000 yen ($6,800). The tax exemption for young children was reduced to help pay for improved child-care leave benefits and means-tested childrearing services. This shift of funding could have an effect on fertility opposite to what is intended. The reason is that, although paid child-care leave and subsidized child-care services may indeed increase the fertility of full-time working women, they may also draw more women into full-time jobs, and the fertility of the women newly drawn into full-time jobs is likely to fall as a result, because full-time working women are subject to opportunity costs when they have children. The overall impact could be to lower Japan's TFR rather than raise it.

This does not mean that the government should back away from paid child-care leave and subsidized child-care services, because these are beneficial regardless of whether they raise fertility, inasmuch as they increase women's ability to realize their individual potential and lead more satisfying lives. But if raising fertility is the goal, large income tax deductions for children may be a more effective means, as well as an economically more efficient means, of achieving the goal. Whether this is actually so is an empirical question in need of further research.

Regarding tax deductions for children, it should be mentioned that currently in Japan the employer prepares the employee's tax return (except for the part dealing with outside income), including the parts of the return that take into account tax exemptions for children. As a result, most Japanese taxpayers have little or no idea what the income tax benefits of children are. If the intent is to raise fertility, the tax forms should be revised so that individual taxpayers have to indicate on the tax form the number of child tax exemptions and the amount thereby subtracted from taxable income, and this should be done in such a way that the amount of the tax reduction is obvious to the taxpayer. Alternatively, the employer could still fill out this part of the form, but the form could be revised to prominently indicate the tax benefit from children so that the employee sees it when he or she signs the tax form. Until something like this is done, the fertility-raising effect of child tax exemptions is unnecessarily reduced.

A likely objection to income progressivity in pronatalist incentives is that it is inequitable and unjust to give those who are already better off larger financial incentives. But this is not really so. Larger incentives for those with higher income will always be much less than the direct economic cost of a child, and very much less than the opportunity cost of a child (lost income to the mother), which is not only very large for full-time working women who resign their jobs to have children, but also higher, on average, the more educated a woman is. Moreover, if the financial incentives are large enough to motivate large numbers of highly educated high-income women to temporarily drop out of the labor force for several years to have two or three children, the result would probably be to reduce household income inequalities, not to increase them, because these women would incur huge income losses over their lifetime. In this regard, it should be borne in mind that one of the major reasons why household income distributions have been becoming more unequal in industrial countries in recent years is the increase in the proportion of families with few or no children where the husband and wife both work, are highly educated, and have high incomes (the extreme case being "double income/no kids" or "DINKS" couples, as economists call them). When these considerations are taken into account, progressivity in childbearing incentives appears more justifiable from an equity standpoint.

THE BIG PICTURE

Japan's Child Care and Family Care Leave Act allows up to one year of child-care leave to care for an infant under one year of age, but most women would probably consider that one year of child-care leave is not enough. Although data are not available on this point, it seems likely that most Japanese women would prefer to have two children in fairly quick succession, with about a three-year interval between them, and then return to work when the youngest child is about three years old, when the mother would feel more comfortable about putting the child in a day-care facility. In other words, most women would probably prefer a six-year leave. This is probably why the previously cited government White Paper that simulated the opportunity cost of children under different scenarios specified a six-year period for temporarily dropping out of the labor force to have children.

Requiring employers to grant six years of child-care leave with return rights and other benefits would, however, place a very heavy burden on employers.

(The government is currently considering extension of the leave to three years.) The problem of the length of the leave highlights the dilemma facing policy-makers, which is how to implement two major imperatives:

1. Restructuring the Japanese economy to be more efficient and competitive in the global economy.
2. Restructuring Japanese society to be more marriage-friendly and family-friendly in order to raise fertility.

The trick is how to do this so that the second imperative does not undermine the first, and without jeopardizing women's hard-won gains in education and employment. Experience to date suggests that this will not be easy, and that it will be very costly to both the government and firms to raise fertility back up to the replacement level.

Finally, it is instructive to consider Japan's situation compared with that of other economically advanced countries with very low fertility. In addition to Japan, approximately 30 countries in the world, mostly in Europe, currently have a TFR of less than 1.5 children per woman. Very few of these countries have been able to bring fertility back up to 1.5, and none of them has been able to bring it back up to anywhere near the replacement level of 2.1 (Caldwell et al. 2002; Caldwell and Schindlmayr 2003; Lutz 2005). This international experience provides some additional perspective on why the Japanese government has not yet been able to reverse the fall of fertility, despite more than a decade of effort to do so.

(*Note*: The authors thank Rikiya Matsukura for research assistance and Andrew Mason, Minja Kim Choe, John Caldwell, and Leah Retherford for comments on an earlier draft.)

2

Low Fertility in Europe: Causes, Implications, and Policy Options

Hans-Peter Kohler, Francesco C. Billari,
and José Antonio Ortega

Global population is at a turning point. At the end of 2004, the majority of the world's population is believed to live in countries or regions of below-replacement fertility, and the earlier distinct fertility regimes, "developed" and "developing," are increasingly disappearing in global comparisons of fertility levels (Wilson 2001, 2004). Several aspects of this convergence toward low fertility are particularly striking. First, the spread of below-replacement fertility to formerly high fertility countries has occurred at a remarkably rapid pace and implied a global convergence of fertility indicators that has been quicker than the convergence of many other socioeconomic characteristics.

Second, earlier notions that fertility levels may naturally stabilize close to replacement level—that is, fertility levels with slightly more than two children per woman—have been shattered. Sustained below-replacement fertility has become commonplace, and Europe has been a leader in the trend toward low and very low fertility. Europe also witnessed in the last 15 years the emergence of unprecedentedly low fertility levels with a total fertility rate (TFR) at or below 1.3 children per woman. Kohler and others (2002) have labeled these patterns as *lowest-low fertility* to emphasize the dramatic implications of these unprecedentedly low levels of fertility: for instance, if they persist over a long time in a contemporary low-mortality context, TFR levels at or below 1.3 imply a reduction of the annual number of births by 50 percent and a halving of the population size in less than 45 years. There have been no cases of sustained lowest-low fertility prior to 1990 (see figure 2.1). In the early 1990s, Italy and Spain were the first countries to attain and sustain lowest-low fertility levels, and in 2002 there were 17 lowest-low fertility countries in Southern, Central, and Eastern Europe with a total population of over 278 million persons. As a matter of fact, the median total fertility rate—that is, the TFR level below

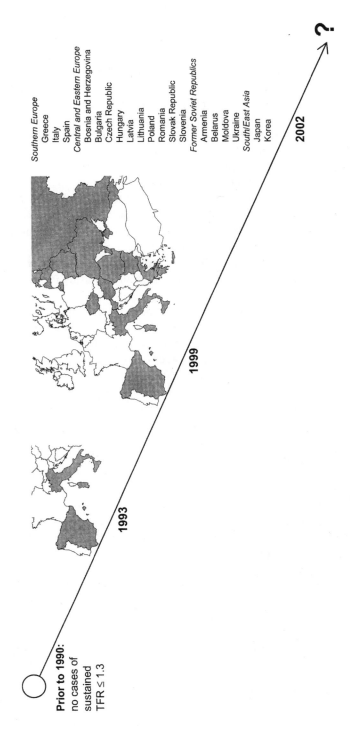

Figure 2.1. The emergence and spread of lowest-low fertility in Europe during 1990–2002.

Prior to 1990:
no cases of
sustained
TFR ≤ 1.3

1993

1999

2002

?

Southern Europe
    Greece
    Italy
    Spain
Central and Eastern Europe
    Bosnia and Herzegovina
    Bulgaria
    Czech Republic
    Hungary
    Latvia
    Lithuania
    Poland
    Romania
    Slovak Republic
    Slovenia
Former Soviet Republics
    Armenia
    Belarus
    Moldova
    Ukraine
South/East Asia
    Japan
    Korea

which 50 percent of the populations in Europe live—is currently 1.31, only slightly above lowest-low fertility.

Third, recent fertility trends have been accompanied by a remarkable divergence of European countries in terms of their fertility levels and future population trends, with current patterns ranging from countries that stabilized at moderately below-replacement fertility levels to lowest-low fertility countries with TFR declines below 1.3 (see figure 2.2). For instance, several European countries that were among the first to experience sustained below-replacement fertility in the late 1960s and early 1970s, including Denmark, France, the Netherlands, and the United Kingdom, exhibited relatively high fertility in 2002. Moreover, the Dutch, Danish, and French TFRs have *increased* during the last decade to levels of 1.72 (the Netherlands), 1.77 (Denmark), and 1.89 (France) (Council of Europe 2003), and several other European countries exhibit even higher TFRs. These trends are in sharp contrast to the pervasive TFR declines in Southern, Central, and Eastern Europe to levels below 1.3, leading to pronounced differences across European countries in their future demographic trajectories.

Fourth, as a consequence of below-replacement fertility that has prevailed for several decades, starting in the 1960s and 1970s, low birthrates in Europe have begun to generate negative population momentum, that is, a new force for population shrinkage over the coming decades due to the fact that past below-replacement fertility will soon result in declining numbers of potential parents (Lutz et al. 2003). A continuation of this trend could substantially exacerbate the future aging of the population, reinforce a future decline in the population size, and constrain the effectiveness of policy interventions aimed at increasing the number of births.

In this chapter, we investigate the emergence and persistence of low and particularly lowest-low fertility in Europe, analyze the demographic patterns and socioeconomic determinants, and address the factors that underlie the divergence of fertility levels in Europe and developed countries more generally. The central thrust of our argument is that the emergence of lowest-low fertility in Europe is due to the combination of four distinct demographic and behavioral factors. First, *economic and social changes* have made the postponement of fertility a rational response for individuals. Second, *social interaction processes* affecting the timing of fertility have rendered the population response to these new socioeconomic conditions substantially larger than the direct individual responses. As a consequence, modest socioeconomic changes can explain the rapid and persistent *postponement transitions* from early to late age patterns of fertility that have been associated with recent trends toward low and lowest-low fertility. Third, *demographic distortions of period fertility measures*, caused by the postponement of fertility and changes in the parity composition of the population, have reduced the level of period fertility indicators below the associated

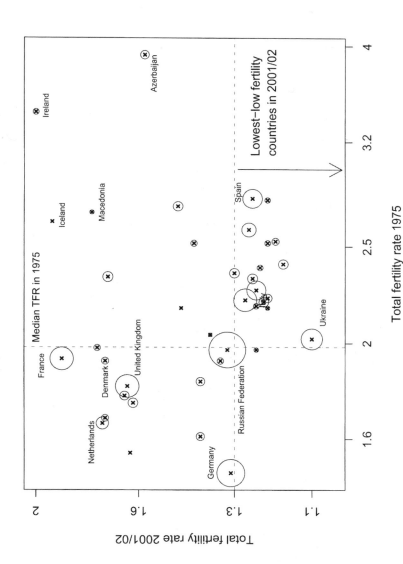

Figure 2.2. Comparison of the total fertility rate in Europe in 1975 and 2002.
Note: The '×' mark gives the exact position of a country, while the area of circle is proportional to the country's population size in 1990.
Source: Council of Europe (2003); see Table A.1.1 for list of countries and data.

level of cohort fertility (for discussion of this technical aspect, see Bongaarts and Feeney 1998; Kohler and Ortega 2002). Fourth, *institutional settings* in Southern, Central, and Eastern European countries have favored an overall low quantum of fertility. Moreover, this institutional setting has caused particularly large reductions in completed fertility in lowest-low fertility countries due to the delay of childbearing.

PATTERNS OF LOW AND LOWEST-LOW
FERTILITY IN EUROPE

Against the background of these recent changes in the demographic landscape in Europe and other developed countries, there is little doubt that the emergence and persistence of lowest-low fertility entails profound consequences for virtually all aspects of society. Some of these implications of Europe's low and lowest-low fertility pattern on the population size and structure are illustrated in figure 2.3, using the UN medium population forecasts for Europe, Bulgaria, Denmark, France, Germany, Italy, and the Russian Federation. The different countries included in these analyses are representative of the major fertility patterns and welfare regimes in contemporary Europe. The United States is also included in these analyses for comparison. Figure 2.3 shows that, while the United States and a small number of European countries are projected to grow in the next decades, Europe as a whole is projected to decline. Some countries such as Bulgaria, Russia, and Italy are likely to experience substantial declines in their population size. These different trends in population size in Europe are mostly due to fertility trends that differ drastically across European countries. France and Denmark, for instance, are expected to have moderately high fertility, with TFRs above 1.7 children per woman, continuing their most recent experiences. Most other European countries are projected to have lower—and often much lower—fertility in the next decades, and Europe as a whole is projected to experience a TFR of below 1.5 until about 2020.

These fertility trends in combination with increases in longevity imply that population aging—as measured for instance by the increase in the median age of the population and the old-age dependency ratio—will occur across Europe. Europe's median age, for instance, is projected to increase from 37.7 years in 2000 to 47.9 in 2040. The old-age dependency ratio is projected to increase from 22 persons age 65 years and older per 100 persons age 15–64 (2000) to 44 persons age 65+ per 100 persons age 15–64 (2040). However, there is likely to be considerable heterogeneity in this population aging across Europe. The median age in 2040 in figure 2.3 ranges from 44.4 years (France) to 52.7 years (Italy), and the old-age dependency ratio ranges from 37 (Russia) to 63 (Italy). Demographically speaking, therefore, European countries are

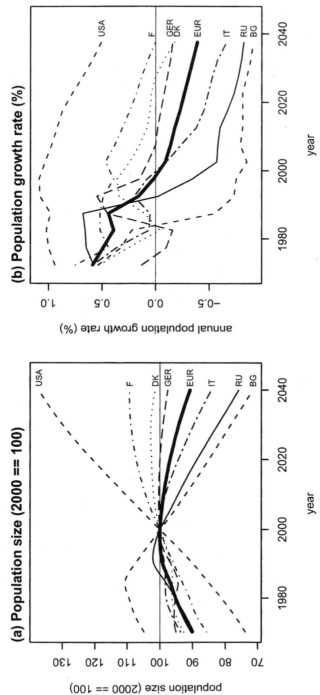

Figure 2.3. UN projections (medium variant) for Europe, United States, Bulgaria, Denmark, France, Germany, Italy and the Russian Federation. *Notes*: The different demographic measures are defined as follows: *Population size*: De facto population in a country, area, or region as of 1 July of the year indicated. *Population growth rate*: Annual average exponential rate of growth of the population.

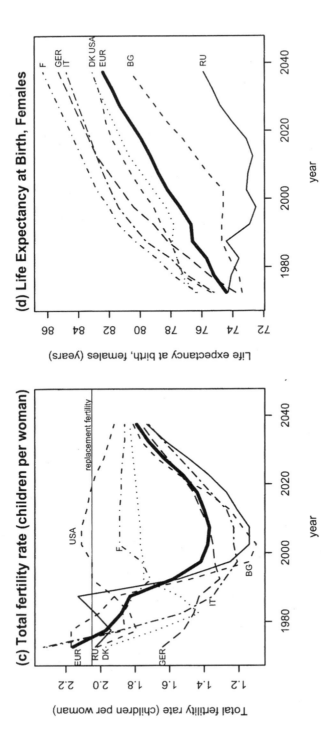

Figure 2.3. (*Continued*)

Notes: *Total fertility rate (TFR)*: The average number of children a hypothetical cohort of women would have at the end of their reproductive period if they were subject during their whole lives to the fertility rates of a given period and if they were not subject to mortality. It is expressed as children per woman. *Life expectancy*: The average number of years of life expected by a hypothetical cohort of individuals who would be subject during all their lives to the mortality rates of a given period. It is expressed as years.

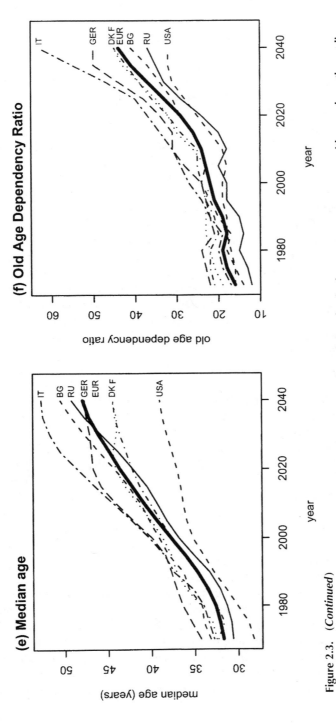

Figure 2.3. (Continued)

Notes: Median age: Age that divides the population in two parts of equal size; that is, there are as many persons with ages above the median as there are with ages below the median. Old age dependency ratio: The ratio of the population aged 65 years or over to the population aged 15–64.

pulled apart by a differential extent of population aging. In addition, the above trends in Europe are in striking contrast to those in the United States. While the U.S. population will also age in the next decades, this process will occur in the context of a growing population, a relatively high level of fertility, and substantial immigration. In comparison with Europe, therefore, the U.S. increases in the median age or the old-age dependency ratio during the next decades will be rather modest.

The implications of population aging, and the societal changes associated with this trend, are going to be most pronounced in countries with very low fertility. These countries are likely to experience a dramatic transformation of their age pyramids (see figures 2.4 and 2.5), and the social and economic organization of individuals and families in these highly aged societies is an uncharted territory in demographic history. The implications of these changes will reach across all aspects of society and individual lives. Lowest-low fertility, for instance, is going to substantially alter the structure and age composition of the labor force as well as of the young and old population, and female—and probably also male—labor supply patterns will change due to the combination of low and late fertility. Lowest-low fertility will also transform a wide range of social relations, which are frequently taken for granted, due to the fact that low fertility, fewer siblings, and increases in childlessness diminish the potential of family networks to provide social, psychological, and economic support. The increased diversity in living arrangements and the changes in the timing of fertility will also have important consequences for income distribution, the welfare of small children, and life changes across individuals and households.

Despite the clear need for more information and evaluation of these developments, the demography of lowest-low fertility is still in its infancy. The emergence of sustained lowest-low fertility first occurred in Southern, Central, and Eastern European countries. According to the Council of Europe (2003), 17 countries attained lowest-low fertility levels by 2002 (see table 2.1): three in Southern Europe (Greece, Italy, and Spain), 10 in Central and Eastern Europe (Bosnia and Herzegovina, Bulgaria, Czech Republic, Hungary, Latvia, Lithuania, Poland, Romania, Slovak Republic, and Slovenia), and four in the former Soviet Union (Armenia, Belarus, Moldova, and Ukraine). The first countries to reach lowest-low fertility levels were Spain and Italy, in 1993. They were then joined by Bulgaria, the Czech Republic, Latvia, and Slovenia, in 1995, and by the remaining lowest-low fertility countries between 1996 and 2002. In addition, several other countries in Central and Eastern Europe and the Balkans have very low TFR levels, and Croatia (1.34), Estonia (1.37), and Russia (1.32) will possibly join—or rejoin, in the case of Russia—the group of lowest-low fertility countries. Moreover, other European countries with traditionally low fertility, such as Austria (1.34), Switzerland (1.4), and Germany (1.31), are candidates that may soon join the group of lowest-low fertility countries.

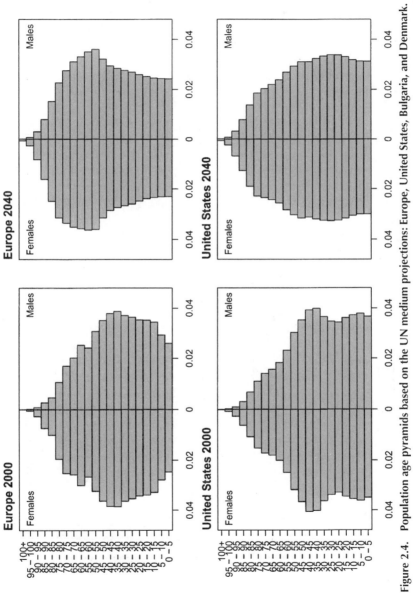

Figure 2.4. Population age pyramids based on the UN medium projections: Europe, United States, Bulgaria, and Denmark.

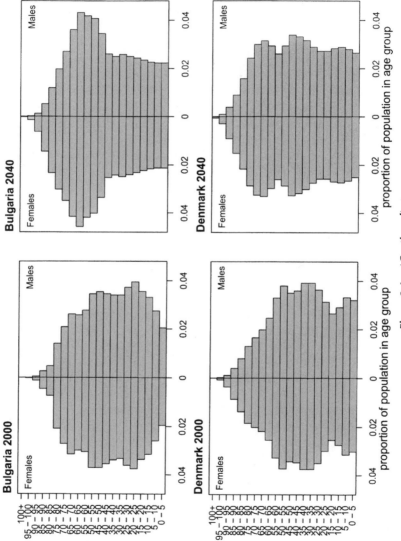

Figure 2.4. (Continued)

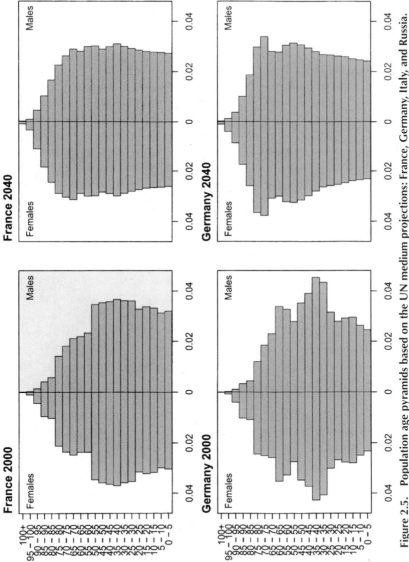

Figure 2.5. Population age pyramids based on the UN medium projections: France, Germany, Italy, and Russia.

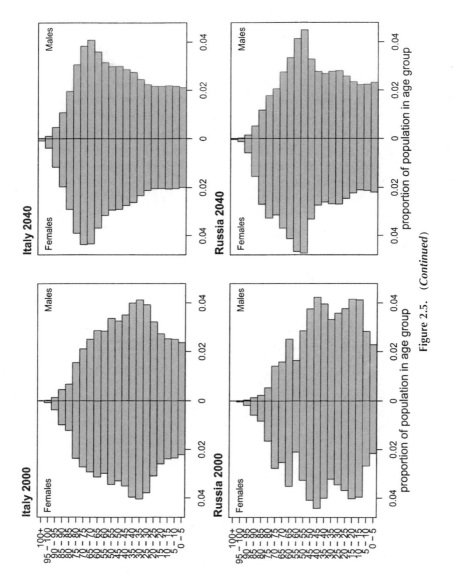

Figure 2.5. (*Continued*)

Table 2.1. Total Fertility Rate (*TFR*) in Lowest-Low Fertility Countries, Candidate Countries, and Selected Other Countries

	TFR				Most recent year TFR *fell*	
	1980	*1990*	*2000*	*2002*	≤2	≤1.3
Lowest-low fertility countries						
Southern Europe						
Greece	2.23	1.39	1.29	1.25[a]	1983	1998
Italy	1.64	1.33	1.24	1.27	1977	1993
Spain	2.20	1.36	1.24	1.25	1982	1993
Central and Eastern Europe						
Bosnia and Herzegovina	1.93	1.71	1.34	1.23	1984	2002
Bulgaria	2.05	1.82	1.30	1.21	1987	2001
Czech Republic	2.10	1.90	1.14	1.17	1983	1995
Hungary	1.91	1.87	1.32	1.30	1980	1999
Latvia	1.90	2.01	1.24	1.24	1991	1995
Lithuania	1.99	2.03	1.39	1.24	1992	2001
Poland	2.26	2.05	1.34	1.24	1992	2001
Romania	2.43	1.84	1.31	1.26	1990	2001
Slovakia	2.31	2.09	1.30	1.19	1992	2000
Slovenia	2.10	1.46	1.26	1.21	1981	1995
Former Soviet Republics						
Armenia	2.33	2.63	1.11	1.21	1993	1999
Belarus	2.04	1.90	1.31	1.22	1990	2001
Moldova	2.41	2.39	1.30	1.21	1994	2000
Ukraine	1.95	1.89	1.09	1.10	1989	1997
East Asia						
Japan				1.29[b]	1975	2003
Korea	2.83	1.59	1.47	1.19[b]	1984	2001
Lowest-low fertility candidates in Europe						
Andorra	–	–	1.32	1.36	–	–
Austria	1.65	1.46	1.36	1.40	1973	–
Croatia	1.92	1.67	1.40	1.34	1968	–
Estonia	2.02	2.04	1.34	1.37	1991	1997[c]
Germany	1.56	1.45	1.38	1.31	1971	1992[c]
Russian Federation	1.86	1.90	1.21	1.32	1990	1996[c]
Switzerland	1.55	1.58	1.50	1.40	1972	–
Selected other countries						
Denmark	1.55	1.67	1.77	1.72	1973	–
France	1.95	1.78	1.88	1.89	1975	–
Netherlands	1.60	1.62	1.72	1.73	1973	–
United Kingdom	1.89	1.83	1.64	1.64	1974	–
United States	1.81	2.08	2.06	2.01	1995[d]	–

Notes: a = 2001; b = 2003; c = fertility has increased to levels above 1.3 by 2002; d = fertility has increased to levels above 2.0 by 2002.
Sources: Council of Europe (2003); Martin et al. (2003); Mathews and Hamilton (2002).

Table 2.2. Mean Age at First Birth (MAFB) in Lowest-Low Fertility Countries, Candidate Countries, and Selected Other Countries

	Mean age at first birth (MAFB)				Annual increase in MAFB		
	1980	1990	2000	2002	1980–1990	1990–2000	Year of onset
Lowest-low fertility countries							
Southern Europe							
Greece	24.1	25.5	27.3[c]	–	0.14	0.20	1983
Italy	25.0	26.9	28.7[b]	–	0.19	0.26	1978
Spain	25.0	26.8	29.1	–	0.18	0.23	1979
Central and Eastern Europe							
Bosnia and Herzegovina	23.3	23.6	–	–	0.03	–	–
Bulgaria	21.9	22.2	23.5	23.9	0.03	0.13	1992
Czech Republic	22.4	22.5	25.0	25.6	0.01	0.25	1991
Hungary	22.4	23.1	25.1	25.6	0.07	0.20	1980
Latvia	22.9	23.0	24.4	24.9	0.01	0.14	1992
Lithuania	23.8	23.2	23.9	24.3	-0.06	0.07	1994
Poland	23.4	23.3	24.5	25.0	-0.01	0.12	1991
Romania	22.5	22.7	23.6	24.1	0.02	0.09	1991
Slovakia	22.7	22.6	24.2	24.7	-0.01	0.16	1991
Slovenia	22.9	23.7	26.5	27.2	0.08	0.28	1985
Former Soviet Republics							
Armenia	22.1	22.8	23.0	–	0.07	0.02	1994
Belarus	–	22.9	23.4	23.5	–	0.05	1997
Moldova	–	–	–	23.0	–	–	–
Ukraine	–	–	–	–	–	–	–

East Asia							
Japan	26.4	27.0	28.0	28.3	0.06	0.1	–
Korea	–	–	–	–	–	–	–
Lowest-low fertility candidates in Europe							
Andorra	–	–	–	–	–	–	–
Austria	23.4	25.0	26.4	26.7	–	0.14	1984
Croatia	23.2	24.1	25.5	25.9	0.07	0.14	1978
Estonia	25.0	22.9	24.0	24.6	-0.03	0.11	1991
Germany[e]	25.0	26.6	28.2	28.4[d]	0.16	0.16	1972
Russian Federation	23.0	22.6	23.0[b]	–	-0.04	0.06	1994
Switzerland[e]	26.3	27.6	28.7	28.9	0.13	0.11	1971
Selected other countries							
Denmark	24.6	26.4	27.5[a]	–	0.18	0.18	1967
France	25.0	27.0	27.9	28.0[c]	0.20	0.09	1973
Netherlands	25.7	27.6	28.6	28.7	0.19	0.10	1972
United Kingdom[e]	–	27.3	29.1	–	–	0.18	–
United States	22.7	24.2	24.9	–	0.15	0.07	1974

Notes: a = 1996; b = 1997; c = 1999; d = 2001; e = birth-order within current marriage.
Source: Council of Europe (2003); Martin et al. (2003); Mathews and Hamilton (2002).

Despite these very low levels of fertility, demographic analyses suggest that the decline in the desire to have at least one child has *not* been a primary driving force in the emergence of lowest-low fertility in the Southern, Central, and Eastern European countries (Kohler et al. 2002). While childlessness is likely to rise, it is projected to remain at relatively modest levels. Calculations by Kohler and others (2002), for instance, suggest that a cohort experiencing the fertility pattern observed during the mid/late 1990s attains a childlessness of 16–19 percent in Italy and Spain and of 13–19 percent in Bulgaria, Czech Republic, and Hungary (for related calculations, see also Sobotka 2004a,b). These levels of childlessness are comparable to the corresponding estimates for Sweden and the Netherlands in the late 1990s and are quite modest in a historical twentieth-century perspective or when compared to the childlessness observed in some other countries, as for instance Germany, where more than a quarter of the women in the 1965 cohort are estimated to have remained childless (Sobotka 2004b).

These findings on childlessness therefore suggest that even in lowest-low fertility contexts, the biological, social, and economic incentives for children are sufficiently strong that most women, or couples, desire to have at least one child (see, for example, Foster 2000; Kohler and Behrman 2003; Morgan and King 2001). Nevertheless, while first births are not necessarily foregone in lowest-low fertility countries, they are delayed to an increasingly late age. For instance, the mean age at first birth in all lowest-low fertility countries is higher in 2000–2002 than in 1990 (see table 2.2). In the Southern European countries, postponement has been very pronounced, with annual increases in the mean age at first birth exceeding 0.2 per year. Combined with a relatively high initial mean age, this postponement has led to some of the highest mean ages at first birth in the world. In the Central and Eastern European (CEE) countries, the patterns are not so uniform. An extremely rapid trend in postponement has occurred in Slovenia, the Czech Republic, and Hungary. Other countries, like Bulgaria, Estonia, Latvia, and Romania, have experienced a moderate postponement trend, with increases in the mean age at first birth at around 0.1 per year, and these countries continue to have a very young mean age. Similar patterns also prevail in other countries of the former Soviet Union like Russia, Belarus, and Armenia.

FERTILITY-RELATED PATTERNS OF HOUSEHOLD AND UNION DYNAMICS

The trend toward delayed childbearing—especially for first births—has occurred not only in lowest-low fertility countries, but also in almost all countries across Europe. This almost universal transition toward a late pattern of childbearing, however, implies that the extent to which specific socioeconomic and institutional contexts in different European countries accommodate late childbearing has become an essential determinant of cross-country variation in fertility levels. To better understand this interrelation between institutional contexts and patterns of childbearing, we must begin with a series of descriptive aggregate analyses, to revisit the relation between low and lowest-low period fertility on the one hand, and key fertility-related behaviors—such as leaving the parental home, marriage, and women's labor force participation—on the other. These analyses can improve our understanding of the demographic, socioeconomic, and institutional context that is associated with the emergence—or non-emergence—of lowest-low fertility in European countries, and show the basic demographic and socioeconomic patterns that are associated with low and lowest-low fertility in contemporary Europe.

LEAVING THE PARENTAL HOME

Leaving the parental home is one of the crucial nodes of the life course and a central event in early adulthood. First, it generally implies the formation of a new household and greater autonomy for young people in all aspects of social life and personal decision-making, including many fertility-related decisions. Second, and most important for our context, childbearing in developed countries almost invariably takes place after young adults have left their parental home, and home-leaving constitutes a central correlate of fertility and union formation in Europe and other industrialized countries.

In a pioneering study, Kiernan (1986) investigates home-leaving in six Western European countries in 1982. The study identifies Denmark as the country with the earliest home-leaving, followed by West Germany, France, the Netherlands, Ireland, and the United Kingdom. In a follow-up investigation, Fernández Cordón (1997) examined the living arrangements of young adults over time in Spain, Greece, Italy, France, Germany, and the United Kingdom between 1986 and 1994. These longitudinal analyses revealed that Italy had the highest share of young people co-residing with their parents during early adulthood, while the United Kingdom had the smallest share. Moreover, Corijn (1999) found that cohorts in most European countries born around 1950 and 1960 were postponing the transition out of the parental home. This common trend toward delayed home-leaving, however, co-exists with substantial variation in the timing of it across countries: Italy and Spain are among the countries with a late separation from the parental home, while Austria, the Netherlands, and Sweden are among the countries with an early pattern.

Despite this overall heterogeneity in patterns of home-leaving, however, there is an important regularity with respect to the relation of home-leaving and lowest-low fertility. In particular, retrospective survey data—which are the only available data source for this purpose—reveal that the timing of home-leaving is quite homogeneously concentrated at relatively late ages among lowest-low fertility countries. In an international comparison of the timing of home-leaving for cohorts born around 1960, for instance, Italy, which was the first country to experience lowest-low fertility in the early 1990s, has the highest age for home-leaving, both for men and for women, with 26.7 years and 23.6 years respectively. Some Central and Eastern European countries, including those with lowest-low fertility, are not very distant from the latest-late pattern of Southern European countries. On the other hand, Sweden represents the opposite side of the ranking regarding age at home-leaving, with 20.2 years for men and 18.6 for women, resulting in a difference of more than 6.5 years (males) and 5 years (females) in the timing of home-leaving across European countries (see Billari et al. 2001).

FERTILITY AND MARRIAGE: A SHIFTING RELATIONSHIP?

In a well-known study, Hajnal (1965) traces an East–West divide in historical family systems in Europe, the so-called Hajnal line that connects the cities of Trieste in Northeastern Italy and St. Petersburg in Western Russia. To the west of this line, the family formation pattern is dominated by a neo-local nuclear family with relatively late marriage and a significant proportion of individuals who never marry. To the east of Hajnal's line, marriage has been early and universal, and the family is often an extended one. This divergence of marriage pattern along Hajnal's line continued after World War II and persists until the present time. It is particularly pronounced between Central and Eastern Europe on the one hand, and Southern Europe on the other (Monnier and Rychtarikova 1992). Countries to the west of Hajnal's line reveal greater heterogeneity and diversity in contemporary marriage behaviors that do not easily cluster into a single pattern (Reher 1998).

   Even if historical patterns are an important aspect shaping present marriage behaviors and family organizations, the emergence of lowest-low fertility is associated with an important shift in the relationship between marriage and fertility between the mid 1970s and the beginning of this decade. In particular, it has traditionally been argued that cumulated fertility is inversely related to age at marriage, and variations in the age at marriage have often been an important explanatory factor of aggregate fertility differences across countries. For instance, a linear relationship between total fertility and the age at first marriage has been shown to be a surprisingly good approximation, and Billari and others (2000) estimate that a one-year increase in the age at marriage would bring down the number of female children ever born by about 0.08 in Italian cohorts born around 1950.

In contrast to this positive association between marriage and fertility, the recent emergence of lowest-low fertility, especially in Southern Europe, is associated with a situation in which long-term partnership commitments—symbolized by a high prevalence of legal marriage and low prevalence of divorce—apparently represent an obstacle for the progression to (relatively) high fertility levels. To illustrate this association, we compare on the left-hand side of figure 2.6 the level of period total fertility with the period total first marriage rate (TFMR). In order to indicate the relevance of individual countries for the relationships in figure 2.6, the data points are surrounded by circles that have an area proportional to a country's population size. In 1975, as figure 2.6a shows, marriage and fertility were still closely intertwined, and there was a positive correlation between the total fertility and the total first marriage rate. The correlation radically changed at the end of the 1990s. In particular, after lowest-low fertility emerged, the positive correlation between the total fertility and the TFMR vanished, and countries with high fertility levels no longer exhibit high marriage propensities (see figure 2.6b). A similarly shifting relation occurs also with respect to fertility and divorce (see figures 2.6c and 2.6d). In 1975, a higher level of divorce in European countries was associated with lower levels of fertility in cross-sectional comparisons, and the period total divorce rate (TDR) exhibited a negative correlation with the level of total fertility (see figure 2.6c). This correlation reversed itself in 2001–2002: countries with high TDR levels exhibited higher fertility levels than countries with a low total divorce rate (see figure 2.6d). In figure 2.7, we can additionally note that the relationship between the extent of out-of-wedlock childbearing and the level of fertility has reversed along with the shifting centrality of marriage. In particular, a cross-sectional comparison of European countries in 1975 reveals a negative correlation between the level of extramarital fertility and total fertility. In 2001–2002, this correlation becomes positive, and along with this reversal, the Southern European countries, Italy and Spain, stand out as combining both lowest-low fertility and the lowest prevalence of nonmarital fertility.

In summary, the above analyses reinforce the argument that the emergence of lowest-low fertility during the 1990s has been associated with fundamental shifts in the relationships between fertility and marriage. In particular, there has been an increasing disconnection between marriage patterns and fertility levels after the emergence of lowest-low fertility in the 1990s in cross-sectional analyses of European countries, and marriage formation and dissolution are no longer important predictors of national fertility levels in cross-sectional analyses of European countries during the late 1990s (see also Heuveline et al. 2003). Moreover, the above analyses show that the aggregate cross-country

(a) Total fertility and first marriage: 1975

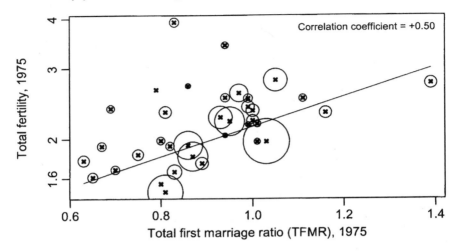

(b) Total fertility and first marriage: 2001/02

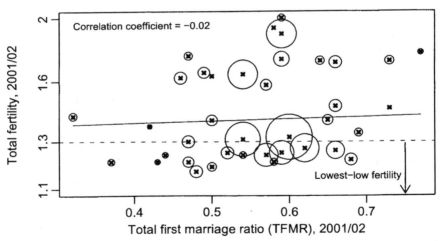

Figure 2.6.   Relationship between total fertility, marriage, and divorce in 1975 and 2001–02.

Notes: The '×' mark gives the exact position of a country, while the area of circle is proportional to the country's population size in 1975 or 2002. The regression line included in the figures is obtained from a weighted regression with weights equal to the population size.

Source: For data: Council of Europe (2003); see Table A.1.1 for the data and list countries.

(c) Total fertility and divorce: 1975

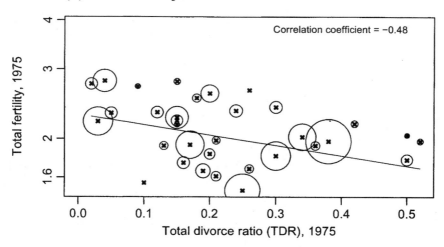

(d) Total fertility and divorce: 2001/02

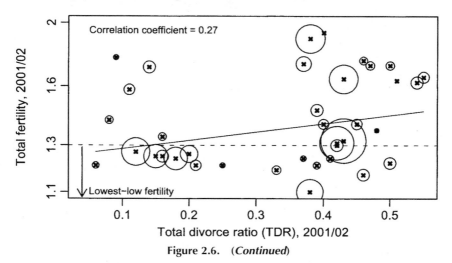

Figure 2.6. (*Continued*)

relationship between partnership formation/dissolution and levels of fertility has become quite indeterminate in the late 1990s, which is strikingly different from the strong relations between fertility and union formation and dissolution that prevailed 20 years earlier. In addition, further analyses—not reported here in detail—reveal important differences in home-leaving, union formation, and dissolution between lowest-low fertility countries (see also Billari et al. 2001).

(a) Total fertility and extra-marital births: 1975

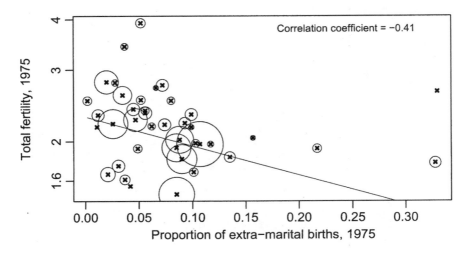

(b) Total fertility and extra-marital births: 2001/02

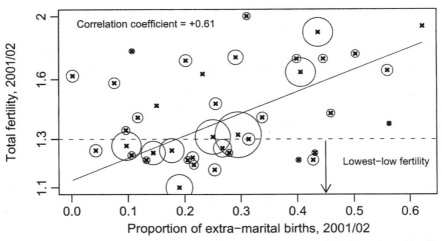

Figure 2.7.   Relationship between the proportion of extra-marital births and total fertility in 1975 and 2001/02. See notes to figure 2.6.
Source: Council of Europe (2003).

On the one hand, the Southern European pattern is characterized by late separation from the parental household, a low prevalence of cohabitation and
extramarital fertility, and a high centrality of marriage with long-term commitments and low rates of divorce. On the other hand, the Central and Eastern

European pattern is more diverse and characterized by earlier home-leaving, lower rates of marriage, and higher rates of divorce and extramarital fertility than the Southern European pattern.

FERTILITY-RELATED PATTERNS OF LABOR FORCE PARTICIPATION

In addition to witnessing a changing relation between fertility and marriage or divorce, experience in the 1990s has also challenged the conventional wisdom about the aggregate-level relation between total fertility and women's labor force participation. In particular, conventional economic theory predicts that increases in the wage rate of women lead to increases in women's labor force participation and decreases of fertility, due to increased opportunity costs of children in combination with a low income elasticity of the number of children (see Becker 1981; Cigno 1991; Willis 1973). At the macro level, this relation has been translated into the hypothesis that total fertility and female labor force participation rate (FLFPR) should be inversely related in cross-country studies.

We will now consider the empirical evidence for this hypothesis as part of an overall attempt to depict the socioeconomic context of lowest-low fertility trends. In particular, several recent studies have documented that the cross-country correlation between the total fertility level and FLFPR has changed its sign in Organization for Economic Cooperation and Development (OECD) countries during the mid 1980s and early 1990s (Ahn and Mira 2002; Engelhardt et al. 2004; Kögel 2004; Rindfuss et al. 2003). This finding is also confirmed in regression-based analyses (Brewster and Rindfuss 2000; Esping-Andersen 1999), where the labor force participation of women has a *positive*, and significant, influence on the total fertility in cross-sectional analyses of OECD countries in the 1990s, while comparable analyses for the 1970s reveal a negative influence.

This reversal is clearly shown in figure 2.8, which plots total fertility levels against female labor force participation rate (FLFPR) for 1975 and 1996 on Western Europe, where the labor force participation of women has traditionally been very different between countries: Austria, Belgium, Denmark, Finland, France, West Germany, Ireland, Italy, Luxembourg, Netherlands, Norway, Sweden, Switzerland, United Kingdom, Greece, and Spain. In 1975, countries with a high FLFPR, such as Sweden or Denmark, exhibited low fertility in a European comparison, while countries with low FLFPR, such as Italy or Spain, had relatively high fertility. In 1996, high FLFPR is associated with high fertility countries, such as Denmark and Sweden, while lowest-low fertility countries, such as Italy and Spain, are characterized by a quite modest

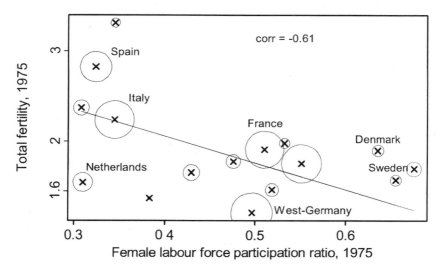

(a) Total fertility and labour force participation: 1975

corr = -0.61

Spain
Italy
France
Denmark
Netherlands
Sweden
West-Germany

Total fertility, 1975

Female labour force participation ratio, 1975

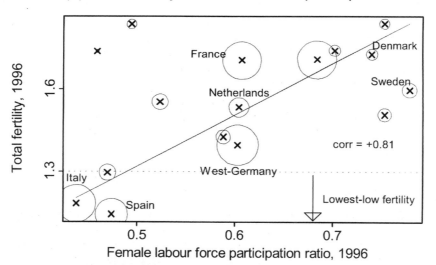

(b) Total fertility and labour force participation: 1996

France
Denmark
Netherlands
Sweden
corr = +0.81
Italy
West-Germany
Lowest-low fertility
Spain

Total fertility, 1996

Female labour force participation ratio, 1996

Figure 2.8. Relationship between the labor force participation of women and total fertility in 1975 and 1996. See notes to figure 2.6.
Source: Kögel (2004).

participation of women in the labor market. It is also important to note that changes in fertility levels—rather than changes in the labor force participation of women—have been more prevalent in the countries dealt with in figure 2.8, and, as shown, the relative country positions with respect to female labor force participation rates have been remarkably constant during the period 1975–1996.

The above findings about the changing association between total fertility levels and women's labor force participation has spurred several additional analyses that investigate this issue further. Ahn and Mira (2002), for instance, emphasize the relevance of Mediterranean countries in the above pattern because the emergence of lowest-low fertility is an important factor contributing to the reversal of the correlation. Brewster and Rindfuss (2000) also emphasize the role of institutional arrangements, such as different family policies, child-care systems, or welfare-state typologies, and they stress the altered social norms regarding the combination between childrearing and labor force participation of women. Specifically, lowest-low fertility in Southern Europe has occurred in a context with a very low compatibility of childbearing with women's labor market participation, due to difficulties in entering and reentering the labor market and the limited flexibility of working hours (Bettio and Villa 1998; Del Boca 2002).

EXPLAINING THE EMERGENCE OF LOWEST-LOW FERTILITY: INCENTIVES, SOCIAL INTERACTIONS, AND INSTITUTIONAL FACTORS

After characterizing the basic patterns of European low fertility and their relation to marriage, divorce, and labor force participation, we explore in this section the socioeconomic conditions and individual-level determinants that underlie this transformation of the demographic landscape in Europe. We initially focus on the delay of childbearing that we have emphasized in our earlier analyses as one of the central demographic aspects in understanding lowest-low fertility. The basic starting point of our discussion is the observation that fertility is a dynamic process over the life course. When individuals progress through their life course and make plans for the future, they can decide— possibly sequentially—how many children they have in total, which is denoted as the *quantum of fertility*, and they can also decide when they have these children, which is denoted as the *timing* or *tempo of fertility*.

Individuals have considerable control over the timing of fertility. Specifically, due to the widespread availability of reliable contraception in most lowest-low fertility countries, we can assume that births are looked for, or at least not intentionally avoided. In such a context, there are different reasons why individuals may not have an extra child for the moment: one may plan to have a child at a later time, one may plan not to have a child at all, or one might not have a clear idea about these future plans. It is important that this decision to postpone childbearing can be revised afterward. There is no irreversible commitment associated with plans to delay fertility, at least within the biological and medical limits that determine the ages of childbearing. This flexibility is in sharp contrast to the transition into parenthood, which is generally irreversible once a child is born. This asymmetry between the irreversibility of childbirth and the reversibility of future plans about the timing of fertility provides an incentive to postpone the decision of having children. A postponement can reduce the uncertainty about the costs and benefits of children, and also the uncertainty associated with the economic situation and the stability of partnerships in early adulthood.

THE SOCIOECONOMIC BACKGROUND OF DELAYED CHILDBEARING IN LOWEST-LOW FERTILITY COUNTRIES

The socioeconomic context of decisions about timing of parenthood varies substantially across lowest-low fertility countries, and there is a striking difference between Southern European and Central/Eastern European (CEE) countries. In Southern European countries, per capita income levels are at medium to high levels with steady growth, and these countries have also experienced low inflation (table 2.3). At the same time, the entry into the labor market for young adults is extremely difficult (table 2.4). The three lowest-low fertility countries in Southern Europe had the highest youth unemployment rates in the European Union in 1999, and this situation has been essentially unchanged since 1989. Unemployment rates are also higher for females than for males, in contrast to Northern European countries. The link between unemployment and low fertility is also supported by the observation that the only Southern European country with relatively high fertility is Portugal, with considerably lower unemployment rates than its Mediterranean counterparts.

The chronic high unemployment situation in Southern Europe has discouraged young adults from entering the labor market and made higher education more attractive, and it has deteriorated working conditions to sometimes precarious situations with mostly low-paid temporary jobs. In addition, there is a crowding-out process in which more-educated young people are displacing less-educated people from their traditional positions (e.g., Dolado et al. 2000). The labor market uncertainty and poor economic prospects in early adulthood also facilitate the commonly observed behavior of prolonging the stay in the parents' household until relatively late ages. In both Italy and Spain, for

Table 2.3 Economic Indicators and Gross University Enrollment Ratios for Lowest-Low Fertility Countries

Country	Economic Indicators				Gross University Enrollment[a]			
	GNI per capita[b] 1999	GDP average growth[c] 1990–1999	GDP growth[c] 1999	Average inflation 1990–1999	Women 1989	Women 1999–2000	Men 1989	Men 1999–2000
Greece	12.1	2.2	3.4	6.2	25.3	56.2	24.4	53.2
Italy	20.2	1.4	1.4	3.4	29.1	52.8	30.3	40.7
Spain	14.8	2.2	3.7	3.1	33.8	62.3	36.3	53.0
Bulgaria	1.4	−2.7	2.4	116.5	28.2	50.1	24.4	35.7
Czech Republic	5.0	0.8	−0.2	7.7	13.9	29.1	17.7	28.2
Estonia	3.4	−1.3	−1.1	15.5	26.5	62.6	25.7	43.3
Hungary	4.6	1.0	4.5	17.4	14.9	40.5	13.7	33.1
Latvia	2.4	−4.8	0.1	9.2	29.0	62.4[d]	20.4	37.9[d]
Romania	1.5	−0.8	−3.2	61.4	8.4	24.3[e]	8.6	20.8[e]
Slovenia	10.0	2.4	4.9	9.9	27.8	61.3[d]	22.3	45.7[d]
Armenia	0.5	−3.2	3.3	32.5	23.8[f]	14.0[e]	23.8[f]	10.5[e]
Belarus	2.6	−3.0	3.4	169.6	50.3	56.2	45.5	43.7
Russia	2.3	−6.1	3.2	52.0	58.9	73.0	48.4	57.4
Ukraine	0.8	−10.7	−0.4	69.8	45.8[f]	46.0[d]	45.8[f]	40.4[d]

Notes:
[a] Gross university enrollment ratio is the total enrollment in university education, regardless of age, divided by the population of the age group which officially corresponds to university education.

[b] GNI per capita = gross national income per capita in thousand US$.

[c] GDP = gross national product.

[d] Calendar year 1998–1999.

[e] Calendar year 1996.

[f] Enrollment ratio pertains to males and females combined.

Sources: World Bank, Data and Statistics, www.worldbank.org; UNESCO, Institute for Statistics, www.unesco.org.

Table 2.4   Youth Unemployment Rates (Under Age 25) in Southern Europe

Country	Women 1989	Women 1999	Men 1989	Men 1999
Italy	38.5	38.3	25.9	28.6
Greece	34	39.3	17	21.4
Spain	42.6	37.3	24.4	21.7
Portugal	15.8	11.1	8.3	7.5
EU (15)	19.6	19.2	14.4	16.7

Source: OECD, Employment Statistics, www.oecd.org.

instance, the successful entry into the labor force tends to accelerate household and union formation (Billari et al. 2002).

There is also considerable heterogeneity in the determinants of low fertility and postponement among Eastern European countries and former Soviet republics. While all of these countries share the common experience of the transition from a planned to a market economy, the success of this transition and the economic hardship during the transformation have varied considerably. Some of these tremendous differences in income levels and economic outcomes during the transition period are documented in table 2.3. Most of the CEE countries with lowest-low fertility, and in particular those in the former Soviet Union, have experienced a decline in output over the transition period. Many countries have also experienced a substantial surge in inflationary pressures during the economic crisis. This is especially the case in the former Soviet Union and countries such as Bulgaria or Romania. In addition, income levels have been very volatile in all transition countries in table 2.3, and the median income fluctuated from year to year by as much as 25 percent (Forster and Toth 1997; Lokshin and Ravallion 2000). Similarly, labor turnover has been very frequent and leads to common spells of unemployment. For instance, 57 percent of Russian women during 1994–1998 were very concerned about the possibility of not being able to provide themselves with the bare essentials in the following year (Kohlmann and Zuev 2001; see also Kohler and Kohler 2002).

The structure of wages and employment has also been transformed in Central and Eastern European transition countries. The returns to human capital have considerably increased as compared to the pre-transition period, and young cohorts can expect reward levels for skills that approach—or are comparable to—the returns in Western European countries (e.g., Munich et al. 1999; Newell and Reilly 2000; Orazem and Vodopivec 1995; Rutkowski 1996). In contrast, there has been a decline in the returns to experience for low-educated people. As a result, poverty is particularly common among the low educated and those having more than two children (Grootaert and Braithwaite 1998; Milanovic 1998).

POSTPONEMENT AS A RATIONAL RESPONSE TO
SOCIOECONOMIC INCENTIVES

Based on the sketch we have just given in regard to socioeconomic background, we must now consider the individual-level determinants of delayed childbearing in lowest-low fertility countries. In particular, an important commonality of the socioeconomic context in lowest-low fertility countries is a high level of economic uncertainty in early adulthood. This uncertainty provides an incentive to delay decisions that imply long-term commitments, such as the decision to have children, and it provides an incentive to invest in education and human capital.

In the Southern European countries, the uncertainty is basically due to youth unemployment and/or job instability. High unemployment risks simultaneously lower the opportunity costs of pursuing higher education and create incentives for education due to the increased employment opportunities. Higher education has thus become the primary pathway for individuals to increase their chances of finding a stable job with a sufficient wage (Lassibille et al. 2001; Sá and Portela 1999). In the CEE countries, the uncertainty is due to the overall economic insecurity and hardship caused by the transition. Moreover, the economic transition has increased the returns for education. The combination of these factors has rendered human capital investments very attractive, since these investments provide insurance against poverty and enable access to more stable employment with relatively high salaries. The main problem in attaining education faced by individuals in Eastern Europe is that the opportunity costs may be too high in some of the poorest countries. Parents may have problems financing higher education of their children, since they are also affected by the transition, and credit constraints may preclude access to loans in order to cover tuition and consumption during studies.

The university enrollment ratios in table 2.3 reflect the drastic increase in higher education in Southern European countries, where half of the women pursued university studies in the late 1990s. Central and Eastern European countries share this general trend toward increased enrollment ratios, particularly for women. Estonia, Slovenia, Latvia, and Bulgaria have strongly increased their enrollment ratios to levels comparable to Western countries. The levels in the Czech Republic, Hungary, and Romania have also increased, but since these countries started at much lower levels, they are still lagging behind. The only deviations from the trend toward increased higher education are among the former Soviet republics.

A comparison of the evolution of university enrollment with the mean age at childbearing is very illuminating. The countries with marked increases in higher education tend to be identical to the countries with the most pronounced delays in the mean age at first birth. This association between delays in childbearing and increases in individuals' human capital investments is consistent with our hypothesis: increasing returns to education induce young adults—and particularly young women—to study for a longer time in the expectation that this improves their ability to cope with the economic uncertainty and to take advantage of the new opportunities created during the transition period. Exceptions to this general pattern seem to be concentrated among countries where the economic situation is worst, and where the coping strategy of higher education and human capital investments is not accessible for important fractions of the population. In addition to the human capital motive for delaying childbirth, the very unstable standards of living in Eastern Europe also lead to a strategic postponement in which children—and similar decisions implying long-term commitments—are deferred in the expectation that the uncertainty about future prospects is reduced over time.

Changes in social policy are an important additional factor in the former socialist countries. In the socialist period, many countries had developed a system of incentives that rewarded early childbearing, for instance via easier access to housing and paid maternity leave. These incentives resulted in a reduced age at motherhood, especially during the 1980s (Frejka 1980; Zakharov and Ivanova 1996). During the 1990s, many of these benefit structures have ended, or eroded due to inflation, or were modified, and this fact has also contributed to the postponement of motherhood in the last decade.

A further determinant of the postponement/low-fertility nexus is the delay of childbearing in association with investments in housing and durables. This is especially relevant in Italy and Spain, where the interference of childbearing with educational investments has been much reduced due to the delay of parenthood to very late ages. In these countries, the preponderance of owned property in the housing market and the restricted rental market induces young people to stay at home with their parents until their financial resources are adequate for paying the mortgage (Duce Tello 1995). Since this can take several years after entry into the labor market, the situation can lead to delays in childbearing substantially beyond the completion of higher education.

SOCIAL FEEDBACK EFFECTS ON THE
TIMING OF FERTILITY

The focus on individuals' incentives that render delayed childbearing more advantageous is not sufficient to understand the fertility change in contemporary Europe and other developed countries. In particular, we believe that important social feedback mechanisms reinforce individuals' behavior changes respecting socioeconomic conditions, particularly changes in the timing of fertility. Social feedback exerts important influences on the dynamics of the fertility postponement for at least three reasons (Kohler et al. 2000; Montgomery and Casterline 1996): social learning about the optimal timing of fertility, social feedbacks mediated through the marriage market, and social feedbacks through competition in the labor market.

Social Learning about the Optimal Timing of Fertility

The optimal timing of fertility is a highly complicated problem for women or couples, especially in the context of uncertainty and changing socioeconomic environments. Social learning provides a possibility to simplify and augment decision-making in this context. Childbearing and career experiences of friends are therefore likely to influence women's and couples' decisions about the timing of fertility. For instance, interaction with others can provide information about questions like "How did classmates who had their first child relatively early fare in terms of career and partnership?" and "What is the divergence in social and economic attainment between those who had their children early and those who had them later?" In addition to this possibility to learn from others, social learning also implies an aggregate-level feedback mechanism. In particular, in a population that delays childbearing, social learning from others implies that the experience of friends having children is revealed at an increasingly later age. A woman at some given age, say age 25, therefore faces more uncertainty about the advantages and disadvantages of childbearing in a population that exhibits a late pattern of childbearing than does an identical woman in a population with early childbearing. Higher uncertainty in turn implies a further incentive to delay childbearing. Social learning therefore implies a multiplier effect that reinforces the impact of socioeconomic changes that lead to delayed patterns of childbearing.

Social Feedbacks Mediated through the Marriage Market

In many lowest-low fertility countries, partnership formation and marriage are inherently connected with the transition into parenthood. This is particularly the case in Italy and Spain, where out-of-wedlock childbearing is still relatively rare, premarital cohabitation is not widespread, and the trend toward late childbearing is associated with late home-leaving and late union formation (De Sandre 2000; Delgado and Castro Martín 1998). An important demographic implication of this trend toward late union formation is the induced shift in the composition of potential mates in the marriage market. While the traditional literature on marriage squeezes emphasizes the effect of differential cohort sizes (see, for example, Goldman et al. 1984; Grossbard-Shechtman 1985), similar implications are caused by changes in the age distribution of union formation. In particular, a general delay of partnership formation in the population reduces the marriage market "costs" encountered by individuals who delay marriage/cohabitation: first, it increases the probability of finding a partner at later ages, for instance after finishing more extended education; and second, it increases the expected "quality" of marriageable partners at older ages because the marriage market will be "thicker" and contain more potential mates at any given age.

Socioeconomic changes that provide incentives for delayed childbearing, for instance higher returns to female education or technological innovations facilitating fertility control, therefore affect the timing of marriage in a twofold manner: via a direct effect on individual's incentives to delay, and via an indirect effect through the reduction in the costs of delaying marriage/cohabitation for individuals. The latter aspect again gives rise to a social multiplier effect. (For a formal analysis and application to the United States, see Goldin and Katz 2002.)

Social Feedbacks through Competition in the Labor Market

A further potentially relevant mechanism of social interaction is competition in the labor market that is caused by the presence of high unemployment. In this situation, the labor market can give rise to a social multiplier effect, quite similar to the mechanism operating through the marriage market mentioned above. (For a related formal model, see Kohler 2001, chap. 6.) In particular, social interaction reinforces the effect of unemployment and economic uncertainty toward delayed childbearing. This social multiplier effect arises because women with children tend to have lower labor supply than women without children, especially in those low and lowest-low fertility countries with inflexible labor markets and insufficient supply of day care. In this situation, a delay in childbearing in the population increases the level of childlessness among women at the primary ages for entering the labor market. This increased childlessness leads to an increased female labor supply, which in turn increases the competition and unemployment risks during early adulthood. The postponement of fertility caused by unemployment during early adulthood is therefore exacerbated through a feedback process that increases the overall female labor supply in the age groups that are most affected by economic stress.

It is our contention that, as a result of these social feedback mechanisms, the delay of childbearing follows a postponement transition that shares many characteristics of the fertility transition in Europe or contemporary developing countries (see, for example, Bongaarts and Watkins 1996). This notion of a postponement transition is substantiated in figure 2.9. In this figure, we define the year of onset of the postponement transition as the first in a group of three years during which the mean age at first birth increases by more than .3 years. Within lowest-low fertility countries, this year of onset ranges from 1978

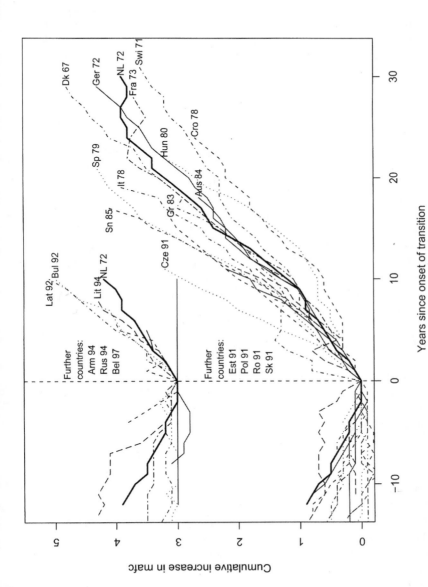

Figure 2.9. Onset and pace of the postponement transition in European countries.
Note: Graph includes all European countries in tables 1.1–1.2, with exception of Andorra, Bosnia and Herzegovina, Moldova, Ukraine, and United Kingdom for which adequate data are missing.
Source for data: Council of Europe (2003); for country codes, see Table A.1.1.

(Italy) to 1994 (Lithuania, Armenia) and 1997 (Belarus) (see table 2.2). The horizontal axis in figure 2.9 plots the years since the onset of the postponement transition, and the vertical axis depicts the change in the mean age at first birth since this onset. In order to avoid a cluttering of the graph, we display some CEE countries with a very recent onset in a subgraph. In addition we include several other European countries for comparison. Particularly interesting in this context is the Netherlands, representing a Western European country with an early onset of the postponement transition (1972) and a moderately high total fertility rate (1.73 in 2002).

Figure 2.9 reflects the substantial increases in the mean age at first birth in lowest-low fertility countries that we have emphasized throughout this chapter. Importantly, the standardization of the time-scale in figure 2.9 reveals several key characteristics that seem to be inherent in the question of postponement of fertility. First, the onset of delayed childbearing in low and lowest-low fertility countries is a break with an earlier regime that is characterized by relative stability in first-birth timing. Second, once initiated, postponement transitions tend to be persistent and irreversible, leading to large changes in the mean age at first birth. Third, the broad characteristics of the postponement transition are similar across a wide range of socioeconomic conditions. For instance, the paths for all countries with an onset of the transition up to 1991—that is, Austria, Croatia, Czech Republic, Denmark, Estonia, France, Germany, Greece, Hungary, Italy, Netherlands, Poland, Romania, Slovakia, Slovenia, Spain, and Switzerland—trace each other closely. This similarity occurs despite the fact that these countries represent very different socioeconomic conditions in Europe, including very different patterns of post-1990 economic crises in Eastern Europe and very different levels in the mean age at first birth prior to the postponement transition. For countries with an onset of the transition after 1993, it is still very early to make inferences about the path of the postponement transitions, but it seems likely that they will follow the other lowest-low fertility countries.

The postponement transition toward late childbearing regimes that we have discussed is in our opinion likely to occur in many European and other developed countries and can therefore be seen as a further step in a long-term transformation of fertility and related behaviors. In particular, our discussion suggests that the long-term trend toward low and lowest-low fertility in Europe is related to three distinct transition processes: the first, demographic transition leading to parity-specific stopping behavior within marriage; the second, demographic transition resulting in ideational changes and in the rise of nonmarital family forms; and most recently, the postponement transition that shifts the timing of fertility toward a late childbearing regime. The postponement transition is therefore a third step that follows the control of marital fertility and the transformation of partnership behaviors, and it implies a delay of parenthood toward later age as the combined result of individual incentives for late child-bearing and social interaction effects that reinforce this trend.

It is also clear that the upper age-limit for childbearing prevents substantial future postponement without changing the age-pattern of parity-specific fertility rates. Yet, in many CEE countries with still relatively early child-bearing, the postponement of birth, even at relatively rapid annual rates such as an annual increase in the mean age at first birth by .2, can continue for at least two to three decades until they reach the late age patterns of fertility currently observed among Northern and Southern European countries. In Western and Southern European countries with an already very late age pattern of childbearing, a differential postponement of fertility across age groups can continue for a considerable time. For instance, borrowing a popular idea on human longevity, one may foresee a rectangularization of fertility patterns. This rectangularization, which needs not only to be a feature of lowest-low countries but of all below-replacement fertility countries, is characterized by a concentration of childbearing in an increasingly narrow age interval. In this scenario, few women will have children prior to, say, age 28 or 29, and child-bearing at parity one and two will be concentrated when women are in their 30s. There will be very few higher parity births, especially among women with a late onset of childbearing.

DETERMINANTS OF THE QUANTUM IN LOWEST-LOW FERTILITY COUNTRIES

There is quite widespread agreement in the literature that lowest-low fertility countries share an institutional setting that implicitly favors a relatively low quantum of fertility. For instance, the lowest-low fertility countries in Southern Europe, Italy and Spain, provide highly insufficient child-care support (Esping-Andersen 1999). In the 1980s, for instance, the share of children below age three with day-care coverage in Southern Europe was 4.7 percent, compared to 9.2 percent in Continental Europe (Austria, Belgium, France, Germany, and the Netherlands) and 31.0 percent in the Nordic countries (Denmark, Finland, Norway, and Sweden) (Esping-Andersen 1999). The labor market is also relatively inflexible in terms of possibilities for part-time work or reentering the labor force after an absence due to childbirth (Del Boca 2002; González et al. 2000; Stier et al. 2001). This hinders the combination of female labor force participation and childbearing. In comparison with other Western European countries, Italy and Spain also have among the lowest levels of state support for families with children in terms of tax allowances or direct transfers (Esping-Andersen 1999). While this deficit is partially compensated for through strong family networks, as for instance through the provision of child care or economic resources by grandparents (Reher 1997), the substitution of family support for public support is likely to be insufficient in contemporary industrialized countries. Moreover, the high integration of young adults in their parents' home and extended family may even discourage union formation and fertility (Dalla Zuanna 2001).

Family roles in the Southern European lowest-low fertility countries have also been slow in adapting to the new role of women (Chesnais 1996). Italy and Spain have highly asymmetric labor divisions within households, which becomes even more asymmetric after the birth of the first child (Palomba and Sabbadini 1993). The countries therefore conform to McDonald's (2000a) argument about gender equity: fertility falls to very low levels when gender equity rises in individual-oriented institutions, like the labor market, while it remains low in family-oriented institutions.

The moderate and very low quantum in Eastern Europe is in part determined by similar institutional factors hindering high parity progression probabilities. In addition, many of the pronatalist—or at least family friendly—policies in CEE countries were discontinued after 1990 (Macura 2000), and an economic crisis has caused a particular deterioration in the high integration of women in the labor market. Furthermore, Eastern Europe is characterized by a persistence of economic insecurity throughout the life course. This is in contrast to Southern Europe, where unemployment and economic stress are concentrated during early adulthood years. In Eastern Europe, the uncertain long-term outlook regarding unemployment, the housing situation, and economic recovery imply that uncertainty not only affects the timing of the first birth but also the transition to the second child and higher parity children.

While the institutional context we have discussed—at least in Southern Europe—has been relatively constant in recent decades, its effect on the quantum of fertility has not. In particular, the effect of this institutional context needs to be investigated with an explicit attention to the rapid postponement that has transformed the age pattern of entering parenthood in lowest-low fertility countries. Specifically, the delay of childbearing has been associated with substantially increased investments in higher education for females (see table 2.3). Similarly, labor-market experience prior to marriage and parenthood are likely to be higher for women with late childbearing than for women with early fertility. A direct consequence of these increased levels of female human capital and labor market experience at the time of childbirth is an increase in the opportunity costs of childbearing in terms of foregone wages.

Such a relation between the timing of fertility and the wage level (measured around first childbirth) is depicted by the broken line in figure 2.10a. The wage level in figure 2.10a has been standardized so that it equals *one* for women with an early onset of parenthood. The level increases with a later age at first birth because the delay in childbearing is generally associated with higher levels

a) Wages, child-costs, and compatibility of fertility and female labor force participation

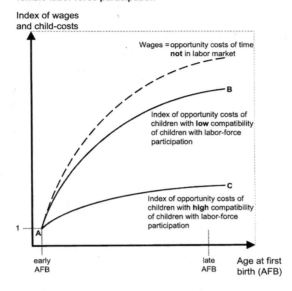

Index of wages and child-costs

Wages = opportunity costs of time **not** in labor market

B

Index of opportunity costs of children with **low** compatibility of children with labor-force participation

C

Index of opportunity costs of children with **high** compatibility of children with labor-force participation

1 ··· A

early AFB   late AFB   Age at first birth (AFB)

b) Postponement effect and compatibility of fertility and female labor force participation

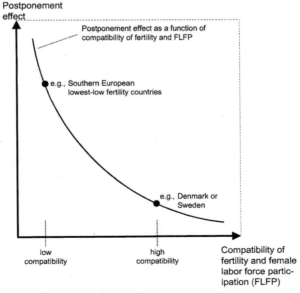

Postponement effect

Postponement effect as a function of compatibility of fertility and FLFP

e.g., Southern European lowest-low fertility countries

e.g., Denmark or Sweden

low compatibility   high compatibility   Compatibility of fertility and female labor force partic- ipation (FLFP)

Postponement effect = (relative) decline in completed fertility associated with an additional delay of childbearing by one year

Figure 2.10.   Postponement of fertility, wages, and child-costs.

of human capital and labor market experience that are rewarded in the labor market. The rise in wages increases the opportunity costs of time spent outside the labor market, and it increases the costs of time-intensive "goods" such as children. The opportunity cost, however, is not as high as the wage level, since there can be some labor force participation. In particular, women with late childbearing can substitute away from "own" child care and into "purchased" child care, such as kindergarten and household help. The implication of this is that the opportunity costs of children increase less steeply with delayed childbearing than does the index of wages. (For the moment we ignore other costs of children that may potentially depend on the age at first birth, such as health costs during pregnancy.)

The extent of this difference between wages and opportunity costs of children, however, depends on the compatibility of childbearing with female labor force participation. In a country with a low compatibility, the ability to arrange flexible part-time work, or the ability to find a position that can be combined with institutional day care, is limited. Hence, the scope for the above substitution from time at home to time in the labor market is restricted. The postponement-induced increase in wages therefore translates into substantial increases in the opportunity costs of children, including also the opportunity costs of additional children after the first child (see line *AB* in figure 2.10a). These higher child costs will tend to reduce the quantum of fertility and the parity progression probabilities after the first birth.

If there is a high compatibility of childbearing and female labor force participation, wage increases associated with late childbearing lead to more modest increases in the opportunity costs of children (see line *AC* in figure 2.10a). In particular, women will be able to shift relatively flexibly their time allocation from time at home to time in the labor market, and this substitution diminishes the effects of increased wages on child costs. In addition, with high levels of female labor force participation there can also be a positive income effect on the demand for children.

The differences between countries with high and low compatibility of work and children have important implications for the causal effects of delayed childbearing on the quantum of fertility. In particular, the higher human capital associated with delayed childbearing translates directly into increased opportunity costs of children. This effect is especially relevant when it is combined with the large delays in childbearing that occur during the postponement transition. In such cases, the postponement-induced increases in child costs are likely to imply substantial declines in an individual's demand for children of birth order two and higher.

Socioeconomic conditions that provide incentives for individuals to delay childbearing, such as uncertainty in early adulthood, therefore indirectly increase the costs of children and have an indirect negative impact on the desired number of children. This effect is particularly strong in the context of inflexible labor markets and insufficient availability of day care that characterizes Southern European lowest-low fertility countries. Moreover, this effect is likely to constitute one of the key reasons why postponement effects, which measure the reduction in completed fertility due to an additional year of delay in parenthood, are particularly strong in Southern Europe (Kohler et al. 2002), and it explains the "falling behind" of cumulated cohort fertility at higher ages in Italy and Spain, as compared to countries such as the Netherlands or Denmark that have combined late childbearing without important reductions in cohort and period fertility (Billari and Kohler 2004).

In summary, the above discussion suggests that the postponement of fertility is not neutral with respect to the quantum of fertility. Quite to the contrary, there is a negative association, and the magnitude of this negative effect of delayed parenthood on the quantum of fertility depends mainly on the compatibility of work and children (figure 2.10b). On the one hand, countries with low compatibility between female labor force participation and childbearing, such as Italy and Spain, are subject to large postponement effects. These countries therefore experience substantial reductions in completed fertility that are causally related to delayed childbearing. On the other hand, in countries with a high compatibility of work and children, as for instance Denmark or Sweden, the increased costs of time at home associated with delayed parenthood can be partially accommodated by increasing the labor force participation. These countries are therefore likely to have a smaller postponement effect, and late childbearing in itself does not imply strong reductions in the quantum of fertility. The above analyses also suggest that differential postponement effects—as depicted in figure 2.10b—constitute an important determinant of the differential reductions in second and higher order fertility in European countries as a result of delayed childbearing. Differences in these postponement-quantum interactions are therefore likely to be an important factor underlying the divergence of fertility levels between low and lowest-low fertility countries in Europe that we emphasized in our beginning section.

THE FUTURE OF LOWEST-LOW FERTILITY—SOME SPECULATIONS

Three questions seem to be of central importance in assessing the future of lowest-low fertility. First, is lowest-low fertility a permanent, long-term phenomenon or is it merely a transient phenomenon that will disappear from the demographic landscape in the near future? Second, has lowest-low fertility already reached its lowest levels, or are future declines in fertility likely? Third, is the emergence of lowest-low fertility likely to be a widespread phenomenon, or will it remain restricted to regions such as Southern, Central, and Eastern Europe, where this pattern is currently concentrated?

Our evaluation of the future of lowest-low fertility indicates that this pattern is unlikely to be a short-term phenomenon that will quickly disappear from the demographic landscape. In our opinion, lowest-low fertility is likely to be a persistent pattern, at least for several decades. We expect that it will prevail for a considerable period in the CEE countries with a TFR below 1.3. In addition, we believe that lowest-low fertility is likely to spread in the near future to several other countries that currently experience a TFR between 1.3 and 1.4 (see tables 2.1 and 2.2). These European "lowest-low fertility candidates" include, for instance, Austria, Germany, Switzerland, and several Central/Eastern European countries like Poland, Lithuania, Slovakia, Russia, and Croatia, comprising overall a population of 248 million people. It is also likely that fertility will decline further in some countries that have already very low levels of fertility. In particular, several Eastern European countries and former Soviet republics have experienced TFR levels below 1.3 without a pronounced postponement of fertility (figure 2.9). Once the pace of fertility postponement in these countries increases, it is likely to depress fertility levels further, perhaps even to TFR levels below 1.0.

At the same time, the periods with the most rapid pace of postponement may have already passed in Southern European lowest-low fertility countries. Annual increases of the mean age at first birth may thus start to decline in the next years, resulting in a possible reversal of fertility trends in Italy and Spain. Some first signs of this pattern are already visible. In the last few years, the Italian and Spanish TFRs have recovered from their troughs of 1.20 (Italy, 1995–1996) and 1.17 (Spain, 1996), and the total fertility rate in both countries increased to 1.3 by 2003. This recovery has been associated with a decline in the pace of fertility postponement during the late 1990s (figure 2.11). A similar reduction occurred in Western and Northern European countries with very advanced ages of childbearing, while Central European and Baltic countries took the lead in the pace of postponement toward the late 1990s—albeit at a younger mean age at first birth than their Western, Northern, and Southern European counterparts (Sobotka 2004b; see also table 2.2).

In a global perspective, it is in our opinion unlikely that lowest-low fertility will remain restricted to Europe. Particularly, Southeast Asian countries might cross the lowest-low barrier. Two important countries, Japan and Korea, joined the group of lowest-low fertility countries during 2000–2003 (tables 2.1 and 2.2; Suzuki 2003), and the regions of Hong Kong and Macao were already experiencing lowest-low fertility levels during the 1990s. These countries are potentially forerunners in a spread of very low fertility levels to Southeast Asia. A recent study on low fertility in urban China (Zhao 2001) has also shown that the one-child policy reduced the total fertility rate of urban China to a level of

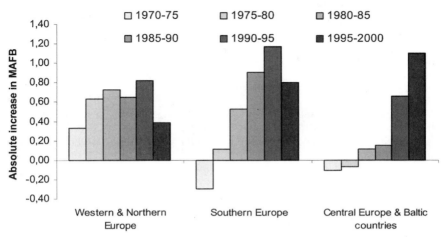

Figure 2.11. The increase in the mean age at first birth in European regions since 1975.
Source: Sobotka (2004b).

1.15 starting in 1980, and the Chinese urban population may already constitute one of the largest lowest-low fertility populations worldwide.

U.S. VERSUS EUROPEAN FERTILITY: WHAT EXPLAINS THE DIFFERENCE?

In striking contrast to the projected population shrinkage due to low fertility and negative population momentum in Europe, the U.S. population continues to be characterized by rapid growth (figure 2.3). Almost 33 million people were added to the U.S. population between 1990–2000, corresponding to a growth of 13 percent during the 1990s, making it the greatest absolute 10-year population increase in U.S. history. The majority of this growth in recent years is attributed to natural increase—that is, an excess of birth over deaths—while net immigration accounted for about 40 percent (Kent and Mather 2002). Moreover, population growth was concentrated in the southern and western parts of the United States. Slow population growth on the state level is primarily concentrated in the northern and eastern parts of the United States, and population decline during the period 1990–2000—mostly as a result of migration losses—occurred almost exclusively in certain rural counties stretching across the Great Plains states from the Mexican border to the Canadian border (U.S. Census Bureau 2001). The U.S. population is also projected to grow by almost 50 percent in the coming decades until 2050 (table 2.5), including a

Table 2.5   Projected Population of the United States, by Race and Hispanic Origin, 2000 to 2050

Population and race or Hispanic origin	2000	2010	2020	2030	2040	2050
Total	282,125	308,936	335,805	363,584	391,946	419,854
White alone	228,548	244,995	260,629	275,731	289,690	302,626
Black alone	35,818	40,454	45,365	50,442	55,876	61,361
Asian alone	10,684	14,241	17,988	22,580	27,992	33,430
All other races[a]	7,075	9,246	11,822	14,831	18,388	22,437
Hispanic (of any race)	35,622	47,756	59,756	73,055	87,585	102,560
White alone, not Hispanic	195,729	201,112	205,936	209,176	210,331	210,283

Notes:
[a] Includes American Indian and Alaska Native alone, Native Hawaiian and other Pacific Islanders alone, and two or more races.
Source: U.S. Census Bureau, "U.S. Interim Projections by Age, Sex, Race, and Hispanic Origin," www.census.gov/ipc/www/usinterimproj/. Internet release date: March 18, 2004.

7 percent growth in the white non-Hispanic population, a 188 percent increase in the Hispanic population, and a 213 percent increase in the Asian population.

While the divergence of fertility trends between the United States and Europe is well known, resulting in predictions about a growing "demographic marginalization" of Europe within the global population (see, for example, Demeny 2003; *Economist* 2002a,b), it is somewhat surprising that the high level of current and projected U.S. fertility is not comparable to that of Canada. Although the United States and its northern neighbor share a long border and overlapping cultures and similar socioeconomic contexts, Canada's total fertility rate was just 1.5 children per woman in 2000, compared with the United States' rate of 2.1. Canada's fertility is more in line with that of Europe, Japan, and Australia than with that of the United States. The most recent divergence in fertility rates between the United States and its northern neighbor originated in the mid 1970s, when fertility in both countries declined to about 1.8. In contrast to the United States, however, where the total fertility rate edged back up to 2.1, the Canadian rate never recovered from the 1970 Baby Bust. Moreover, while minority populations in the United States—especially Hispanic immigrants—have higher fertility rates than many of the minority groups in Canada, the higher fertility rate of blacks and Hispanics by itself explains only about 40 percent of the differences in total fertility rates (Belanger and Ouellet 2002; Kent and Mather 2002).

A frequently cited explanation for higher American fertility is that the United States is more racially and ethnically diverse than other more developed countries. The largest U.S. minority groups tend to have higher fertility than the white non-Hispanic majority, and foreign-born women tend to have higher fertility than U.S.-born women. Because minorities and immigrants make up an increasing share of the U.S. population, these racial and ethnic differences may keep fertility at the same relatively high level for decades to come. Still, the racial and ethnic diversity of the United States explains just part of the fertility gap between the United States and other developed countries. The TFR for non-Hispanic whites was about 1.8 for most of the 1990s, and inched up to 1.87 in 2000—lower than the TFR for Hispanics and blacks, but still higher than the rate in other more developed countries.

The key to understanding the relatively high U.S. fertility seems to lie in the relatively young age pattern of fertility, the only modest pace of fertility postponement, and the relatively high compatibility of childrearing and labor force participation (Morgan 2003; see also tables 2.1 and 2.2). In terms of day care for children, U.S. business and volunteer organizations have been increasing the availability of child care, with federal and state governments playing a relatively minor role in that regard (Rindfuss et al. 2003). Also, family use of child care is viewed positively in the United States. The proportion of all U.S. adult respondents agreeing that "a preschool child suffered if the mother works" declined from 68 percent in 1977 to 48 percent in 1991; for women of childbearing age, it declined from 73 percent in 1970 to 34 percent in 1991 (Rindfuss et al. 1996). By comparison, in West Germany in 1996, 76 percent of the adult population said that they thought small children suffered when their mothers went to work (European Commission 1998).

The nature of the job market is also an important factor in the level of fertility rate. One strategy available to parents is that of staggering their working hours so that at any given time only one parent is working. In 1997, among dual-earner U.S. couples with children under 14 years of age, 31 percent were found to include at least one parent who worked other than a fixed daytime, Monday through Friday schedule (Presser 1999). And a related matter has to do with the hours when grocery and other stores are open. In many countries, there has been a shift toward stores staying open longer hours, thus making it easier for working parents to shop for necessities. In addition, based on a review of available time-use data for developed countries, Joshi (1998) reports that additional hours in paid work for women are counterbalanced by fewer hours spent on home production tasks and, to a lesser extent, by declines in leisure time and sleep. Such a pattern is particularly pronounced in the Nordic countries, the United Kingdom, and the United States. As a result of this high degree of flexibility in the U.S. labor market, American women are found to exit the labor market after the birth of a first child for much shorter periods than is the case for German women or women in other low fertility countries (Diprete et al. 2003; see also Adsera 2004). Government aid in countries such as Germany often make up for a substantial part of this difference, but the net costs of children tend to remain smaller for American women due to their exits from the labor market. Indeed, greater cost and longer exits from the labor force are more associated with lower rates of first birth in West Germany than in the United States. High unemployment and market rigidities also make the reentry into the labor market after a maternity leave more difficult in Germany (or Europe) as compared to the United States, and career-oriented women who are aware of such difficulties may choose not to have children—or to have fewer children—rather than risk their careers through child-related disruptions in their labor market participation.

In summary, we ask again: why is America different? The United States has a much higher total fertility rate than other developed countries. Recently, the United States has also experienced stronger productivity growth, much higher levels of immigration, but lower life expectancy, than European countries. Other important differences include the facts that Americans work more hours per week, take shorter vacations, tend to retire at older ages, and experience a much lower incidence of long-term unemployment. It could be argued that U.S. fertility trends simply trail behind Europe and Japan temporarily, and that the TFR in the United States will fall to historically low levels in future years, as has occurred in so many other wealthy countries in recent decades. However, the situation in the United States compared to most other high income countries differs in at least two respects (Technical Panel on Assumptions and Methods 2003). First, population composition favors a higher fertility level, since some of the largest immigrant and minority groups within the United States have fertility levels that are higher than the national average. For example, the TFR among Hispanics in the United States was 2.75 in 2001, 35 percent higher than the national average of 2.03. The TFR of 2.10 for non-Hispanic blacks in the same year was slightly above the national level, while non-Hispanic whites, Asians/Pacific Islanders, and American Indians had below average fertility levels. Since Hispanics and non-Hispanic blacks together comprise roughly a quarter of the U.S. population, their higher fertility levels are an important source of the nation's relatively high TFR. Second, U.S. fertility generally is relatively high. Notably, the TFR of non-Hispanic white women, which averaged 1.77 to 1.87 during the period 1990–2001, is above the national average for most other high-income countries.

The heterogeneity of the U.S. population is therefore one factor that contributes to the relatively high level of fertility in the United States. But it does not constitute the primary explanation. Instead, an overriding factor is greater ability of U.S. women to combine work and childbearing, thanks to a variety of institutional factors. In general, women (and couples) are deterred from having children when the economic cost—in the form of lower lifetime wages—is too high. In the United States, compared to other high-income countries, this cost is diminished by an American labor market that allows more flexible work hours and makes it easier for women to leave and then reenter the labor force. The importance of this factor is shown by the positive relationship between measures of women's labor force activities and levels of fertility across wealthy countries in recent years (figure 2.8). Thus, it appears that, despite a lack of U.S. public financial support for families with children, the flexibility offered to individuals through the market facilitates integration of work and traditional family life.

HOMEOSTATIC RESPONSES TO LOW FERTILITY

In light of the striking contrast between European and U.S. fertility trends, it is essential to ask: Which processes or policy interventions might reverse Europe's low fertility? While policies targeted at increasing the number of children born to women and couples must be considered, and such options will be discussed in the next section, we must first ask: Is it possible that low fertility will reverse itself without policy intervention? The leading economic model suggesting this possibility is the so-called "Easterlin hypothesis" (Easterlin 1980), which predicts an inverse relation between cohort sizes and fertility level. In particular, this theory predicts that—under conditions of restrictive immigration—declining cohort sizes result in higher levels of fertility because young adults in small cohorts experience easier transitions into the labor market due to lessened competition. This is potentially relevant for the European low fertility context, since persistent lowest-low fertility not only leads to a rapid aging of the population, with well-known problems for social security and related government assistance programs, but also to substantially reduced relative cohort sizes. For instance, the first lowest-low fertility cohorts born early in the 1990s in Italy and Spain are about 41 percent smaller than the cohorts born 25 years earlier. In the next 10 to 20 years, when these smaller cohorts begin higher education, or begin to enter the labor and housing markets, they are likely to face substantially more favorable conditions than their older predecessors of 25 years before, who have contributed importantly to the emergence of lowest-low fertility in the 1990s.

Such a positive effect of cohort size, first proposed by Easterlin in the context of the U.S. Baby Boom (see Easterlin 1961), seems particularly likely, given the limited international migration into lowest-low fertility countries. Positive experiences in the labor and housing market during early adulthood may contribute to an increase in both period and cohort total fertility rates. This is speculative, of course, but smaller cohort size may nevertheless be important, since it is likely to be one of the few demographic factors with homeostatic implications that could lead to a reversal of lowest-low fertility.

POLICY RESPONSES TO LOW AND
LOWEST-LOW FERTILITY

Government policies are a possible alternative to the speculative self-correcting mechanisms just discussed. Various terms are used to describe governments' attempts to influence demographic developments such as population aging. Most commonly, these government interventions are referred to as "population policy" and can include measures that are designed to have an impact on the population structure, of which birthrate or fertility rate is the most prominent indicator. Many authors also employ the term "family policy" to emphasize that government policies often do not aim at specific goals in terms of the population size and structure, but are concerned with family well-being and resultant activities that are directed toward families with children. Although the policy objectives of both terms seem to differ considerably—family on the one hand and population on the other—the actual definitions of family policy and population policy do not make clear distinctions. Since family policies are an integral part of welfare-state policies, it is also useful to draw on the literature on European welfare-state regimes in reviewing and classifying family policy in Europe.

According to Esping-Andersen (1999), European countries can be grouped into four distinct welfare-state regimes according to the intentions of their social policies and the principles on which they are based: "universalistic welfare states" (the Nordic countries), "conservative welfare states" (continental European countries), "liberal welfare states" (Anglo-Saxon countries), and—somewhat contested—"Southern European welfare states" (Mediterranean countries). Universalistic welfare states are characterized by welfare-state policies that are targeted at individual independence and social equality between individuals (not families). Conservative welfare states direct their welfare-state policies toward status maintenance and the preservation of traditional family forms, and they often rely heavily on familialism—that is, on the family as a provider of welfare. Liberal welfare states encourage market-based individualism through minimal social benefits and through subsidizing private and marketized welfare schemes, and social benefits are usually means tested and poverty related. The Southern European welfare states are often considered part of the conservative welfare-state regimes; but their stronger familialism merits them being viewed as a separate welfare-state regime (Neyer 2003).

While different welfare regimes embrace very different philosophies and fertility-related welfare policies, the different regimes are only weakly associated with differential fertility levels in Europe: the Nordic countries with their universalistic welfare regimes tend to have relatively high fertility in Europe, and the Southern European welfare regime is associated with lowest-low fertility. The Anglo-Saxon welfare regime is associated with moderately high fertility, while the conservative welfare regimes comprise a wide spectrum of fertility levels including ranging from Germany (TFR = 1.31 in 2001) to France (TFR = 1.89 in 2002).

The largest pressures to respond with policy changes to low and lowest-low fertility currently exist in the conservative and Southern European welfare regimes. The specific population or family policies that have been proposed in this context can be classified in two ways (Grant et al. 2004). First, they can be classified as preventive policies aimed at affecting the demographic behaviors that are believed to lead to adverse outcomes. These preventive policies can be indirect, such as economic policies, gender policies, and education policies, or direct, such as migration policy, family support, reproductive health policy, and family-friendly employment policies. Second, specific population or family policies can be classified as ameliorative policies aimed at accommodating or ameliorating the consequences of low fertility, population decline, and population aging. These policies would include, for instance, social security reform, labor force policy, health care policy, or policies dealing with the elderly.

Various preventive and ameliorative policy responses to low and lowest-low fertility have been widely discussed and are often the subject of heated debate. A detailed discussion of these policies is beyond the scope of this chapter. Instead, we will focus our discussion on two specific subsets of the overall policy responses to population aging in Europe: immigration and policies directed toward increasing the level of fertility.

IMMIGRATION

European countries have long depended on immigrants to supply labor in times of economic prosperity. In recent years, however, while removing restrictions to mobility within the European Union, European governments have tightened controls over immigration from outside the EU. This has lead to various complex and often uncoordinated systems of incentives and disincentives to influence international flows of population. Contemporary immigration policy in Europe is thus aimed at restricting the number of new immigrations and limiting the perceived "social discohesion" that is thought to come with them; such policies usually have no direct population objectives (Grant et al. 2004). The impact of contemporary European policy on population dynamics is, nonetheless, quite relevant and significant, and such policy has resulted in quite distinct international migration patterns among the European countries.

International migration policies and patterns are almost certain to change as a result of European population aging and population decline. But it is appropriate to ask whether a policy favoring increased immigration would ameliorate the consequences of very low fertility with respect to population growth, working-age population growth, and changes in the support ratio. The United Nations (2000) in their report on replacement migration concluded that the potential of immigration to substitute for domestic births is rather limited. Replacement migration refers to the international migration that would be needed to offset declines in the size of population and working-age population, as well as the overall aging of a population. A key finding of the UN report is that if retirement ages remain essentially where they are today, increasing the size of the working-age population through international migration is the only short- to medium-term option for reducing declines in the support ratio. However, such a policy would not reverse the process of aging.

In table 2.6, the first column shows the numbers of migrants assumed for the UN medium-variant population projection (see also figures 2.3 to 2.5). For example, the total number of migrants for the United States for the 50-year period 2000–2050 is 38 million, and the average annual number is 760,000. For

Table 2.6 Replacement Migration in Europe: Total Immigrants for Period 2000–2050 and Average Annual Number of Immigrants for Different Replacement Goals (in thousands)

Scenario	1	2	3	4
	Medium variant	Constant total population	Constant age group 15–64	Constant ratio of 15–64 to 65 years or older persons
A. Total number for period 2000–2050				
France	325	1,473	5,459	89,584
Germany	10,200	17,187	24,330	181,508
Italy	310	12,569	18,596	113,381
Russian Federation	5,448	24,896	35,756	253,379
United Kingdom	1,000	2,634	6,247	59,722
United States	38,000	6,384	17,967	592,572
Europe	18,779	95,869	161,346	1,356,932
European Union	13,489	47,456	79,375	673,999
B. Average annual number for period 2000–2050				
France	7	29	109	1,792
Germany	204	344	487	3,630
Italy	6	251	372	2,268
Russian Federation	109	498	715	5,068
United Kingdom	20	53	125	1,194
United States	760	128	359	11,851
Europe	376	1,917	3,227	27,139
European Union	270	949	1,588	13,480

Source: United Nations (2000).

Europe, the total immigration is 18.8 million, and 376,000 annually. Except for the United States, the numbers of migrants needed to maintain the size of the total population (second column in table 2.6) are considerably larger than those assumed in the medium variant of the UN projections. In Italy, for example, the total number of migrants in the medium variant is 12.6 million (or 251,000 per year) versus 0.3 million (or 6,000 per year). For the European Union, the respective numbers are 47 million versus 13 million (or 949,000 per year versus 270,000 per year). In order to keep the working-age population (15 to 64 years) at a constant size, the numbers of migrants needed would be even larger (third column in table 2.6). In Germany, for instance, the total number of needed migrants would be 24 million (or 487,000 per year) in order to maintain a constant working age population, versus 17 million (or 344,000 per year) that would be necessary to maintain a constant overall population size. Expressed in terms of migrants per million inhabitants in 2000, Italy would require the highest number of immigrants—at 6,500 annual immigrants per million inhabitants, in order to maintain its working-age population, followed by Germany, with 6,000 needed annual immigrants per million inhabitants; the United States would require the smallest number of immigrants, approximately 1,300 per million inhabitants. Finally, the numbers of immigrants necessary to keep constant the ratio of those age 15–64 to those age 65 or older—that is, the support ratio—are extraordinarily large (fourth column in table 2.6). For the European Union, the total number required would be 674 million (or 13 million per year), and for Italy, the figure would be 113 million (or 2.3 million per year).

Most analysts consider the levels of immigration that would be required to keep the population size, the size of the labor force, or the support ratio at a constant level as unrealistic for Europe. Therefore, immigration to Europe—even if its level increases in future decades—is unlikely to prevent population and working-age decline and rapid population aging, particularly in European countries with very low fertility levels. Still, it does seem likely that increases in immigration levels—even if they do not prevent population aging and decline—will be a widespread response of low fertility European countries, in combination with measures to increase the level of fertility, discussed below. Furthermore, internal migration within an enlarging European Union is likely to become more important in this context; in particular, internal EU migration is likely to contribute to population aging and decline in migrant-sending countries, as well as to ameliorate population aging and decline in migrant-receiving countries. While the most important migrant-sending countries within the European Union will also experience declines in population size and are unlikely to be long-term sources of migrants, the potential future joining of Turkey to the European Union will likely substantially affect migration streams, due to Turkey's relatively young age structure and substantial projected population growth.

POLICIES TO INFLUENCE FERTILITY

The only viable long-term strategy to limit the extent of national population aging and the decline of population size will be an increase in the level of fertility. Several such policies are already in place—although not always with an explicit goal to increase fertility (Grant et al. 2004). In particular, especially in Western Europe, governmental efforts to affect fertility have been generally implicit policy measures to influence family formation decisions with financial incentives, such as tax exemptions, or to provide family-friendly facilities, such as for child care. Explicit population policies directed at increasing fertility, also called "pronatalist" policies, are less common in European countries. In the past, pronatalist policies were widely implemented in the former socialist regimes of Eastern Europe as part of a strict procreative goal; currently, explicit policies intended to boost fertility, or at least to prevent it from falling, are pursued in some other European countries, such as France.

Despite the small number of countries that pursue explicit pronatalist policies, a growing number of countries in Europe view their low birthrates, with the resultant population decline and aging, as a serious crisis that could jeopardize the basic foundations of the nation and threaten its survival (Chamie 2004; Stark and Kohler 2002, 2004). Attempting to raise birthrates, governments are thus increasingly seeking to address the underlying causes of low fertility and to adopt policies, programs, and incentives to encourage couples, and women, to increase their childbearing. Maternity and paternity leave, child care, after-school programs, part-time employment, job security, and cash allowances and other financial incentives are among the measures that have been adopted or are being seriously reviewed by governments. Growing governmental concerns about fertility decline, and resultant consequences, are shown by a number of recent magazine and newspaper articles that quote leading national politicians (Chamie 2004). For example, France is reported to be offering a monetary reward for each new baby: "The French Prime Minister, Jean-Pierre Raffarin, announced last week that a bonus of 800 Francs ($895) will be awarded mothers for each baby born after January 1, 2004. The bonus is part of a series of measures to encourage families to have more children" (*British Medical Journal*, May 10, 2003). Italy is also offering cash to boost its birthrate: "The 2004 budget package includes a one-time one-thousand-Euro ($1,200) payment to Italians on the birth of their second child, a measure set to run from December 1 until the end of 2004. . . . Mayor Rocco Falivena, of Laviano, digging deep into town coffers, is offering couples ten thousand Euros ($11,900) for every newborn baby" (*Reuters*, December 7, 2003). The government of Estonia has also taken steps: "Worried about a declining population, Estonia's president has urged the country's 1.4 million residents to make more babies. 'Let us remember that in just a couple of decades the number of Estonians seeing the New Year will be one-fifth less than today,' President Arnold Ruutel said in

Table 2.7 Government Views on the Level of Fertility and Policies on Fertility Level

Year	Number of countries	Percentage			
Government views on the level of fertility					
		Too low	Satisfactory	Too high	Total
1976	29	24	76	0	100
1986	29	31	69	0	100
1996	43	42	56	2	100
2003	43	63	37	0	100
Policies on the level of fertility					
		Raise	Maintain	Lower	No intervention
1976	29	24	24	0	52
1986	29	28	21	0	52
1996	43	37	9	2	51
2003	43	47	9	0	44

Source: United Nations (2004).

a speech broadcast live on national television Wednesday" (*New York Times*, January 2, 2003).

A more detailed look at how countries perceive their national fertility levels is provided in table 2.7. Between 1976 and 2003, the proportion of European countries that viewed their level of fertility as *too low* increased from 24 percent to 63 percent, reflecting a sharp shift away from an approving assessment of fertility patterns. During the same period, the proportion of countries with a policy aimed at raising fertility levels increased from 21 percent to 44 percent. Countries reporting having a policy of "no intervention" included Germany, Italy, Norway, Portugal, Spain, and Switzerland; these countries, however, do have family or social policies that may lead to higher fertility, although they are not labeled pronatalist. The remaining European countries have implemented a broad range of policies and measures to raise fertility levels.

Looking forward, McDonald (2000b) has proposed the following comprehensive "toolbox" of public policies to impact low and lowest-low fertility:

Financial incentives:
- *Periodic cash payments*, usually in the form of regular payments to parents for each child.
- *Lump-sum payments or loans*, including payments at the time of birth of a baby (baby bonus, maternity benefit), at the time a child starts school, or at some other age.
- *Tax rebates, credits, or deductions* based on the presence of a child.
- *Free or subsidized services or goods*, including education at all levels, medical and dental services, public transport, and recreation services such as sports, entertainment, leisure, or artistic activities.

- *Housing subsidies*, including periodic cash payments such as housing benefits, lump-sum cash payments as first-time home-buyer grants or mortgage reductions at the birth of each child, tax rebates or deductions for housing costs, or subsidies to housing-related services.

Work and family initiatives:

- *Maternity and paternity leave*, including the right of return to a position following leave related to the birth of a child.
- *Child care*, including the provision of free or subsidized child care as part of the family-friendly employment policies, including for those who are not employed.
- *Flexible working hours* and short-term leave for family-related purposes.
- *Anti-discrimination legislation* and gender equity in employment practices.

Broad social change supportive of children and parenting:

- *Employment initiatives that improve the job prospects of young men and women*, especially also in the part-time sector.
- *Child-friendly environments*, including traffic calming, safe neighborhood policies, public recreational facilities such as playgrounds, and provision for children in places of entertainment and in shopping centers in order to build a child-friendly environment.
- *Gender equity*, including non–gender-specific workplace policies, gender-neutral tax-transfer policies in social insurance, support of workers with family responsibilities irrespective of gender, removal of institutional remnants of the male breadwinner model of the family, acceptance of fathers as parents by service providers, and more general recognition and support to fathers as parents.
- *Marriage and relationship supports*, including the provision of greater encouragement in the formation of relationships, relationship education, relationship counseling, and possibly economic incentives to marry, such as through housing assistance.
- *Development of positive social attitudes toward children and parenting*, including a clear and simple message that people desiring children will be supported by society without creating inequities to the childless, voluntary or involuntary.

In addition to these policies, there are many alternative policy suggestions aimed at increasing fertility levels. Policy proposals are abundant, albeit not always realistic in the face of limited government resources. Recent examples that expand beyond the above toolbox, for instance, include tempo policies that aim at reducing the pace of fertility postponement, or perhaps even reversing the trend (Lutz et al. 2003; Lutz and Skirbekk 2004), a proposal to restructure the Italian system of transfers so that each newborn child becomes an "account holder" that receives and gives transfers throughout life (Livi Bacci 2004), and linking fertility and economic security at old age (Demeny 1987).

The above policy proposals to impact fertility are comprehensive, ambitious, and potentially also controversial in terms of a country's welfare-state philosophy. Some elements of the proposals will, however, almost certainly be implemented in European low fertility countries, or, if already implemented, extended. Nevertheless, it is important to keep in mind that, even if some of these population policies are implemented and are effective in terms of increasing individual and couple fertility, future declines in the number of women, and couples, in childbearing ages will limit their impact on the number of births and on population aging (see also Demeny 2003). Figure 2.12, for instance, shows the number of European women in primary ages of childbearing (age 20–35) for Europe, the United States, Bulgaria, Denmark, France, Germany, Italy, and the Russian Federation (based on UN median projection, year 2000 = 100). In Europe and in all the European countries included in figure 2.12, the number of women in primary childbearing ages is projected to decline between the years 2000 and 2040. This decline is close to 35 percent for Europe, and it exceeds 50 percent in Italy and Bulgaria. Moreover, the decline until about 2025 is

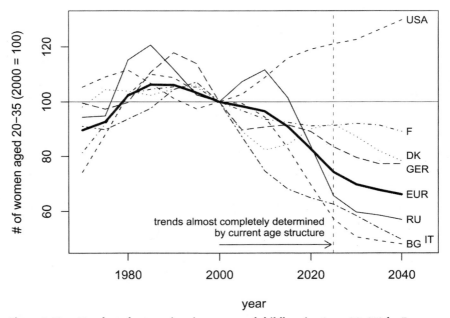

Figure 2.12. Number of women in primary ages of childbearing (ages 20–35) for Europe, United States, Bulgaria, Denmark, France, Germany, Italy, and the Russian Federation (year 2000 = 100, based on UN medium projection).

almost completely determined by the current age structure of the population (except for migration). Thus, it can be implied that the annual number of births would continue to decline, even if government fertility policies resulted in large increases in the number of children born per woman. This negative population momentum (Lutz et al. 2003) occurs because low fertility levels result in successively smaller birth cohorts, and past periods of low and lowest-low fertility were already manifest in the population age structure in 2000 (see figures 2.4 and 2.5). Of course, females who were not born during a period of low fertility in the past will not become mothers 20 to 35 years later; the negative population momentum thus reinforces the effect of low fertility. As a result of this negative momentum that is already built into the current European population age structure, fertility policies—even if effective on the individual level—will potentially have only a limited effect on slowing population aging or on reversing the decline of the population size.

EVALUATION OF CURRENT POPULATION POLICIES

Several evaluations of the effect of family and population policies on the level of fertility have been conducted in recent years (see, for example, Gauthier 1996, 2002; Gauthier and Hatzius 1997; Grant et al. 2004; Pampel 2001; Sleebos 2003), although virtually all of these studies fall short of a sophisticated policy evaluation based on experimental studies. Keeping this important limitation in mind, there seems to be a consensus among studies that family and population policies have only a moderate and long-term effect. For instance, Sleebos (2003) concludes that the impact of any specific policies on women's or couple's reproductive decisions depends on a broad range of factors, and detailed studies are necessary to evaluate these policies. A qualitative assessment, based on the currently available empirical evidence, of the effectiveness of various policies for changing fertility behavior in OECD countries is given in table 2.8. Some studies have documented that the impact of family policies is more significant on the timing of fertility than on the total number of children achieved over a full reproductive cycle (Barmby and Cigno 1990; Ermisch 1988). Several studies reviewed in Sleebos (2003) investigated the effect of family cash benefits on total fertility rates and suggested a weak but positive relation; the estimated impact, however, was small. Gauthier and Hatzius (1997) estimate that a 25 percent increase in family allowances would increase fertility rate by about 0.6 percent in the short run, and by about 0.4 percent in the long run—that is, an increase in the total fertility rate of 0.07 children per woman. Several studies for Austria, Canada, Hungary, Italy, the Netherlands, Norway, Sweden, and the United States all conclude that work/family reconciliation measures, such as maternity or parental leave and child-care subsidies, have

Table 2.8   Qualitative Findings from Empirical Studies on the Impact of Policies on Fertility

	Total fertility rates	Timing of births	Specific birth order	Age of mothers	Other individual characteristics
Family cash benefits	Small positive effects in most countries		Contradictory results on whether effects of policies are larger for first or subsequent births	Small positive effects, or contradictory results, on the effects of welfare benefits on teenage births (but evidence limited to few countries)	Some evidence that effects of policies differ among ethnic groups
Tax policies	Positive effects in the US and Canada	Larger effects of policies on the timing of births than on completed fertility			
Family-friendly policies	Positive effect of part-time and flex-time work; weak or contradictory effects of maternity leave		Small or no effect on probability of having a first child		
Child-care availability	Positive effect, weak in some countries				Some evidence that effects of child-care availability and costs differ according to the employment status of mothers

Source: Sleebos (2003).

a positive impact on fertility. Again, the estimated effect is small. Hyatt and Milne (1991) estimate that a 1 percent increase in the real value of maternity benefits would increase total fertility rate in Canada between 0.09 percent and 0.26 percent. In contrast, Gauthier and Hatzius (1997) report that neither the duration nor the benefits provided by maternity leave explain much of the variation in total fertility rates across OECD countries.

Availability of jobs suited to the needs of mothers favors fertility. Castles (2003) reports a positive link between the percentage of employees working flex-time and total fertility rates across OECD countries. Del Boca (2002) also finds in Italy a positive relationship between availability of part-time jobs and fertility rates, and Adsera (2004) finds that a large amount of public employment, by providing employment stability, and generous maternity benefits linked to previous employment, such as those in Scandinavia, boost fertility of women age 25–34.

Results of the impact of child care on total fertility rates also vary, partly depending on the form of child care. Some studies have documented a strong positive relationship between total fertility rates and formal child-care availability (for example, Castles 2003; Rindfuss et al. 2004), particularly for children below the age of three, while other analyses have found no effect of child-care availability on a decision to have a first child (Hank and Kreyenfeld 2000). These inconsistent findings about the availability of child care may in part be due to a lack of control in existing studies for the determinants of child-care provision. In an important recent study that addresses this limitation, Rindfuss and others (2004) use fixed-effect analyses of child-care availability data from 1973 to 1997 for Norway's 435 municipalities, and show a strong, statistically significant, positive effect of child-care availability on the transition to motherhood. In addition, utilizing a "natural experiment" provided by the introduction of a policy in Spain that provides working mothers with a monthly child-care benefit amounting to 100 euros for each small child, Sánchez-Mangas and Sánchez-Marcos (2004) show that the introduction of this policy resulted in an increase in the labor participation of mothers with small children. For low- and medium-educated women, for which the policy seems to be most effective, more than 40 percent of the 3.5 percentage-point increase in Spanish female labor force participation during 2002–2003 can be attributed to the policy change.

In summary, the studies reviewed in Sleebos (2003) provide mixed conclusions as to the effects of various policies on fertility behavior. Similar conclusions were obtained also in other evaluations of family/population policy effectiveness (Gauthier 1996; Grant et al. 2004). On balance, Sleebos (2003) concludes that the evidence supports a weak positive relation between reproductive behavior and a variety of policies. Moreover, an important conclusion from the study is that policy measures that may potentially affect reproductive behavior will manifest their influence only in the long term. Thus, a consistent application of different measures over time is likely to be more important than abrupt introduction of big pronatalist measures, which might be reversed at some later stage. Moreover, policies targeted at an increased compatibility between childbearing and labor force participation, as well as policies aimed at reducing uncertainty in early adulthood due to high unemployment and related factors, are most promising in our opinion, based on the theoretical framework and empirical evidence provided in this chapter. Finally, consistent also with our assessment of policy effectiveness and the existence of a negative population momentum, Sleebos (2003) concludes that policy-makers should not expect too much from pronatalist policies, and knowledge about the effects of policies and their complementarities in many areas is still too limited to guide the design of cost-effective interventions.

CONCLUSION

Low and lowest-low fertility is likely to be a considerable challenge for many developed countries in the next decades. Our analyses in this chapter allow us to draw some first conclusions about the causes and implications of, and potential policy responses to, low and lowest-low fertility in Europe. First, our portrait of contemporary European fertility patterns identifies a systematic pattern of lowest-low fertility that is characterized by a rapid delay of childbearing, a low progression probability after the first child (but not particularly low levels of first-birth childbearing), a "falling behind" in cohort fertility at relatively late ages (in Southern Europe), and a reversal in the relative ranking of lowest-low fertility countries in a European comparison of total fertility levels (Billari and Kohler 2004). At the end of the 1990s, therefore, there emerges a clear clustering of European nations, separating them into countries with low fertility levels and countries with lowest-low fertility, and this clustering is mirrored in many fertility-related behaviors, such as women's labor force participation, the diffusion of cohabitation or out-of-wedlock childbearing, and other dimensions.

Second, lowest-low fertility countries are themselves heterogeneous and cluster into two distinct patterns. On the one hand, Southern European lowest-low fertility countries, including foremost Italy and Spain, exhibit latest-late home-leaving behavior, a limited spread of nonmarital cohabitation, a low share of extramarital births, a limited diffusion of divorce, and a relatively low share of women participating in the labor force. These countries also exhibit a more marked postponement of first births and a lower recuperation of fertility at higher ages. On the other hand, Central and Eastern European countries exhibit relatively earlier household independence and union formation. These countries also have higher nonmarital fertility and divorce rates, and first births take place earlier than in Southern European lowest-low fertility countries.

Third, we have argued in the previous sections that lowest-low fertility, defined as a period TFR below 1.3, is caused by a combination of the following demographic and socioeconomic factors:

- *Socioeconomic incentives to delay childbearing* that make postponed fertility a rational response to high economic uncertainty in early adulthood, increased returns to education, shortages in the labor market, and similar factors.
- *Social feedback effects on the timing of fertility* that reinforce the adjustment of an individual's desired fertility to socioeconomic changes. In particular, social feedback effects can give rise to postponement transitions that lead to rapid, persistent, and generally irreversible delays in childbearing across a wide range of socioeconomic conditions.
- *Institutional settings*, characterized by labor market rigidities, insufficient child-care support, and a prevalence of relatively traditional gender roles, favor an overall low quantum of fertility and lead to reductions in completed fertility that are causally related to the delay in childbearing.

The postponement of fertility therefore does not only lead to a delayed pattern of childbearing. It also implies important negative effects on the quantum of fertility and on completed fertility, and this effect is particularly strong in the institutional context that is characteristic of lowest-low fertility countries. While the above factors are not necessarily unique to lowest-low fertility countries, we believe that lowest-low fertility countries are characterized by a combination of all three factors in a particularly pronounced fashion. Lowest-low fertility is therefore the outcome of an interaction of demographic and behavioral factors that each in itself would lead to lower fertility. In combination and interaction, however, these factors reinforce each other and lead to lowest-low fertility. It is also noteworthy that substantial childlessness has not been a driving force leading to reduced fertility in the group of countries currently classified as lowest-low fertility countries.

Fourth, the emergence of lowest-low fertility during the 1990s has been accompanied by a disruption or even a reversal of many well-known patterns that had formerly been used to explain cross-country differences in fertility patterns. For instance, the cross-sectional correlations of European countries between total fertility level on the one hand, and the total first marriage ratio, the proportion of extramarital births, and the female labor force participation ratio on the other, have reversed during the period from 1975 to 2001–2002 (see table 2.9). In 2002, there no longer was evidence that divorce levels were negatively associated with fertility levels. Hence, there have been crucial

Table 2.9   Total Fertility, Total First Marriage Ratio, Total Divorce Ratio, and Proportion of Extramarital Births in Europe

	Total fertility		Total first marriage ratio		Total divorce ratio		Proportion of extramarital births	
	1975	*2002*	*1975*	*2002*	*1975*	*2002*	*1975*	*2002*
Andorra	–	1.36	–	–	–	–	–	–
Armenia	2.79	1.21	–	0.37^i	0.15	0.06	2.80	13.20
Austria	1.83	1.40	0.75	0.50	0.20	0.45	13.50	33.80
Azerbaijan	3.92	1.58	0.83	0.57	–	0.11	5.20	7.60
Belarus	2.20	1.22	–	0.68	–	0.50^i	7.40	21.40
Belgium	1.74	1.62	0.89	0.46	0.16	0.54	3.10	0.21^e
Bosnia and Herzegovina	2.38	1.23	0.69^b	–	–	–	5.60	10.60
Bulgaria	2.22	1.21	1.00	0.47	0.15	0.21	9.30	42.80
Croatia	1.92	1.34	0.82	0.69	0.13	0.16	4.90	9.60
Czech Republic	2.40	1.17	0.99	0.48	0.30	0.46	4.50	25.30
Denmark	1.92	1.72	0.67	0.73	0.36	0.47	21.70	44.60
Estonia	2.04	1.37	0.94	0.42	0.50^b	0.48	15.70	56.30
Finland	1.68	1.72	0.70	0.64	0.26	0.50	10.10	39.90
France	1.93	1.89	0.86	0.59	0.17	0.38^i	8.50	43.70^i
Georgia	2.52	1.42	0.99^b	0.32^i	–	0.08	0.20	45.90
Germany	1.48	1.31	0.81	0.54	0.25	0.42^i	8.50	25.00^i
Greece	2.32	1.25^i	1.16	0.52^h	0.05	0.16^g	1.20	4.30^i
Hungary	2.35	1.30	1.00	0.47	0.24	0.42	5.60	31.40
Iceland	2.65	1.93	0.79	0.58^i	0.26	0.40^h	33.00	62.30
Ireland	3.43	2.00	0.94	0.59^f	–	–	3.70	31.10
Italy	2.21	1.27	0.95	0.62	0.03	0.12^i	2.60	9.70^h
Latvia	1.97	1.24	1.01	0.44	0.52	0.37	11.70	43.10
Lithuania	2.18	1.24	1.01	0.54	0.42^a	0.41^i	6.20	27.90
Luxembourg	1.55	1.63	0.80	0.50	0.10	0.51	4.20	23.20
Macedonia	2.71	1.77	0.86	0.77^i	0.09	0.09	6.60	10.70
Malta	2.17	1.46	–	0.73^i	–	–	1.10^b	15.00
Moldova	2.52	1.21	1.11^b	0.58	–	0.39	8.00	20.50^h
Netherlands	1.66	1.73	0.83	0.59	0.19	0.37	2.10	29.10
Norway	1.98	1.75	0.80	0.47	0.21	0.46	10.30	50.30
Poland	2.26	1.24	0.93	0.57	0.15	0.18	4.70	14.40
Portugal	2.75	1.47	1.39	0.66	0.02	0.39	7.20	25.50
Romania	2.60	1.26	0.97	0.66	0.20	0.20	3.50	26.70
Russian Federation	1.97	1.32	1.03	0.60^d	0.38	0.43^d	10.70	29.50
Serbia and Montenegro	2.33	1.71^i	0.81	0.66^i	0.12	0.14^i	9.90	20.20^i
Slovakia	2.53	1.19	0.94	0.50	0.18	0.33	5.20	21.60
Slovenia	2.17	1.21	0.99	0.43	0.15	0.25	9.90	40.20
Spain	2.80	1.25	1.05	0.59^i	0.04^c	0.15^e	2.00	17.70^h
Sweden	1.77	1.65	0.63	0.49	0.50	0.55	32.80	56.00
Switzerland	1.61	1.40	0.65	0.65	0.21	0.40	3.70	11.70
Ukraine	2.02	1.10	–	–	0.34	0.38	8.80	19.00
United Kingdom	1.81	1.64	0.87	0.54^h	0.30	0.43^f	9.00	40.60

Notes: a = 1970; b = 1980; c = 1981; d = 1996; e = 1997; f = 1998; g = 1999; h = 2000; i = 2001.
Source: Council of Europe (2003).

changes in the relationship between traditional determinants of fertility—such as marriage, divorce, home-leaving, and women's labor force participation—and fertility *before* and *after* the emergence of lowest-low fertility. Perhaps most importantly, there is a clear indication that a high prevalence of marriage and institutionalized long-term partnership commitments are no longer associated with higher fertility in cross-sectional comparisons. While the detailed analysis of the determinants of this reversal is beyond the scope of this chapter, one fundamental cause can probably not be disputed: the reversal in cross-sectional associations between fertility and related behaviors is in part due to the different demographic factors driving fertility change. Initially, the decline toward low fertility was importantly related to stopping behavior, that is, a reduction of higher parity births. More recently, the postponement of fertility—particularly for first births—has emerged as a crucial determinant of differences in fertility levels among developed countries.

Fifth, the relatively high overall fertility in the Unites States, near replacement levels, cannot be fully explained, as is often done, by the higher fertility of Hispanic and African American subpopulations. Instead, the key to understanding the relatively high U.S. fertility lies in the relatively young age pattern of fertility and the only modest pace of fertility postponement, as well as in a relatively high compatibility between childrearing and labor force participation or other opportunities/constraints on fertility. This high compatibility is not the result of extensive welfare-state policies targeted at families and children, but of a market-based system that combines a very flexible labor market, flexible work schedules, privately supplied day care, and high female labor force participation.

Sixth, the policy options available to European low and lowest-low fertility countries are limited. The existing empirical evidence provides mixed conclusions as to the effects of various policies on fertility behavior. On balance, the evidence supports a weak positive relation between reproductive behavior and a variety of policies, but policy measures that may potentially affect reproductive behavior manifest their influence only in the long term. Policy measures that aim to make women's participation in the formal labor force compatible with childrearing are in our opinion among the most promising alternatives. The effectiveness of such measures, however, is likely to be limited due to a negative population momentum that results from decades of below-replacement fertility in many parts of Europe since the 1960s and 1970s. Even if policies are effective in raising women's or couple's fertility, and even if levels of immigration into Europe increase, a loss of demographic weight within the global population, a decline in the population size during the coming decades, and a substantial aging of the population are therefore safe predictions for the Europe of the twenty-first century (Demeny 2003). It is clear that current social and economic programs and institutions are not sustainable in light of these trends, and an individual's life courses already have been—and will continue to be—transformed in response to reductions in fertility and increases in longevity. Adjusting to the demographic reality of the twenty-first century will therefore constitute a major challenge for policy-makers and companies on the one hand, and for individuals and families on the other. Whether an adjustment to these trends will be successful and whether the trends lead to a reduced well-being of individuals, if appropriate policies are implemented, are still open questions.

Part II

THE UNITED STATES AND THE BABY BUST

3

The U.S. Baby Bust in Historical Perspective

Herbert S. Klein

In many ways, the term "Baby Bust" as applied to the United States is an anomaly, because the fertility decline this country has experienced since 1964 has followed closely long-term secular trends in American fertility. In fact, the Baby *Boom* of the 1946–1964 period was the deviant experience; the Baby Bust was to be expected, however abrupt and steep the transition to lower fertility, which dropped below replacement for the U.S. white majority in 1972. The exuberance of fertility in the immediate post–World War II period was an exceptional phenomenon, quickly replaced by long-term trends that would leave the native-born U.S. population below replacement fertility level (2.1) at the beginning of the twenty-first century, tracking the norm for most advanced industrial societies of the world.

There is little question that the U.S. fertility decline from 1964 to the present was part of a systematic secular trend that went back to the early nineteenth century (see figure 3.1). The United States, in contrast to most of the world's population, experienced fertility decline well before the decline of mortality. The so-called Demographic Transition model, which postulated that fertility only began a secular decline after a secular decline in mortality, was not the norm for the American population. American birthrates, which had been high by Western European standards in 1800, slowly declined by 1900 to the relatively low fertility rates of most of the Western European countries at that time. There were temporary spurts of high fertility, as for example just after the Civil War, but these had little impact on the trend. Although there were initially regional and racial differences in birthrates, most of these differences progressively declined over the course of the nineteenth century. Consistently, the western frontier birthrates of native-born Americans—which were the highest nationally—declined over time to the levels of the low eastern seaboard native

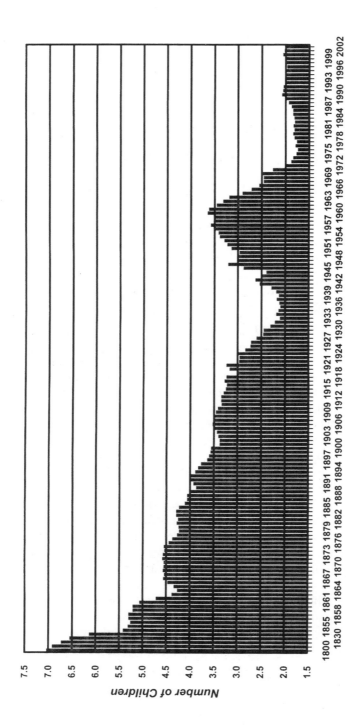

Figure 3.1.   Total fertility rate for the U.S. white population, 1800–2002.
Sources: Coale and Zelnik (1963), table 2; and from 1960 to 2002, CDC, *National Vital Statistics Reports* 52, no. 17 (March 18, 2004): 7.

U.S. populations. Equally, all immigrant groups arrived with higher fertility rates than the native-born populations, and they quickly adapted to the lowest fertility patterns of the native born, by the second generation. Finally, even high African American birthrates declined over time, though they did not reach native-born white rates.

From 1900 to 2005, this same secular decline in fertility continued and matched that of all the advanced industrial nations of the world, although the Great Depression of 1929–1940 represented a slight deviation from the trend, as severe economic conditions forced couples to produce fewer children than desired. The combination of economic and military constraints forced fertility below desired levels to 1945. The post–World War II economic boom, and the delayed childbearing caused by war and economic depression, were factors that explained the short-term deviation of fertility trends known as the Baby Boom of 1946–1964, when fertility rose significantly and the age of first marriage and first births to married women fell to their lowest levels in the modern period.

Many have argued that historically unique factors created the Baby Boom. New postwar government social and educational programs, tremendous economic growth with new levels of occupational mobility, and the rise of a suburban housing market all encouraged higher than historical trends in birthrates. As the rates of occupational mobility returned to the norm, and the desired family sizes were reached, the next cohort of women entering the marriage market quickly reverted to long-term trends. The age of first marriage for women went back to the higher pre-1940 norms and has slowly increased in every year since 1960. Equally, the average age of mothers at first births has also risen every year since 1960.

What is even more impressive about the post-1960 period is that fertility has declined consistently, even as marital fertility has lost its role as the primary determinant of national fertility rates. Traditionally, out-of-marriage births had been well below 10 percent of all births in the United States, as in most Western European countries prior to the middle of the twentieth century. But beginning in the period of the Baby Bust, not only have fertility rates returned to long-term trends, but the origins of births has changed profoundly as never before in our history. What is revolutionary, in fact, about the post-1960 fertility is not the level of fertility, but that fertility is being carried out within a rapidly changing family structure. The rise of single-parent households and the secular rise in births outside marriage are parts of a social change that is new to the United States, though the phenomenon has been occurring at roughly the same time in most advanced industrial nations. But even despite the real revolution in the role of the family in fertility, births within and outside marriage continue to decline.

FERTILITY IN THE NINETEENTH CENTURY

In 1800, the United States still had very high fertility—higher in fact than the Western European countries. The crude birthrate was estimated to be approximately 55 births per thousand resident population in 1800, which was equivalent to a total fertility rate of just over seven children per woman who had completed her fertility. At this time, most of the Scandinavian countries and the United Kingdom had a crude birthrate in the upper 20s and lower 30s per thousand population. By 1860, this same resident white population in the United States had reduced its birthrate to 42 per thousand births and lowered its total fertility rate to 5.2 children, a decline of over a quarter (Haines 2000; Coale and Zelnik 1963). This was still a third higher than the equally declining French rate (at 3.5 children total fertility), but was closing on the relatively high English fertility rate of 4.9 children at that time (Chesnais 1992).

This long-term decline of fertility occurred in a nation that was almost 80 percent rural and one that experienced a death rate that was either stable or rising. In Europe, only France went through this process of declining fertility rates preceding any serious decline in mortality. Almost all other major Western European nations imitated the English example, which maintained stable birthrates for most of the nineteenth century and only began to experience declining fertility long after mortality had begun to decline. Thus, the United States and France differed from the pattern that demographers have labeled the "Demographic Transition" and which was the experience of most world populations from the nineteenth century to today. In this transition in the advanced European states, death rates declined and stabilized at lower than fertility rates in the late eighteenth and early nineteenth centuries for a variety of reasons related to better nutrition and sanitation. The experience of declining mortality occurred in the developing countries in the mid twentieth century and was due both to better sanitation and nutrition and to the use of modern medicines after 1950. Initially, the resident population experiencing this change usually maintains its traditional high levels of fertility that were associated with higher levels of mortality. It is only after two or three generations that the growing rate of natural increase of the local population—reaching 2 percent per annum in the developed countries of Europe in the nineteenth century, and over 3 percent per annum in the developing countries in the late twentieth century— leads most people to begin restraining fertility. As pressure slowly builds on land and resources because of the increasingly rapid growth of the population, natives respond by reducing their fertility rates, which in turn leads to a decline in the natural growth rates. This was the pattern in Europe from the late nineteenth to the early twentieth century and was repeated in the developing world countries from the mid twentieth century until the early decades of the twenty-first century. Here, the model society used is England, where increasing urbanization and population density led the local population to begin to curtail fertility only in the last quarter of the nineteenth century, long after its late eighteenth-century decline in mortality.

Demographers have suggested that the initial pre-1860 fall in fertility in both France and the United States was related to the increasing pressure of population on land and agricultural resources. The adoption of partible inheritance under the Napoleonic codes and the increasing subdivisions of agricultural properties are suggested as possible causes in the French situation, along with the long and massive wars suffered by the French in the late eighteenth and early nineteenth century. Paradoxically, declining land availability is also suggested as the primary cause in the case of the United States. Though the American frontier was ever expanding, the majority of the population resided in the old eastern seaboard states, and there, available land resources were on the decline. It was estimated that population density in the original 13 colonies in 1790 was just nine persons per square mile. By 1820, this had doubled to 20 persons per square mile and doubled again to 42 persons per square mile by 1860. In contrast, the new frontier areas added to the Republic by the 1810s held less than one person per square mile, and those added subsequently to 1860 never reached the density of the original 13 colonies in 1790. This density reflects a declining availability of agricultural land that in turn was the primary factor affecting fertility before the Civil War. After 1860, both in France and the United States, the continuing decline in fertility is tied more to the traditional causes suggested in the classic model; increasing urbanization and industrialization in both countries raised the costs of children in terms of housing and education, at the same time that more possibilities for consumption opened for adults in the industrializing world.

In the pre-1860 period, when the rural population was still well over 80 percent in the United States, the response of eastern seaboard residents to increasingly limited land resources was to marry later and leave a higher ratio of women outside the marriage market. The former action resulted in the decline in marital fertility. This decline in fertility, first noted as early as the late eighteenth century in New England, began to appear in the Middle Atlantic colonies in the nineteenth century. On the frontiers, early marriage and high marital fertility were still the norm, but this ever moving frontier population made up only a small share of the total national population and did not seriously influence the national figures. Not all regions experienced fertility decline at the same rate. The Middle Atlantic colonies received the most foreign immigrants, and these foreign-born immigrants had higher fertility rates than the native born. Thus, the rate of decline was slower there than in New England. Of the older coastal seaboard regions, the South declined the least, falling mortality rates somewhat making up for a declining fertility, and reproductive rates remained above the national average for the entire period to 1860.

It should be stressed that fertility in the United States, although declining, was still quite high and positive. Its decline, however, quickly translated into lower natural growth rates. In the 1800–1810 period, the rate of natural increase in the resident white population was estimated at 2.92 percent per annum—a rate that even today would be considered high for a rapidly growing, developing nation—but this rate dropped slowly but steadily to 1.99 percent in the decade of 1850–1860. Had it not been for immigration, it is estimated that the 1860 population in the United States would have been a quarter smaller than it was on the eve of the Civil War, but it would still have grown impressively (Klein 2004, chap. 3).

By the late nineteenth century, as the United States industrialized and the urban population became ever more important, fertility decline accelerated and finally reached Western European levels by the last decade of the century. Whereas the total fertility dropped 25 percent from 1800 to 1855, it declined by a third between 1855 and 1900. The post–Civil War decline in fertility is now thought to have been more related to the demand for education, housing, and employment that was associated with increasing urbanization and industrialization then occurring in the North American society and economy. The escape valve of the frontier migrations, with their usually higher rates of fertility, was coming to an end, and the frontier would cease to exist altogether by the end of the century. The increasing density of western settlement began moving western population fertility rates toward those of the eastern seaboard. The movement of the national population off the farms and into the cities was also beginning to affect rates of reproduction quite dramatically, as was true in the rest of the industrialized world. Whereas land tenure was considered the most important factor influencing the trend in declining rates in the first half of the nineteenth century, by the second half of the century these new factors of urban residence and nonfarm occupations were beginning to be more important.

Though there was the usual spike in postwar birthrates in the late 1860s and early 1870s, general fertility rates thereafter continued their long-term secular decline for the rest of the century. This declining fertility rate of native-born whites was somewhat compensated for by the arrival of European immigrants, who now accounted for between a third and a quarter of the total growth in the national population in the last quarter of the nineteenth century. Although immigrants tended to have higher birthrates than native North Americans in the first generation of arrivals, the experience in the nineteenth and twentieth century was that by the second generation, their birthrates approached that of the natives. Given their relatively modest importance within the national population, foreign-born first-generation residents had only a moderate effect on long-term fertility trends. The same can be said for the African American fertility rates, which remained higher than that of the whites throughout the nineteenth century (see figure 3.2) but which accounted for only a small proportion of total births, since African Americans represented only 14.1 percent of the population in 1860 and just 11.6 percent in 1900. By the late 1870s, the total fertility rate in the United States dropped to 4.5 children per woman and finally and permanently reached a rate at or below that of the advanced European countries and in line with England itself. The only exception, and a unique one, was that of France, which had the advanced world's lowest rates of reproduction for the entire century (see figure 3.3).

But the question that is difficult to answer for the nineteenth century is how this change in fertility actually occurred. Given the fact that births outside marriage remained low in all Western societies in the nineteenth century, marital fertility was the crucial area in which change occurred. In populations where contraception was not being systematically practiced, one way of reducing fertility was to raise the age of marriage for women and have more women reach the end of their fertile years without being married, thus eliminating several years of potential fertility and reducing the number of potential mothers. From small samples of nineteenth-century population, this seems to have been the case in the earlier period but not in the second half of the nineteenth century. It would appear that the age of first marriage for women was moderately rising throughout most of the nineteenth century, though the ratio of women never married was relatively stable. Nevertheless, it has been estimated that three-quarters of the decline in fertility in the nineteenth century came from changes in marital fertility rates (due to changes in child spacing and the earlier termination of fertility among married women), and only about a quarter was due to changes in marriage rates—that is, in the age of marriage and the ratio of women ever married (Sanderson 1979).

Data from the Mormon genealogical records suggest that just this possibility actually occurred among Mormon families in the nineteenth century. It would appear that once optimal family size was reached, the spacing of children quickly increased and the age of the woman when her last child was born declined. The Mormon data suggest that there was little difference in spacing in the birth of the earliest children, but that when some ideal level was reached, the spacing to the last child increased substantially, and the mother's age when she had her last child declined. All this suggests voluntary attempts to control fertility that resulted in last children being significantly different from what one could expect on biological grounds (Anderson and Bean 1985).

In this move toward lower fertility, native-born whites were leading the way with declining extended family organizations and declining family size of the nuclear family. This model was quickly adopted by the arriving immigrants. However, not all resident groups moved at the same pace among even the native-born whites. Evidently elites were more concerned with wealth issues than the poor, and initially the Protestants were more willing to control fertility

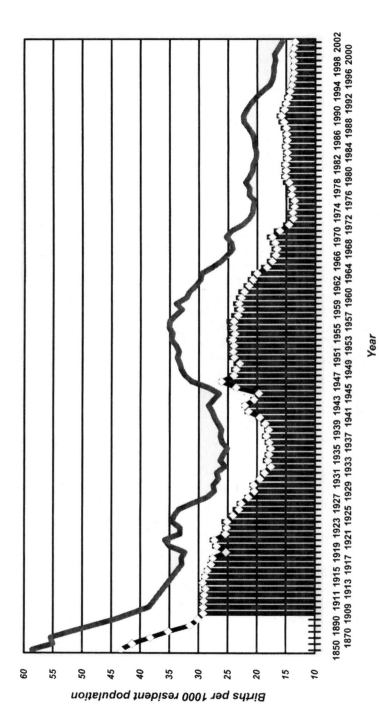

Figure 3.2. Crude birthrate by race, 1850–2003 (To 1964 black = nonwhite. From 1964 black = blacks only).

Sources: For 1909–1979, CDC, NCHS, Vital Statistics of the United States, 1997, vol. 1 "Natality," table 1.1, and *National Vital Statistics Report* 50, no. 5 (February 12, 2002): 27. For 1980–2003, National Center of Health Statistics, Health, United States, 2004, table 3, 109; data for every decade 1850–1900 from Haines (2000), table 4.2.

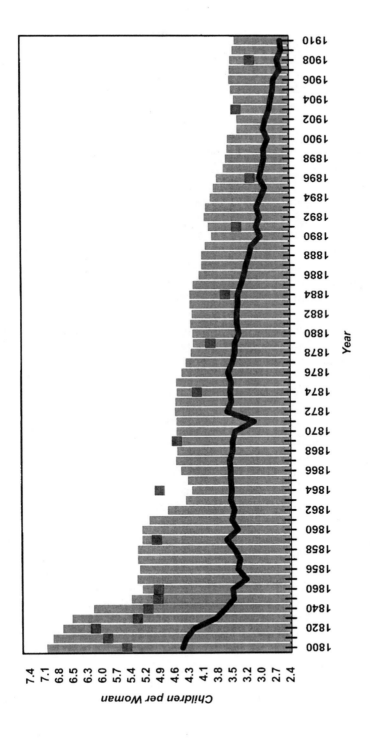

Figure 3.3. Estimated total fertility rate of U.S. white women compared to England and France, 1800–1910.
Sources: Coale and Zelnik (1963), table 2; Chesnais (1992), tables 11.1 and A2.2; Haines 2000, table 8.2.

than were the Catholics. Immigrants were slower to change than natives, and rural persons were slower to adapt than were the urban residents, though all were moving in the same direction throughout the North Atlantic world by the last quarter of the nineteenth century.

FERTILITY IN THE TWENTIETH CENTURY

The trend of declining fertility, which by the late nineteenth century had brought U.S. rates in line with most of Northwestern Europe, continued to move in the same direction in the new century, but at a slower pace and with some sharp variations around the trend, due to external events that would influence reproduction on the part of the resident population. The three most important external factors influencing fertility were the Great Depression and the two major wars fought by the United States in the first half of the twentieth century. The economic crisis led to mass unemployment and the decision of many families to postpone childbearing for economic reasons. The two world wars in turn extracted a large share of the young males from the United States and forced their temporary withdrawal from both the marriage and fertility markets. This initially had a negative influence on childbearing decisions of American families. But in the immediate postwar years, postponed marriage would cause a temporary rise in fertility due to pent up demand for marriage and children that had been blocked by war. This was only modestly important in influencing fertility rates after World War I, but it was to be especially important after World War II, which saw the mobilization of over double the number of young adult men into the armed forces in the 1941–1945 period than had occurred in World War I.

Thus, in 1914, the total fertility rate was already declining from earlier late nineteenth-century highs and had fallen to 3.3 children per woman who had completed her fertility—a drop of .2 children since 1900. This rate then steadied during the World War I years, and progressively declined through the 1920s. The rate reached its low point of just 2.1 children—the number of children considered the bare necessity to replenish the resident population—in the middle of the Great Depression in 1936. Fertility would then slowly reverse its long-term decline but would climb to only 2.4 children by 1945. In the immediate post–World War II period, a relative boom in births occurred, pushing the fertility rate temporarily back up to very high levels. By 1957, at the peak of the postwar Baby Boom, the total fertility rate reached 3.6 children for women who had completed their fertility, a figure even higher than the 1900 rate. But this extraordinary reversal lasted only for a decade, and the century-long trend of decline would continue, as economic growth led families to space their children at longer birth intervals or delay first births even later into marriage.

This longer spacing between children and delaying of first births explains the surprising finding that the decline in fertility in the period to 1945 was occurring at the same time that the age of first marriages for women and men was progressively declining, which should have increased fertility. In 1900, for example, age at first marriage for men was 27.6 years and for women 23.9 years—both at the high end compared to nineteenth-century rates. By 1940, the age at which men married was two years younger than this, and for women it was three years less than their 1900 rates. Moreover, these ages at marriage were lower than the norm in Europe at this time except for France, which it greatly resembled. At the same time, the percentage of women never married only modestly changed during this period, slowly rising from 7.8 percent of the women who reached age 45–54 in 1910 to a peak of 9.1 percent by 1920, and then the percentage declined to just 8.7 percent in 1940, a trend in declining "spinsterhood" that would continue to the 1980s. Women would continue to marry at ever younger ages in every decade to 1960, in that year reaching a record-setting 20.3 years of age—a level not seen since the colonial period (Haines 1996). Given the still quite low rates of illegitimate births (just 8.2 percent of all births for all women in 1930–1934, then dropping to 7.0 percent of all births in 1940–1944), marital fertility itself was seriously declining in this period, despite the increasing time women spent in marriages (Bachu 1999). This was clearly due to the increased use by men and women in this century of birth-control practices within marriage.

The difference between African American and white rates of fertility changed little over the period from 1914 to 1945. Though African Americans would also experience a significant decline in fertility rates, this decline was too modest to close the fertility rate gap between the races. In fact, convergence between the two rates would not seriously occur until after 1980. But in one area of fertility, African American women began to experience change, well in anticipation of white women. Already by 1930–1934, almost a third of first births for African American women were illegitimate, while only 5.9 percent of all births occurred outside marriage for white women. Though illegitimate birthrates fell for both races in the period to 1944, after 1945 the rates would reverse and begin their long steady climb, here in the United States and in all the advanced nations of Europe. But the pace of growth was much more rapid among African American women than white women.

One group that was slow to show a drop in fertility was Native American Indians. Though there was variation from tribe to tribe, Native Americans had the nation's highest level of women ever married and the nation's highest total fertility rate in 1900—on the order of six to seven children per woman who had completed her fertility. But they also had higher mortality rates than any other group in the population, and their high fertility seemed to be maintained more by early and universal marriage of women than by higher fertility within marriage. In fact, Indian women probably had a higher ratio of diseases that affected fertility, which may account for their very long spacing between childbirths—much longer than for native-born whites or African Americans. But as their economic situation finally stabilized with the end of the frontier changes in the 1890s, and the slow but progressive immunization of their children and adults in the first decades of the twentieth century, the very high mortality rates for American Indians finally began to fall and in turn would lead to ever higher growth rates in their total population. Given the delayed pattern of these mortality changes, fertility decline was also delayed among American Indians. The result was that population expanded quite rapidly at 1.33 percent per annum for the continental American Indian population between 1900 and 1960, by which time the population was double that of the 1900 low point. Though fertility slowly declined, even as late as 1940 the total fertility rate was 4.5 children for American Indian women who had completed their fertility— two children more than for African American women and almost three more children than U.S. white women had in that year (Shoemaker 1999).

In contrast to the African American and American Indian patterns, there was rapid convergence between foreign-born immigrant and native-born white birth patterns during this period. Soon after their arrival, foreign-born white women began to move quickly toward the native-born white woman norms. In a study of native and foreign-born whites in Chicago from 1920 to 1940, it was found that the total fertility rate gap between the native- and foreign-born population was constantly decreasing. Moreover, this narrowing occurred for all income groups, and it was most rapid for the richest immigrants. In fact, by 1920, wealthy immigrants had a lower rate of fertility than wealthy native-born whites (Kitagawa 1953). The same occurred in Detroit between 1920 and 1930, when the foreign-born women in all age groups lowered their fertility much more rapidly than did the native-born white women, and this was the most important factor driving down overall birthrates in the city (Mayer and Klapprodt 1955). In a detailed analysis of Italian immigrants to the United States in the late nineteenth and early twentieth centuries, Livi-Bacci found that immigrant families were quickly adapting to the reduced native-born white birthrates. In fact, he found that younger mothers (under 34 years of age) who had been born in Italy, and who had fertility rates almost double that of native-born whites in 1920, had fertility rates at or below that of the native-born whites by the late 1930s. He also estimated that between 1910 and 1940, the fertility of almost all immigrant groups of all ages (except for the Italians and the Mexicans) fell more rapidly than for native-born white women, though none fell below the fertility rate of the native-born white women. But at the younger ages for these foreign-born women (that is, from 15 to 34 years of age), he

estimated that half of the major immigrant groups in these same 30 years had
already achieved lower fertility rates than those obtained by the native-born in
this age category (Livi-Bacci 1961).

In the United States as a whole, it is estimated that of the three basic groups
of the population—that is, native-born whites, non-whites, and foreign-born
whites—the latter decreased at double the rate of the other two groups. Whereas
between 1920 and 1929, fertility among U.S. native-born white women 15–44
years of age was estimated to have fallen by 20 percent, the rate fell by almost a
third for the foreign-born and just 18 percent for African Americans (Thompson
and Whelpton 1933). In another study of fertility by origin, it was found that the
period 1910–1914 showed the largest gap in fertility rates between native-born
and foreign-born white women since such data was available, from 1875–1979.
But then the gap decreased so rapidly that by the period 1925–1929, the fertility
of the foreign-born population was actually below that of the native-born white
women for the first time ever (see figure 3.4). Moreover, this pattern of initially
higher fertility rates of the foreign-born and their progressive decline to or
below the level of the native-born is noted in every study and for every group
arriving in the United States during the nineteenth and twentieth centuries,
including even for the Mexicans in the most recent period. No matter if the
immigrants came from Europe in the early 1900s or from Latin America or
China in the 1980s, the pattern held over time and place.

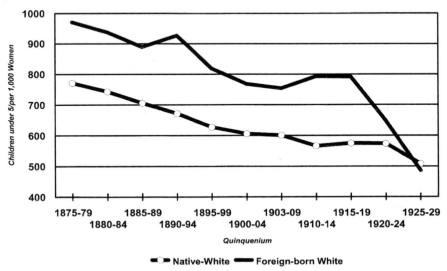

**Figure 3.4.   Fertility ratio for white population by origin, 1875–1929 (children under
5 per 1,000 women 20–44).**
Source: Easterlin (1961), 906, table A3.

THE BABY BOOM

Unquestionably, the event that most defined this period in the popular perception and even in the historical literature was the sudden postwar shift to higher fertility that created what has come to be called the Baby Boom. Because this boom in births was immediately followed by a return to low fertility, which has been called the Baby Bust, it has meant that those born during this period were a well-defined cohort that could be easily identified as they grew older, and they have come to be known as the generation of the Baby Boomers. The question that intrigued the demographers at the time was: Why had this massive shift occurred and was it permanent? Was the United States, now one of the world's wealthiest societies, about to enter a new era and create a unique model of high fertility in an advanced industrial society, something no other comparable society was experiencing? While everyone expected a temporary postwar shift in fertility, initially it seemed as if this might be a permanent change in U.S. attitudes toward fertility and family life. But it is now seen that this shift in the direction of greater fertility was to last for only some 18 years, though its impact on the nation was to last until well into the twenty-first century as the Baby Boom generation worked its way through the labor market and into retirement ages in the first decades of the new century.

Numerous reasons are suggested for the massive U.S. Baby Boom. First of all, the Great Depression years had driven fertility rates to levels below trend and clearly reflected economic constraints on what people wanted in terms of family size. The easing of that economic crisis on the eve of World War II allowed the fertility rates to start moving slowly upward, though they were then temporary repressed by the withdrawal of so many men from the marriage market because of national conscription. The return of these men after 1945 then allowed the rate to rise again. But the fact that the fertility rate began rising ever faster at the end of the 1940s and throughout the decade of the 1950s, not peaking until the early 1960s, was the result of a shift in expectations and possibilities on the part of the young women and men who were then entering into marriage.

The factors that clearly changed U.S. traditional family expectations, according to Easterlin, were the unprecedented postwar economic expansion combined with rapid socioeconomic mobility. This new economy favored young adults as never before. First of all, a rapidly expanding postwar labor market was absorbing a generation that had originated in the low fertility period of the late 1920s, creating a tight labor market that in turn would push up wages. There was also a massive government subsidization of adult education in the immediate postwar years, through the GI Bill, which resulted in a major increase in years of schooling for a large share of the population that would never otherwise have been able to afford such schooling. These two factors help to explain a major shift of young workers into higher-status and better-paying jobs. It is now estimated that median male income in the decade from 1947 to 1957 grew at 5 percent per annum in current dollars. That increasing income and the increasing availability of government credit for home mortgages also explain an explosion of home ownership—from 44 percent of the total population owning their own homes in 1940 to 64 percent in 1980 (Easterlin 1961).

In 1945, millions of returning U.S. World War II veterans brought with them a pent-up desire for family formation and children. New levels of family income, new availability of federal credit for middle- and lower-class home ownership, the introduction of cheap mass-produced tract housing, and increasing economic mobility due to the movement to higher-status employment on the part of the younger population, all had their impact on temporarily reversing fertility trends. The housing space and available income for providing for more children were now available, and Americans responded to these opportunities by lowering the age at which they married, beginning their families at an earlier age, and opting for marriage more frequently, thus increasing their overall fertility (see figure 3.5).

In 1940, the mean age at first marriage for men was 24.3 years of age, and for women it was 21.5 years. By 1956, the mean first-marriage age had declined to 22.5 years for men and to just 20.1 years for women—the men's mean first-marriage age being probably the lowest ever recorded for men in the United States, and the women's mean first-marriage age being the lowest ever recorded for U.S. women in the twentieth century and probably one of the lowest such ages ever. The age trend downward was not sustained in the ensuing years; age at first marriage began slowly rising again and reached 25 years for women by the end of the century.

At the same time, the ratio of women age 20–24 who were married reached an all-time high of 70 percent in 1960, a rate that would quickly decline again to just 32 percent by 1990 (Haines 1996). The number of women who remained unmarried throughout their lives dropped considerably, to lowest levels, during the period of the Baby Boom. Whereas in 1900 almost a third of U.S. women over 15 years of age were never married, by 1950 the rate had fallen to 18 percent, and to 17 percent by 1960—again, rates that would be reversed during the following years.

Moreover, the median age of first births dropped to its lowest level in the immediate post–World War II period. In 1930, women had their first child at 21.3 years of age. By 1956, that age had declined to 20.3 years, its lowest recorded level in the century, though this, too, would reverse in subsequent years, as the median age of mothers having their first child reached 25 years by the end of the twentieth century.

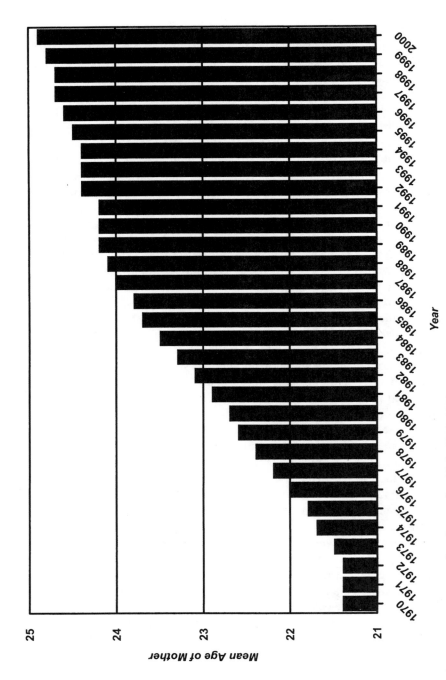

Figure 3.5.   Mean age of mothers at first birth, 1970–2000.
Source: *National Vital Statistics Reports* 51, no. 1 (December 11, 2002): 6.

Finally, the spacing between marriage and first child, and then between the first and second children, dropped to their lowest levels during the first half of the 1960s, again beginning a long-term reversal by the second half of that decade (Klein 2004, chap. 6).

All of these changes in behavior explain how the new Baby Boom level of fertility was achieved. The total number of children produced by women who had completed their fertility went from a low average of 2.1 children in 1936 to an extraordinary high average for a modern industrial society of 3.6 children in 1957—a rate not seen in the United States since 1898. This caused the median age of the U.S. population to drop to 28.1 years by 1970, the lowest median since 1930 and far below the median of 35 years for all sexes found in the census of 2000. At the same time, the ratio of the U.S. economically active population dropped below 60 percent in 1960 for the first and only time in the twentieth century because of the large Baby Boom jump in births. All this had a direct impact on creating a very large cohort of the population that slowly worked its way through the population pyramid, becoming a most conspicuous cohort, since the generations that followed were produced by lower birthrates. These distinctions can be seen in the age pyramids for the period. In 1940, the low births during the Great Depression truncated the younger ages of what should have been a normal pyramid (see figure 3.6); by 1950, a big increase in births was showing up as a very large increase in the two youngest age groups (0–9), and this child and infant base kept expanding during the next decade. Then came the decline in fertility; the age pyramid of 1980 in its bottom ages began to look again like the one of 1940. The big difference from 30 years previously, however, was the bulge in the teen and young-adult ages caused by the huge influx of Baby Boomers working their way through the age structure. By 1980, this Baby Boom group was being replaced by a smaller birth cohort of 0–14 years old and, in turn, was bulging out at the ages 15–24, and moving steadily toward middle age and retirement by the beginning of the twenty-first century.

THE BABY BUST AND RETURN TO TREND

The Baby Boom was just that—a deviation that was due to a set of unusual factors that all came together at the same time to reverse long-term trends in fertility decline. After just two decades, Americans were back again to marrying later, producing children later, and having fewer children. Whereas Gallup polls found a majority of women desiring four children in 1945, 1957, and 1966, by 1971, women who desired this number of children were in the minority. Equally, the opinion surveys showed that attitudes toward sex were changing abruptly during this period; those who opposed premarital sex, for example,

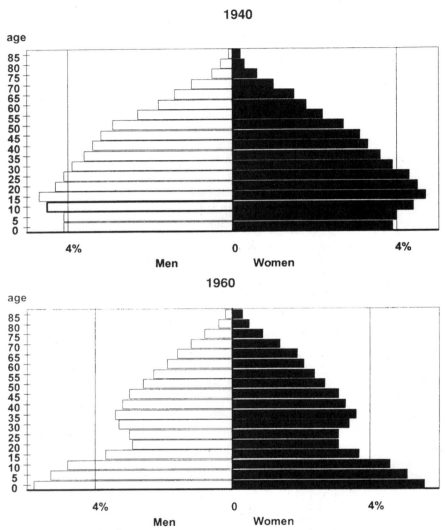

Figure 3.6.   Age pyramids of U.S. population, 1940–2000.
Source: Hobbs and Stoops (2002).

dropped from 68 percent in 1969 to 48 percent in 1973 (May 1988). Given this sea change in attitudes, along with changing economic conditions, each succeeding generation after the 1960s reduced its fertility to such an extent that native-born white Americans quickly reached the low fertility norms of the advanced industrial world and, by the last decades of the twentieth century, differed little from their peers in Northern Europe. By 1972, the total fertility rate

1980

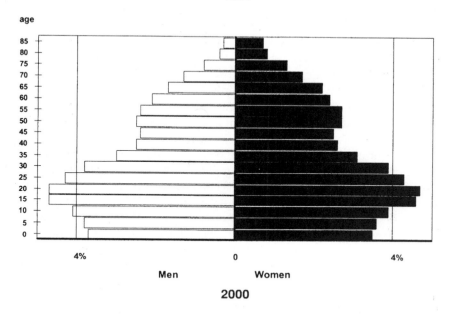

Men   Women

2000

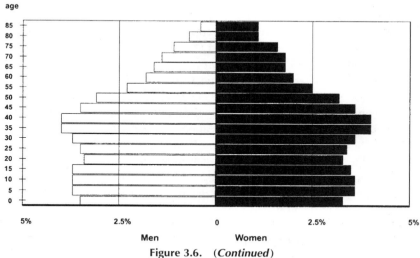

Men   Women

Figure 3.6. (*Continued*)

of white non-Hispanic women who had completed their fertility dropped for the first time to below replacement level—just 1.9 children per woman, a rate that, though fluctuating and even falling to 1.6 children in 1978, would not, to the present day, return to the theoretical replacement level of 2.1 births per woman (U.S. Census Bureau, *Statistical Abstract of the United States* 2004, 63).

Along with declining fertility generally, there was a profound change in the role of the family in fertility. Although the family values and the dominant role of young married mothers in the fertility of Americans reached its peak during the Baby Boom, the post-1964 period was a time not only of historically low rates of fertility, but a time when the American family was beginning to lose its overwhelming importance in society and even in controlling fertility itself. Between rising rates of divorce and births outside marriage, the family began to lose its role as the predominant determinant of fertility and of household organization. Births out of wedlock progressively reduced the importance of marital fertility over time, and the rising rate of divorce was one of the key factors favoring the increasing importance of single-parent households with young children. In turn, the increasing reluctance of young women to marry also influenced the rise of single-person households in the United States. Thus, as early as the 1970s, the United States was beginning to experience a profound change in its basic social structure. During the years 1965–1969, the ratio of births outside marriage to total births remained at or below the historic rate of 10 percent, but by 1969–1975 such births were up to 15 percent of all births, and by 1975–1979 had reached over a quarter of all births and was still rising. Moreover, the parents of extramarital children now had a greater tendency not to marry either before or after the birth of the child. During the pre-1970 period, half the parents of extramarital children later married, but only a third did so in the late 1970s, and that rate kept dropping. Similarly, divorce rates doubled between 1900 and the 1960s—going from four divorces per 1,000 married women in 1900 to nine divorces per 1,000 married women by 1960. Then, from 1967 through 1975, no-fault divorce laws were adopted in almost all the states, and the divorce rate during the post-1960 period jumped to an average of 20 per 1,000 married women by the end of the century. Between 1950 and 1980, the number of divorced persons in the adult population 15 years or older grew at a steady rate of 5 percent per annum, accounting for over 7 percent of the total adult female population and 5 percent of the male population by 1980 (see figure 3.7). One estimate suggested that by 1967, half the marriages contracted in that year would end in divorce, while a more recent estimation gives a slightly lower figure, suggesting that four out of 10 marriages contracted in the year 2000 will end in divorce.

Much of the divorce increase was due to major changes in socioeconomic mobility and the national economy in the post-1960 period, as well as to some basic changes in attitudes toward the role of women in society. Female labor force participation rates began to climb during this period, and women began entering professions at a rate never before seen. In 1950, only 34 percent of adult women were in the labor force. By 1970, the figure was 43 percent, and by 1978, half the adult women were working outside the home, a rate that increased every year thereafter, reaching over 60 percent by the beginning of the twenty-first century (see figure 3.8).

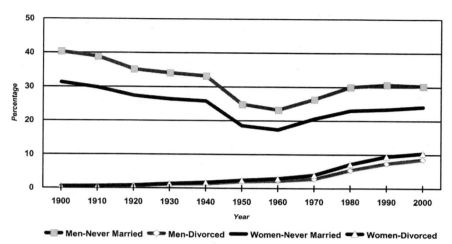

Figure 3.7. Marital status of persons 15 years or older, 1900–2000.
Sources: For 1900–1990, Census of 1990, table 1418; Census 2000, "QT-P18. Marital Status by Sex, Unmarried-Partner Households, and Grandparents as Caregivers: 2000."

Equally, as might be expected after an unusually rapid growth and restructuring of the economy in the immediate post–World War II period, the secular mobility of those years—when most people increased their status above that of their parents—was now replaced by the more traditional circular mobility, when as many people moved down the socioeconomic ladder as moved up.

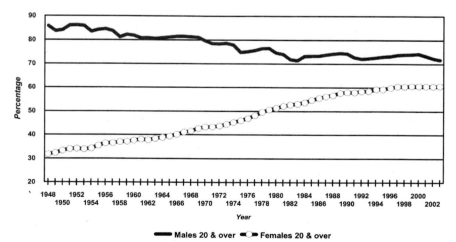

Figure 3.8. Ratio of adults (20 years and older) in the labor force, by sex, 1948–2003.
Source: U.S. Department of Labor, Bureau of Labor Statistics, Labor Force Statistics from the Current Population Survey, table A1, www.bls.gov/webapps/legacy/cpsatab1.htm.

While fertility moved back after 1964 to its long-term secular trend of decline, a pattern common to all industrial societies, women's role within the household and in the marketplace now began to change in profound ways never seen before. Women entered universities in ever larger numbers, thus delaying marriage. In turn, they began to enter professional careers at an unprecedented rate and to keep working at those careers longer than ever before. They also moved with increasing frequency into households either alone or with a companion to whom they were not married. The cause for this change has much to do with the changes in attitude toward the place of women in society that took place in the 1960s and 1970s, when traditional values were rejected by lead elements in the generation that came of age in this period. The introduction of the birth-control pill in the early 1960s was important in this change in giving women control over their own fertility. But even more important was a new attitude toward the equality of women in society. By the 1960s, there came a spate of new federal legislation against sexual discrimination in the workplace.

We can see the demographic results of this evolution of new attitudes toward and by women in many ways. There was, first of all, a major change in the education of women that became manifest in this period. Women had always done well in primary and secondary education. In the mid nineteenth century, when the first comparable data became available, women already were more likely to be secondary school graduates than men, and for most of the period since then, there were more women than men in secondary graduating classes. But it was only in 1980 that women finally became more than half of all college students, and it was only in 1984 that they finally represented the majority in graduate school enrollment as well, though they have yet to pass men in enrollments in post-college professional education.

Women also began to move into the labor market in ever higher numbers, and to remain in the labor market at higher rates than ever before. At the end of the nineteenth century, less than a fifth of all women were in the salaried labor force; by the 1980s, the figure had risen to 60 percent. But this was not a linear trend. In fact, female participation rates and the ratio of single and married women in the labor force probably dropped to their lowest point in the 1920s, and that trend was only reversed in a significant way with the advent of World War II. Both the rates of older women returning to work and younger ones entering the market increased dramatically in the 1960s, and this was one of the forces behind the equal pay movement. Whereas in 1940 only 14 percent of adult women who were married and 46 percent of those who were single were in the work force, by 1980 half the married women and almost two-thirds of the single women were working outside the home (Klein 2004, chap. 6; and Goldin 1990).

Even within marriage, there were important new trends. Ever since the late 1960s, the age of women contracting marriage was once again on the rise, increasing by 4.8 years at the end of the century. Not only were Americans marrying later, but they were not getting married as much as they had in previous eras. Among persons of all races and sexes over 15 years of age, the ratio who had never married was slowly rising, reaching a third of the men and a quarter of the women by the year 2000. Broken down by race, the changes among whites was occurring at a slower pace than among African Americans, though both saw unmarried rates rising. By century's end, some 22 percent of adult white women and 42 percent of adult African American women had never married.

All this, of course, was having its impact on the structure of households and the relation between families and households. Nonfamily households had always existed as a small share of the total households in the United States, though usually made up of elderly persons with no families left. But now, nonfamily households were being formed by young adults, many of whom never married. Moreover, the ratio of two-parent households, even in family households with children, was on the decline, as the ratio of single-parent plus children households was on the rise. The rapidity of this change is evident when one looks beyond this period. As late as 1960, at the height of the Baby Boom, married families made up 74 percent of all households, whereas by the time of the 2000 Census, they accounted for just over half (53 percent) and were on a long-term trend downward (see figure 3.9). In turn, nonfamily households now accounted for 31 percent of all households, having risen from just 11 percent of all households at mid twentieth century. This figure, moreover, was quite high, compared to the other advanced industrial countries.

Married couples were also no longer the norm for even households with children. In the second half of the twentieth century, households with children under 18 years of age probably experienced the most change. The number of two-parent families that made up such households with children was steadily on the decline, falling by 20 percent from 1950 to 2000, and they accounted for just under four-fifths of such households in the 2000 Census. At the same time, families headed by a single parent had climbed in the opposite direction, reaching 27 percent of all such families. Though the trend for all groups was the same, the African American population experienced the fastest decline in dual-parent family households, and by the end of the century, married couples with children accounted for only 39 percent of all black family households with children. But as the general figures indicate, no group was immune to this fundamental shift toward declining two-parent households (see figure 3.10).

Not only were married families and families in general on the decline, but with the consequent rise of single-person and childless-couple households, there were also important accompanying shifts in fertility. Though the extremely low total fertility rates of the mid 1970s were somewhat reversed in the 1980s and 1990s, the total fertility rates barely reached replacement and fluctuated

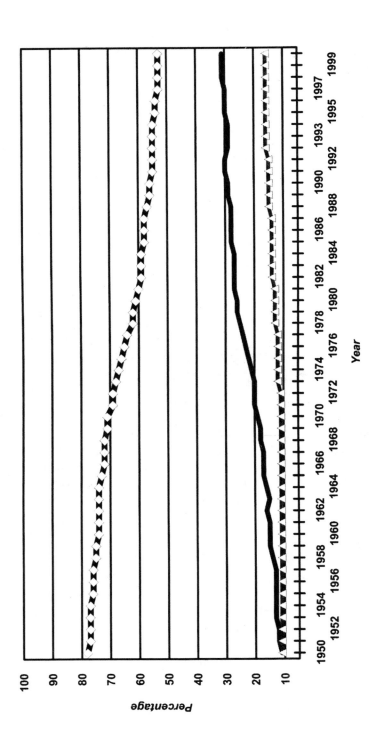

Figure 3.9. Changing nature of households, 1950–2000.
Source: U.S. Census Bureau, table HH-1, "Households, by Type: 1940 to Present," Internet release date: June 29, 2001.

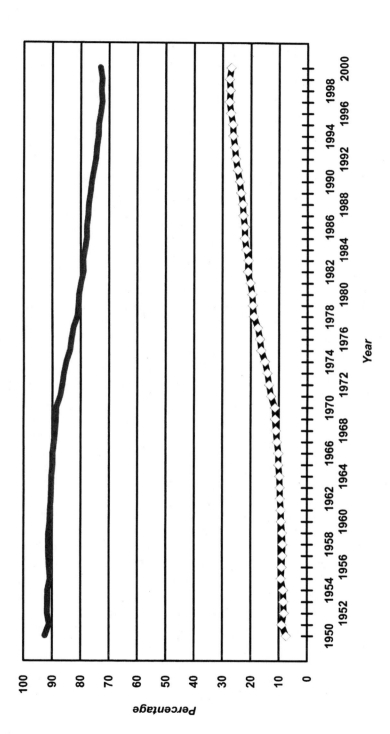

Figure 3.10. Changing nature of families with children, 1950–2000.
Source: U.S. Census Bureau, FM-1, "Families, by Presence of Own Children under 18: 1950 to Present," Internet release date: June 29, 2001.

between 2.0 and 2.1 children per woman who had completed her fertility by the end of the century. In fact, this overall national rate masked a continued severe decline in the total fertility rate of non-Hispanic white women, who by 2000 were averaging just 1.8 children—even lower than the rate they had in the mid 1970s. Among all groups, it was only Hispanic women who were significantly above replacement level (see figure 3.11). Even among Hispanic women, it was essentially Mexican American women, the largest single group, that maintained very high fertility rates. Cuban American women were close to non-Hispanic whites, and Puerto Rican women were closer to the patterns of fertility of non-Hispanic black women (see figure 3.12).

There were also the beginnings of a profound change in the role of marriage in fertility. This was made evident by the rise in births outside marriage. Though all groups experienced this rise, non-Hispanic whites experienced a slower rise than all other groups, but even they had illegitimacy rates of 28 percent by 2000. It is impressive that these were probably the highest recorded rates for any period in American history, and despite all the talk about their declining, the increasing illegitimacy rates in Europe suggest that North America is following European trends. Though rising illegitimacy appeared first among the poorest elements in U.S. society, the fact that wealthier groups also began to experience such rising trends when the economy was stable, if not growing, suggests that by the late twentieth century, the trend was due to changes in cultural norms and attitudes and the changing role of women in society, as can be seen in the shift in the relative rates of illegitimate births by age. In the 1970s, when the issue began to be perceived by the public as one of major concern, it was teenagers who had the highest rates of births outside marriage, and these births seemed to be rising at the time. But by the end of the century, it was older women whose rates of illegitimacy were highest and rising, while those for teenage girls was falling (see figure 3.13), and actually, total teenage rates of births were declining as well (Klein 2004, chap. 7).

That the increase of births outside of marriage was not due to poverty per se can be seen in the fact that the United States was not unique in such a new pattern of births and the declining importance of traditional marriage. Other wealthy countries such as Sweden also experienced the same trend. Although Sweden at midcentury still had a low rate of just 10 percent illegitimate births, by the end of the century, its rate of nonmarital births had reached 53 percent of all births. Even Catholic countries such as Spain and Portugal had arrived at 16 percent and 22 percent illegitimacy rates, respectively, and France was up to 38 percent of its total births being defined as illegitimate by 1996. Although Italy's nonmarital births were still quite low, almost all other advanced industrial countries in Western Europe were experiencing a steady and unabated rise in illegitimate births in this period. Thus, the belief that this was a temporary or uniquely North American development does not appear to be the case. The

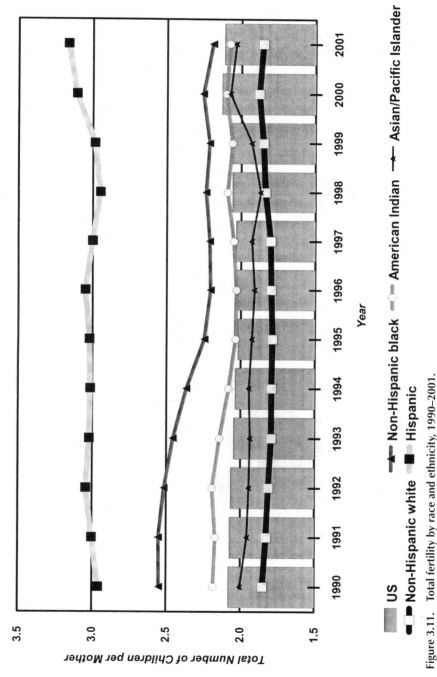

Figure 3.11. Total fertility by race and ethnicity, 1990–2001.

Sources: S. J. Ventura et al., "Births: Final Data for 1997," *National Vital Statistics Reports* 47, no. 18 (1999); J. A. Martin et al., "Births: Final Data for 2001," *National Vital Statistics Reports* 51, no. 2 (2002).

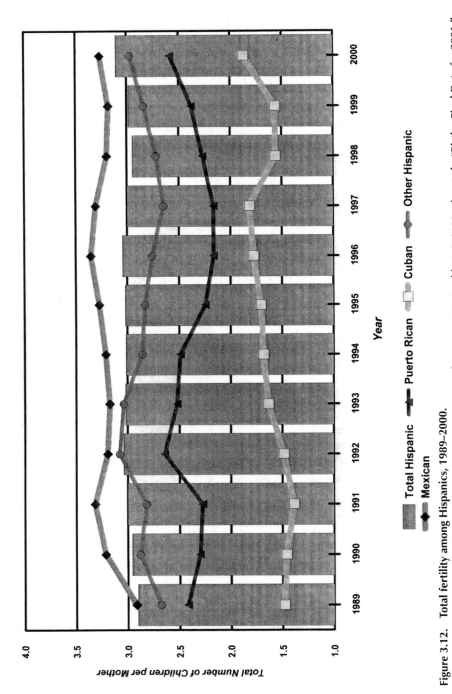

Figure 3.12.   Total fertility among Hispanics, 1989–2000.
Sources: NCHS, *National Vital Statistics Reports* 51, no. 2 (December 18, 2002), 4, table 9; J. A. Martin, et al., "Births: Final Data for 2001."

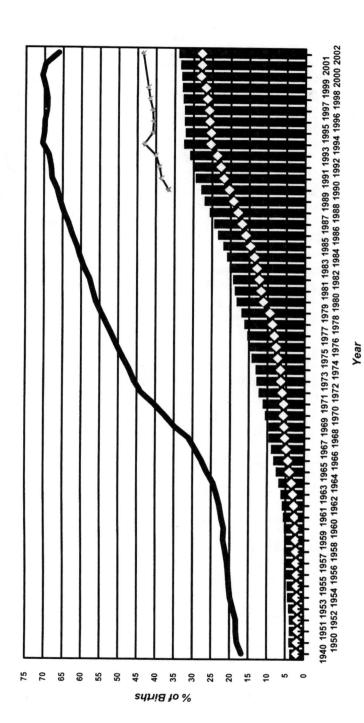

Figure 3.13. Percentage of births to unmarried women by race and ethnicity, 1940–2002.
Sources: CDC, *National Vital Statistics Reports* 48, no. 16 (October 18, 2000), table 4; and *National Vital Statistics Reports* 52, no. 10 (December 17, 2003), table 17.

factors influencing these trends everywhere in the modern industrial world seem to be the same: late marriages, women increasing their participation in the labor force, with resulting higher incomes for women, and changing beliefs about the importance and necessity of marriage—beliefs and changes that seem to be general phenomena affecting all Europe and North America at approximately the same time.

Even among dual-parent households with children, the traditional family with a single male breadwinner working alone to sustain the family was no longer the norm. By the end of the twentieth century, only one in five married couples had just a single male breadwinner working outside the home. Even the traditional family model of the stay-at-home mother was not the norm for families with children. Although the ratio of families with fathers working and mothers staying at home was higher among these families, even in this subsection of married couples, the traditional model no longer accounted for the majority of such families. Among married couples with children, only 28 percent had just a father alone in the workforce, and even for families with children under six years of age, only 36 percent had the mother staying at home with the children and not working. That this pattern will not be reversed anytime soon is indicated by the fact that the trend of male breadwinners as the only support of the family was down for all of this period, and these rates were the lowest recorded in the last part of the century (see figure 3.14). Not only were more women in the workforce—a ratio that was constantly on the rise through the second half of the century—but the vast majority of married

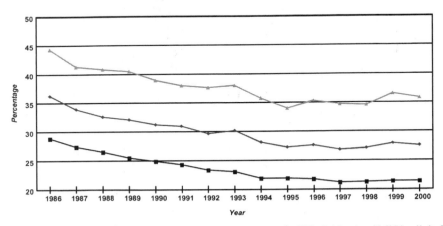

Figure 3.14.   Ratio of married couples with husband only working, by age of children, 1986–2000.
Source: U.S. Census Bureau, Table MC1, " Married Couples by Labor Force Status of Spouses: 1986 to Present, Internet release date: June 29, 2001.

mothers with young children were also working outside the home by 2000. Even for women who had given birth to a child during the previous year, the majority were found to be working outside the home by the end of the year—a rate of 55 percent of them in 2000, whereas the rate was just 31 percent in 1967.

All of these changes had their impact on fertility. Not only was formal marriage no longer the exclusive arbiter of fertility, but more and more women were reducing the number of children they did have. This was not due to women forgoing children. In fact, there was little change in the number of women going childless, which has remained quite steady for the past 40 years. Nor was it due to declining sexual activity, since sexual activity of teenagers was on the rise, and many more women in the 1990s were having sexual relations outside marriage than had been the case just 30 years before. The decline in fertility was due to the fact that women were deliberately deciding to have fewer children. They were marrying later, thus reducing their marital fertility; they were beginning childbearing at ever later ages; they were spacing their children farther apart; and they were terminating their fertility at earlier ages. Not only did the average age of mothers having their first children rise by 2.7 years during the period from 1960 to 1999, but the age rose significantly for every subsequent child being born, while the spacing between children also increased. Although the average age of mothers at first birth for the entire population was now 24.9 years, for non-Hispanic white women, it was 25.9 years. From 1950 to 2000, the number of live births for each age category declined by over half, with the biggest decline occurring in the 25–39 age group. As was to be expected from the fertility declines, the size of families with children was declining as well. The average number of children in families that included children went from 2.4 children in 1965, at the height of the Baby Boom, to just 1.9 children in 2000.

Women were carrying out these changes in their fertility through a variety of methods. They were making more systematic use of contraceptives and legal abortions. It is estimated by the end of the century that almost two-thirds of all women age 15–44 used some form of contraception. Although only a third of the teenagers used some method of birth control, by the time women were reaching the crucial fertility years (after 24 years of age), over 70 percent of them were using contraceptives. This pattern of rising contraceptive use over time was common to all racial and ethnic groups. At the same time, while legal abortion rates rose initially, and reached as much as 43 percent of total live births in the mid 1980s, by the late 1990s they were down to 34 percent of all live births and falling. For whites, the fall was quite dramatic, reaching just a quarter of white births at the end of the century. African American abortion rates, however, once rising to the 65–70 percent range in the earlier years, did not decline; they remained steady throughout the period (see figure 3.15).

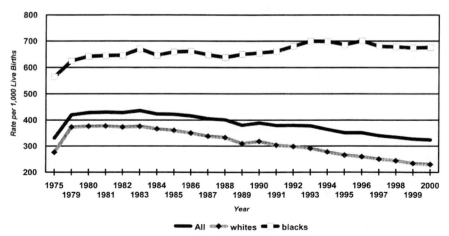

Figure 3.15.   Abortion rate by race, 1975–2000.
Source: U.S. Census Bureau, *Statistical Abstract of the United States: 2004*, 70, table 89.

Although the impact of legal abortion may have repressed the birthrate somewhat in the early years, the decline in abortions at the end of the century has not reversed fertility rates. These have continued to decline, from the 1960s onward. During the period 1980 to 2000, the crude birthrate dropped from 24 per 1,000 resident population to just 15 per 1,000. Almost all groups experienced this decline, but it was non-Hispanic whites who experienced the lowest birthrate for any group in the population, reaching a crude birthrate of just 12.2 births per 1,000 non-Hispanic white residents. African Americans and American Indians, among the highest fertility groups, also experienced similar declines. The one group that stands out against the trend is Hispanics, whose rate actually increased to 25.1 births per 1,000 residents in the national population. Though Cuban American and other non-Mexican American Hispanics tended to have low birthrates, this was balanced by the rate for Mexican Americans, who were both the single most important part of the Hispanic population and who had overwhelmingly the highest birthrates of any group in the country. Thus, particularly in certain urban regions in the coastal and frontier states, Mexican Americans made up for the declining fertility rates of the other native-born populations.

In the context of the declining birthrates of native-born non-Hispanic whites, the net arrival of foreign-born now accounted for 39 percent of the natural growth of the American population. The impact of Hispanic birthrates, while maintaining the positive growth of the national population, only slowed somewhat the aging of the population, a process that was occurring in all the advanced industrial societies. Given the low fertility rates of the dominant non-Hispanic white population, the aged were becoming an ever more impor-tant element in the society. Together with a rising life expectancy, the fertility and mortality trends at the end of the twentieth century were transforming the age structure of the national population in profound ways. First of all, the mean age of the population was progressively rising, along with the share of the population of persons in the older age groups. In the last 20 years before the year 2000, the median age of the U.S. population rose 5.3 years, to reach 35.3 years of age (Hobbs and Stoops 2002). At the same time, there was a steady growth in the portion of the population over 65 years of age—from 11.3 percent in 1980 to 12.4 percent in the 2000 Census. This was still slightly behind the European rate of 15.5 percent, but it is projected that the United States will reach the European rate by 2010 and that the elderly will make up 20 percent of the population as early as 2030 (Kinsella and Velkoff 2001).

FUTURE TRENDS

By the first decade of the twenty-first century, America looked like most of the advanced industrial nations of the world in terms of its fertility patterns. The U.S. native-born non-Hispanic white population had fertility rates below replacement level, similar to most of the populations in the advanced industrial world. But thanks to U.S. minorities, the total fertility rate was still above 2.1 children. In the trends in fertility, illegitimate births, and abortion rates, not only was the United States moving more into conformity with the rest of the world, but its internally divided population was also converging toward these common patterns, whether white, black, American Indian, Asian, or Hispanic.

Will these low rates of fertility continue? Since 1972, the non-Hispanic white fertility rate has been below replacement, but it has fluctuated, going from a low total fertility rate of 1.6 children in 1978 to a current estimated rate of 2.0 children in 2004. In the government's latest projections on fertility by race and ethnic group, both the middle and upper estimates suggest that the national population will return to above replacement levels by 2025, thanks to the still-high—though declining—rate of births for Hispanics and a modest return to higher fertility by all ethnic groups except blacks and non-Hispanic whites. For these two latter groups, only the highest estimates project a potential return to above-replacement rates—and, even then, the rates are at or below 2.3 children (see figure 3.16).

Given that there could be changing attitudes toward births (if not toward marriage) on the part of the major racial and ethnic groups of women in the population, there is no guarantee that fertility will continue to remain at below-replacement levels forever. And given the rising rates of births out of wedlock, it is evident that changes in age of marriage will have much less impact than

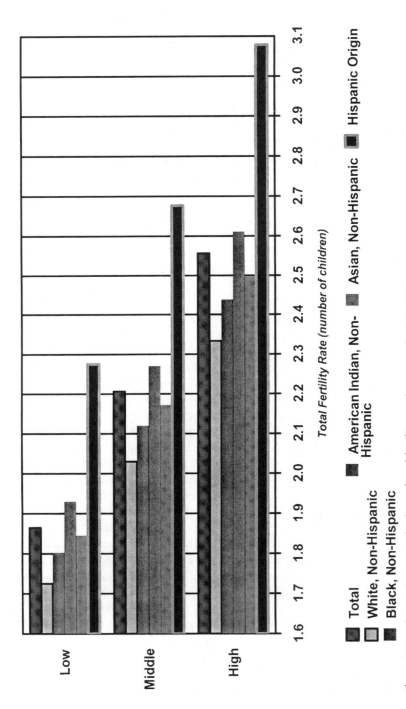

Figure 3.16. Census Bureau projections of total fertility rate by race and origin, 2025.
Source: "Methodology and Assumptions for the Population Projections of the United States: 1999 to 2100," Population Division Working Paper, no. 38 (January 13, 2000), 14.

ever before on fertility, and that the primary determinant will be women's attitudes toward fertility. This could be influenced by a number of both economic and social considerations. Recent studies have suggested, for example, that after a certain period in fertility decline, labor market participation rates and even increases in the educational level of women no longer have an automatically negative correlation with fertility and, in fact, reverse their traditional relationship (Castles 2003). Also, all surveys of women about the desired number of children they wish to have in their lifetimes, both in the United States and in the other advanced industrial countries, continue to suggest that a two-child family is the norm. Yet in all these societies, the desired family size is above the actual fertility rates—the reverse of what was the norm in the pre-transition eras. But demographers are still unsure what this disparity means and whether the desired rate could be promoted by more active pronatalist government policies (see Bongaarts 2001; Livi-Bacci 2001; Chesnais 2001). It is also evident that the fertility rates of all groups have moved in the same direction in recent years, and that even the rate for Mexican American women has started to approach the overall American rates.

The Baby Bust would seem to be the norm for the foreseeable future. Even if present trends were reversed, fertility as currently projected in the most optimistic estimates would rise to only modest levels above replacement.

4

Combating Child Poverty and Enhancing the Soundness of Social Security

Robert G. Lynch

In the great policy debates of the day, far too much is alleged about threats to the retirement security of our eldest citizens, while much too little is said about the crises confronting our children. Ironically, the more successfully we deal with the severe problems confronting our children, the easier it will be to resolve the relatively minor economic threats to the retirement security of our senior citizens. Although there may be challenges in the distant future to its financing, the Social Security program is not in crisis. Its potential financial challenges, furthermore, may be resolved with relative ease.

On the other hand, too many young children—the most vulnerable members of our community—have inadequate access to food, clothing, shelter, health care, and clean, safe, crime-free living environments. Nearly one in five children under the age of six lives in poverty, and the number is growing. In addition, too many of our children do not have access to high-quality educational opportunities or fall far short of achieving their academic potential while in school, making them more likely to enter adulthood lacking the skills to compete in a global labor market. As adults, they are more likely to suffer from poor health and participate in crime and other antisocial behavior; these children are also less likely to grow up to be gainfully employed and contributing to economic growth and community well-being.

Fortunately, there is a growing consensus among experts of all political stripes that high-quality investments in the education and health of young children would have huge long-term economic payoffs—to our children, to the elderly, and to society as a whole. Recent studies of high-quality early childhood development (ECD) programs have consistently found that investing in young children has many important benefits for children, their families, and society at large (including its taxpayers).

148

Specifically, research has shown that investments in high-quality ECD programs generate benefit-cost ratios exceeding three to one—or more than three dollars return for every one dollar invested—well above the one to one ratio needed to justify such investments. Follow-up studies of poor children who have participated in these programs have found solid evidence of markedly better academic performance, decreased rates of criminal conduct, and higher adult earnings than among their nonparticipating peers.

As is demonstrated later in this chapter, a nationwide commitment to providing all 20 percent of the nation's three- and four-year-old children who live in poverty with a high-quality ECD program would have a substantial payoff for governments and taxpayers in the future. As those children grow up, costs for remedial and special education, criminal justice, and welfare benefits would decline. Once they enter the labor force, their incomes would be higher, as would the taxes, including Social Security taxes, they would pay back to society.

A publicly financed, comprehensive ECD program for all children from low-income families would cost billions of dollars annually but would create much larger budget savings over time. By about the 17-year mark, the net effect on budgets for all levels of government combined would turn positive. Within 25 years, by 2030 if a nationwide program were started immediately, the budget benefits would exceed costs by more than a two to one margin, and the net budget savings would continue to grow thereafter.

The timing of these fiscal benefits resulting from a nationwide ECD program should appeal to those concerned about the fiscal difficulties posed by the impending surge of retiring Baby Boomers. The substantial fiscal payoffs from investing in young children would become available to governments just as the wave of new retirements puts the greatest pressure on government resources. For example, the government-wide budget savings in 2030 and in 2050 from ECD investments begun immediately would be enough to offset one-fifth or more of the deficits in the Social Security system projected for those years. This potential contribution to the solvency of the Social Security system would be achieved without raising Social Security taxes or cutting benefits.

This chapter begins by challenging the notion that the Social Security system is in crisis; while there may be some long-term challenges, the system is financially sound for the next 37 years, and any revenue shortfalls thereafter are likely to be relatively minor. The chapter then describes the overall benefits of investment in high-quality early childhood development programs. The effects that a high-quality, large-scale ECD program for all poor three- and four-year-old children is likely to have on future government budgets, the economy, and crime are presented. Finally, the potential benefit to the solvency of the U.S. Social Security system from ECD investment is illustrated.

SOCIAL SECURITY IS NOT IN CRISIS

In a radio address on December 11, 2004, President George W. Bush asserted, "In the year 2018, for the first time ever, Social Security will pay out more in benefits than the government collects in payroll taxes. And once that line into the red has been crossed, the shortfalls will grow larger with each passing year. By the time today's workers in their mid 20s begin to retire, the system will be bankrupt, unless we act to save it." According to Vice President Dick Cheney in a speech delivered at Catholic University on January 13, 2005, "The system is on a course to eventual bankruptcy," and if nothing is done, the government will have to reduce benefits dramatically or "impose a massive, economically ruinous tax increase on all American workers."

In addition, President Bush has argued that the financial exigency confronting Social Security is being largely driven by a serious, growing, and inexorable demographic problem. As he noted in his State of the Union Address of February 2, 2005, "A half-century ago, about 16 workers paid into the system for each person drawing benefits," whereas "right now it's only about three workers. And over the next few decades, that number will fall to just two workers per beneficiary." Thus, "with each passing year, fewer workers are paying ever-higher benefits to an ever-larger number of retirees."

But the assertion of looming bankruptcy is an exaggeration. Similarly, the implication that demographic forces will inevitably undermine the current Social Security system is inaccurate. Let us review what is known about the soundness of the Social Security system.

Each year the Social Security Administration (SSA) publishes a report in which the trustees of Social Security describe the current financial conditions of the system and make 75-year projections that attempt to describe the future solvency of the system. For the past 20 years, Social Security revenues have been greater than the benefits paid, so that the system has been running surpluses and amassing savings. In their 2005 report (Social Security Administration 2005), the trustees of Social Security projected that the program will continue to amass savings by earning more in revenue than it pays out in benefits for the next 13 years. Thus, by 2017 the system will have accumulated over $4.6 trillion in assets, up from about $1.7 trillion in assets in 2004. The assets are held in the Social Security trust fund in the form of U.S. Treasury bonds. These bonds are currently earning about 6 percent interest, and this interest is reinvested in the trust fund. The trustees project that, starting in 2017, Social Security tax revenues will not be enough to cover all the benefits that have been promised. They estimate that for the next 10 years, part of the interest earned on the Social Security trust fund will be needed to cover the promised benefits. The rest of the interest will be reinvested in the trust fund, so that by 2027 the trust fund holdings will have grown to over $6 trillion. Between 2027 and

2041, the trustees project that promised benefits will exceed Social Security tax collections and interest on the trust fund, so that the trust fund itself will have to be gradually liquidated. Once the trust fund is exhausted in 2041, the trustees project that Social Security taxes will continue to be sufficient to pay about 70 percent of the benefits that have been promised through 2079, the last year of their analysis.

In other words, according to the trustees, who include the treasury secretary, the secretary of labor, and the secretary of health and human services, the Social Security system is currently in excellent financial health, running surpluses and accumulating assets. The trustees also project that the system will be able to pay all its promised benefits for the next 37 years, through 2041, and after 2041, it will still be able to pay about 70 percent of promised benefits. Under no circumstances do the trustees foresee "bankruptcy," as most people understand the word: the system never runs out of money and is always able to pay most of its promised benefits. However, the trustees do expect financial challenges that will eventually undermine the system's ability to pay about 30 percent of its promised benefits. They summarize these potential financial challenges by estimating that there is likely to be a long-run (75-year) deficit that is equivalent to 1.92 percent of taxable payroll.

There are good reasons to believe that the projections of the trustees are overly pessimistic. The nonpartisan Congressional Budget Office, using slightly more optimistic economic assumptions, projects that the Social Security system will be able to fully pay all promised benefits for 48 more years, through 2052, and will be able to pay about 80 percent of promised benefits after that (Congressional Budget Office 2004). The CBO projects a 75-year deficit of 1.0 percent of taxable payroll.

The long-term economic and demographic assumptions made by the Social Security trustees and the CBO are probably too pessimistic. Pessimistic projections of future economic and population growth translate into gloomy estimates of the solvency of the Social Security system. Although no one can honestly claim to know with certainty what the economic and demographic outcomes will be over the next 75 years, within the economics profession perhaps the most commonly accepted predictor of future economic performance and trends is past performance and trends. And yet, in a number of critical areas, the projections of the trustees and the CBO for future economic and demographic outcomes fall short of past performance and trends. For example, the trustees project real wages to grow only 1.1 percent, and the CBO assumes only 1.3 percent real-wage growth. But between 1940 and 2003, real wages subject to Social Security taxes increased about 1.5 percent annually, according to the Congressional Research Service (2005).

Faster real-wage growth would improve Social Security's finances. According to the trustees' report (Social Security Administration 2005, 153), each

0.5 percentage point increase in the assumed real-wage growth rate "increases the long-range actuarial balance by about 0.53 percent of taxable payroll." Hence, if real wages were to grow at their historical rate of 1.5 percent over the next 75 years, the trustees' projected deficit would be reduced by 0.42 percentage points, from 1.92 percent to just 1.5 percent of taxable payroll. Although the CBO does not provide precise numbers, they note as well that real-wage growth faster than what they anticipate would reduce the deficits they project.

The trustees also guess that long-run real GDP growth will be about 1.8 percent, or about half the rate of the historical average. They arrive at this GDP growth rate largely by assuming that productivity will grow about 1.6 percent, and population will grow at only 0.2 percent a year. However, over the past century, productivity has grown over 2 percent, and population has grown over 1 percent. In a detailed review of productivity data, economist Robert Gordon (2003) concluded that future productivity growth over the next two decades is likely to fall in the 2.2–2.8 percent range, population growth is likely to amount to about 1 percent, and real GDP should grow about 3.3 percent per year, or just a little short of the 75-year historical average. If Gordon is correct that future productivity growth is likely to settle down at a long-term rate of about 2.5 percent, then the Social Security deficit projections of both the trustees and the CBO are far too dismal. Productivity growth of 2.5 percent is likely to result in wage growth that is considerably faster than what the trustees or the CBO project.

Gordon (2003, 264) further points out that "when the trustees of the Social Security Administration forecast potential GDP growth of only 1.8 percent in the period 2040–80, the most important reason for their surprisingly low growth rate is their projection of population growth at only 0.2 percent a year." Note, too, that the CBO adopted the assumptions of the Social Security trustees with respect to population growth. Population projections are based on assumptions about the fertility rate, the mortality rate, and the number of immigrants. Gordon (2003, 266) argues that the trustees' assumption about future immigration is "by far the most controversial issue in assessing the official Social Security assumptions about future population growth." After reviewing the historical record, Gordon (2003, 267) states, "Somewhat incredibly given this historical perspective, which shows a growth rate of total immigration since 1970 of 3.75 percent a year, the Social Security projections assume not just zero growth in the future, but an absolute decline from 1.4 million total immigrants in 2002 to a steady state after 2020 of 900,000 new immigrants a year." Gordon goes on to argue (2003, 267) that "to project negative growth implies a discontinuity that is without any basis. Labor economists would presumably model the immigration process as the intersection of supply and demand, both of which would be likely to increase in the future as the populations of the immigrant-supplying countries (Mexico, Central America, China, India,

Pakistan, and others) continue to grow, while a growing population and rising income per capita within the United States increase the demand for both skilled and unskilled immigrant labor." The bottom line is that net immigration, and thus population and GDP growth, are likely to be substantially higher than what the trustees (and CBO) project.

Growth in immigration, and therefore in population and in GDP, that is faster than what the trustees assume would ease any potential financial challenge faced by Social Security. The trustees (Social Security Administration 2005, 152) acknowledge that each additional annual 100,000 immigrants beyond the 900,000 they assume "increases the long-range actuarial balance by about 0.07 percent of taxable payroll." Hence, if instead of declining, as the trustees assume, net immigration were to grow at a modest 1 percent annually over the next 75 years, then net immigration would average roughly 2 million people annually. This rate of net immigration would reduce the trustees' projected 75-year deficit by 0.77 percentage points, from 1.92 percent to 1.15 percent of taxable payroll. With greater net immigration, the CBO's projected deficit would also be significantly lower.

Together, an annual real-wage growth of 1.5 percent and an annual average of roughly 2 million net immigrants would largely eliminate the Social Security deficits forecast by the trustees and the CBO. These two plausible modifications in assumptions would reduce the long-run 75-year Social Security deficit projected by the trustees by more than the sum of their individual effects (that is, more than 0.42 percent plus 0.77 percent, or 1.19 percent of taxable payroll). This is due to the fact that higher wages and higher net immigration will interact synergistically to produce greater financial savings.

The trustees recognize the high degree of uncertainty in their projections, although they fail to acknowledge that their assumptions are very pessimistic. In fact, they offer three projections (Social Security Administration 2005): a low cost, a high cost, and an intermediate forecast. All of the trustees' projections provided above refer to their intermediate forecast that they consider to be their best estimate. It is instructive, however, to briefly review their low-cost, or optimistic, projection to get an idea of how easily the financial challenges confronting Social Security could disappear.

Under the low-cost scenario, the 75-year actuarial balance is assumed to be a positive 0.38 percent of taxable payroll, and the trust fund in 2079 instead of being depleted is assumed to hold assets that amount to about five times the value of the benefits promised in 2079. In other words, under the low-cost scenario, Social Security is more than fully funded, and without undermining the solvency of the system, we could afford to immediately and permanently *reduce* payroll taxes, from 12.4 percent to 12.02 percent.

What are some of the main differences between the assumptions underlying the pessimistic intermediate forecast and the rosy low-cost forecast?

Productivity in the low-cost forecast is assumed to be 1.9 percent, still below the historical average, instead of 1.6 percent as in the intermediate projection. Real-wage growth in the low-cost projection is pegged at 1.6 percent, about the historical average, instead of at 1.1 percent, as in the intermediate forecast. And net immigration is projected at 1.3 million, probably considerably less than what we should expect, instead of 900,000 as in the intermediate projection. To wit, relatively minor and reasonable adjustments in the basic economic and demographic assumptions eliminate the projected financing problems of the Social Security system. Thus, Social Security may not be facing any financial challenges, and if it is, we can grow our way out of them.

The excessively pessimistic nature of the trustees' intermediate forecast can be illustrated by examining the changes in the trustees' projections over time. Almost every year between 1997 and 2005, the trustees' day of reckoning, the year in which the trust fund is projected to be depleted, has been moved back: from 2029 in 1997 to 2041 in 2005. Another way the excessively pessimistic nature of the trustees' intermediate forecast can be illustrated is by comparing their population forecast with the population projections widely considered the most authoritative—those of the U.S. Census Bureau. The trustees (Social Security Administration 2005, 77) assume that U.S. population will be only about 384 million in 2050, while the U.S. Census Bureau (2004) assumes that the U.S. population will be much larger, at about 420 million in 2050. Interestingly, the population projection of the Census Bureau for 2050 is nearly identical to the population projection of 424 million in 2050 that the trustees (Social Security Administration 2005, 78) make under their optimistic low-cost scenario. As noted earlier, a larger population would, of course, ease the financial challenges of sustaining Social Security.

But what if the predictions of the intermediate forecast are in fact correct? Are we not then threatened by a serious crisis? No, not really. Even if we do nothing, future Social Security recipients will get more in benefits than do current retirees. If the best estimates of the trustees are correct and we do nothing to fix the looming financial problem, then Social Security will be able to pay only about 70 percent of promised benefits after 2041. But even at 70 percent of promised benefits, the benefits that Social Security will be able to pay after 2041 will be *greater* in today's dollars than what current retirees receive: the real purchasing power of the benefits of future retirees will be higher than that of current retirees.

Under the CBO's projections, the future for retirees is even brighter, as the CBO anticipates that the system will be able to pay about 80 percent of promised benefits after 2052. Thus, for example, the average retiree in 2065 would receive benefits (in 2004 dollars) of $18,300, whereas the average retiree in 2005 receives $13,300 (Congressional Budget Office 2004, 14). This means that in the midst of a so-called "crisis," future retirees can expect to receive

38 percent more in benefits than retirees do today. Of course, relative to prevailing real average wages, the average future retiree would be relatively less well off than the average current retiree, as the CBO expects average real wages to grow more than 38 percent between 2005 and 2065.

But what about the demographic time bomb? How can relatively fewer workers afford to pay ever higher benefits to an ever larger number of retirees? How will two workers be able to support each Social Security beneficiary in the future when we have three workers to support each beneficiary today? Consider that if demography were destiny, Americans would have starved to death long ago. Seventy-five years ago, each farmer had to feed only about eight Americans. Today, each farmer must support well over 100 Americans.

The President has misstated the challenge of supporting retirees in the future. The challenge is not how many workers we have, and will have, per beneficiary, anymore than the food challenge is how many farmers we have per American. Instead, the challenge is a function of two interrelated factors, one demographic and one related to productivity. The demographic factor is how many workers we have, and will have, relative to the population that must be supported (the workers themselves, their dependents, and the beneficiaries). The second factor is how productive these workers are and will be. Today, 1.9 people live off the output of each worker paying into the system (Social Security Administration 2005, pp. 47 and 77). Using the pessimistic demographic assumptions of the Social Security trustees, by 2080 there will be 2.03 people supported by each worker paying into the system, a ratio that will be only about seven percent higher than what it is at present. More importantly, each worker today generates an average of $78,000 in output (in 2000 dollars) or $41,000 in goods and services for each of the 1.9 people that he or she must support (Social Security Administration 2005, 47, 93, and 171). But using the gloomy economic assumptions of the trustees, each worker in 2080 will produce an average of $260,000 of output in 2000 dollars, or $128,000 in goods and services for each person they will need to sustain.

In other words, the relatively fewer workers of the future will produce so much more than today's workers that it will be much easier for the coming workforce to support the population of the future than it is for current workers to support the population of today. Imagine a State of the Union Address by President Bush that would have accurately portrayed the issue this way: "Today, every three workers paying into the system produce $234,000 in output and must support nearly six people. In 75 years, every two workers paying into the system will produce a much larger $520,000 in output and will need to support only slightly more than four people."

Even if the trustees are right, the magnitude of the Social Security "crisis" is small and pales in comparison to other fiscal challenges faced by the government. For example, the trustees estimate that the present value of Social

Security's long-term financial shortfall is $4 trillion. By comparison, the Medicare trustees have estimated that the present value of the 75-year shortfall in just Medicare's prescription drug program alone is more than twice as large, at $8 trillion (Medicare Trustees 2004, 108). So, while there may not be any serious threat to the retirement security of our senior citizens, there is certainly a very serious danger to the health security of our seniors. Likewise, the Center on Budget and Policy Priorities (2004, 2) has calculated that the present value of the 75-year cost of permanently extending President Bush's 2001 and 2003 tax cuts is nearly three times as large, at $11.6 trillion. If Social Security is "in crisis," then what words would be appropriate to describe the financial condition of Medicare or the fiscal consequences of President Bush's proposal to make permanent his tax cuts?

Given the relatively small size of the deficit in Social Security projected by its trustees, the projected deficit can be corrected by fairly small adjustments. For example, to eliminate the deficit, payroll taxes could be raised 1.92 percentage points, from their current rate of 12.4 percent to 14.32 percent. If the CBO's deficit projection were correct, payroll taxes would need to be raised only 1 percentage point, from 12.4 percent to 13.4 percent. These are small tax increases relative to the tax cuts that were enacted in 2001 and 2003 and would leave Americans paying less in total federal taxes in 2005 than they were in 2000.

As Dean Baker and David Rosnick at the Center for Economic and Policy Research have pointed out, "Raising payroll taxes is not the only way to increase the revenue for Social Security. An alternative is to raise the ceiling on taxable wages. Currently (in 2004), no Social Security taxes are paid on income earned above $87,900 in any given year. If the ceiling were raised to $110,000 to cover 90 percent of the country's income from wages (the level set by the Greenspan Commission in 1983), it would eliminate approximately 40 percent of the projected funding shortfall. Using the CBO projections, this change alone would be almost enough to make the program solvent through the seventy-five year planning period" (Baker and Rosnick 2004, 6). If we went further and made all wages above $87,900 subject to Social Security taxes, as are all wages below that level, then the deficit projected by the trustees of Social Security would be eliminated without cutting benefits for anyone or raising taxes on the bottom 94 percent of taxpayers.

Finally, we could make a major contribution to the long-run soundness of the Social Security system by investing in our young children. Aside from strengthening the financial conditions of our public retirement benefit program, such investment would provide a vast array of other benefits. In the next sections, we describe the economic, fiscal, and social benefits of investment in early childhood development and its potential contribution to the solvency of Social Security.

THE NET BENEFITS OF INVESTMENT IN EARLY
CHILDHOOD DEVELOPMENT

At a time of fundamental disagreements in the United States over the nature of the country's economic problems and their solutions, it is rare when a consensus emerges across the political spectrum on both the problems and the appropriate policy solutions. There is almost universal agreement among experts that too many young children have inadequate food, clothing, shelter, health care, and safety. Likewise, there is agreement that too many children do not have access to high-quality educational opportunities, and that too many fall far short of achieving their academic potential while in school. At the same time, there is a consensus among experts that high-quality investments in the education and health of young children would help resolve these problems and have huge long-term economic payoffs, both to our children and to society as a whole.

Although there are many ways to illustrate the deprivation experienced by children, one good indicator of the magnitude of the crisis is the statistics on childhood poverty. In 2003, fully 19.8 percent of all children under the age of six—that is, one out of every five kids, or some 4.7 million children— were living in poverty in the United States. This is up from 18.5 percent, or 4.3 million children, in 2002.

To make matters worse, poor children grow up into adults who are more likely to engage in crime, use illegal drugs, abuse alcohol, neglect and abuse their children, and suffer from poor physical health and a variety of mental illnesses. They are also less likely to be gainfully employed and, thus, less likely to contribute to the growth of our economy.

Poor children who fail to achieve their full academic potential are more likely to enter adulthood without the skills necessary to develop into highly productive members of society able to compete effectively in a global labor market. Less skilled, less productive, and earning less, when these children become adults they will be less able to help us sustain public retirement benefits systems such as Social Security, a challenge we may face in the future. In short, the consequences of childhood poverty on our collective economic health and well-being as a community are profoundly negative and have long-term consequences.

Below, I provide a brief overview of the benefits of high-quality ECD programs and report the benefit-cost ratios that have been calculated for four such programs: the Perry Preschool Project, the Prenatal/Early Infancy Project, the Abecedarian Early Childhood Intervention, and the Chicago Child-Parent Center Program. Next, I present calculations on the effect a high-quality, large-scale ECD program for all poor three- and four-year-old children would have on future government budgets, the economy, and crime. Finally, I illustrate the potential contribution of ECD investment to the solvency of the U.S. Social Security system. In the appendix, I provide a brief description of the methodology used to derive these estimates. For a fuller description of the methodology, the benefits of high-quality ECD programs, and the effects that a high-quality, nationwide ECD program would have on government budgets, the economy, and crime, see Lynch (2004).

OVERVIEW OF THE BENEFITS OF EARLY CHILDHOOD DEVELOPMENT PROGRAMS

ECD programs differ in whom they service and in the types of services they offer. However, most provide language development and other education services, and often include health services (such as immunizations, health screenings, and pre- and post-natal services), social services, and nutrition services, typically for children under age six. In addition, ECD programs often provide adult education and parenting classes for the parents of young children. Good ECD programs, furthermore, have well-educated and trained staffs, low child-to-teacher ratios, and small class sizes.

Consensus about the effectiveness of investments in high-quality ECD programs has not always existed. Early studies showed that children in high-quality ECD programs performed significantly better on IQ tests in the first few years after program participation than did comparable children who did not participate in the programs (see, for example, Deutsch 1967). Thus, there was great initial optimism about the benefits of ECD programs. However, follow-up studies of ECD participants found that their advantage over non-ECD participants in terms of IQ test scores tended to fade as they progressed through school, so that by the end of elementary school, there were no significant IQ test score differences (see, for example, Cicirelli 1969). Thus, initial optimism turned to pessimism, and some scholars concluded that investment in ECD was a waste of money, producing few if any benefits, but costing thousands of dollars per participant.

Long-term studies of ECD participants have found that such pessimism is unwarranted, because exclusive attention on IQ test scores is misplaced, and significant benefits of ECD programs do in fact exist. In general, these benefits include:

- Higher levels of verbal, mathematical, and intellectual achievement.
- Greater success at school, including less grade retention and higher graduation rates.
- Higher employment and earnings.
- Better health outcomes.
- Less welfare dependency.
- Lower rates of crime.
- Greater government revenues and lower government expenditures.

More specifically, assessments of well-designed and well-executed ECD programs have established that participating children are more successful in school and in life after school than children who are not enrolled in high-quality ECD programs. In particular, children who participate in high-quality ECD programs tend to have higher scores on math and reading achievement tests, have greater language abilities, are better prepared to enter elementary school, are more likely to pursue secondary education, have less grade retention, have less need for special education and other remedial coursework, have lower dropout rates, have higher high school graduation rates, have higher levels of schooling attainment, have improved nutrition, have better access to health care services, have higher rates of immunization, have better health, and experience less child abuse and neglect. These children are also less likely to be teenage parents and more likely to have higher employment rates as adults, higher earnings as adults, greater self-sufficiency as adults, lower welfare dependency, lower rates of drug use, show less frequent and less severe delinquent behavior, engage in fewer criminal acts both as juveniles and as adults, and have fewer interactions with the criminal justice system and lower incarceration rates. The benefits of ECD programs to participating children enable them to enter school "ready to learn," helping them achieve better outcomes in school and throughout their lives.

Parents and families of children who participate in ECD programs also benefit. For example, mothers have fewer additional births, have better nutrition and smoke less during pregnancy, are less likely to abuse or neglect their children, complete more years of schooling, have higher high school graduation rates, are more likely to be employed, have higher earnings, engage in fewer criminal acts, have lower drug and alcohol abuse, and are less likely to use welfare.

Investments in ECD programs easily pay for themselves over time by generating very high rates of return for participants, the public, and government. Good programs produce three dollars or more in benefits for every dollar of investment. While participants and their families get part of the total benefits, the benefits to the rest of the public and government are larger and, on their own, tend to far outweigh the costs of these programs. Thus, it is advantageous even for nonparticipating taxpayers to pay for these programs.

There is now a consensus among experts of all political persuasions that investments in ECD programs have huge potential long-term payoffs. Several prominent economists and business leaders (many of whom are skeptical about government programs generally) have recently issued well-documented reviews of the literature that find very high economic payoffs from ECD programs. For example, Nobel Prize–winning economist James Heckman (1999, 22 and 41) of the University of Chicago has concluded: "Recent studies of early childhood investments have shown remarkable success and indicate that the early years are important for early learning and can be enriched through external channels. Early childhood investments of high quality have lasting effects. . . . In the long run, significant improvements in the skill levels of American workers, especially workers not attending college, are unlikely without substantial improvements in the arrangements that foster early learning. We cannot afford to postpone investing in children until they become adults, nor can we wait until they reach school age—a time when it may be too late to intervene. Learning is a dynamic process and is most effective when it begins at a young age and continues through adulthood. The role of the family is crucial to the formation of learning skills, and government interventions at an early age that mend the harm done by dysfunctional families have proven to be highly effective."

The director of research and a regional economic analyst at the Federal Reserve Bank of Minneapolis, Arthur Rolnick and Rob Grunewald (2003, 3 and 16), have come to similar conclusions: "Recent studies suggest that one critical form of education, early childhood development, or ECD, is grossly under-funded. However, if properly funded and managed, investment in ECD yields an extraordinary return, far exceeding the return on most investments, private or public. . . . In the future any proposed economic development list should have early childhood development at the top."

Likewise, after reviewing the evidence, the Committee for Economic Development (2002), a nonpartisan research and policy organization of some 250 business leaders and educators, concluded, "Society pays in many ways for failing to take full advantage of the learning potential of all of its children, from lost economic productivity and tax revenues to higher crime rates to diminished participation in the civic and cultural life of the nation. . . . Over a decade ago, CED urged the nation to view education as an investment, not an expense, and to develop a comprehensive and coordinated strategy of human investment. Such a strategy should redefine education as a process that begins at birth and encompasses all aspects of children's early development, including their physical, social, emotional, and cognitive growth. In the intervening years the evidence has grown even stronger that investments in early education can have long-term benefits for both children and society."

ESTIMATES OF BENEFIT-COST RATIOS FOR ECD INVESTMENT

Four ECD programs have had carefully controlled studies with long-term follow-up of participants and a control group of nonparticipants: the Perry Preschool Project, the Prenatal/Early Infancy Project, the Abecedarian Early Childhood Intervention, and the Chicago Child-Parent Center Program. All but

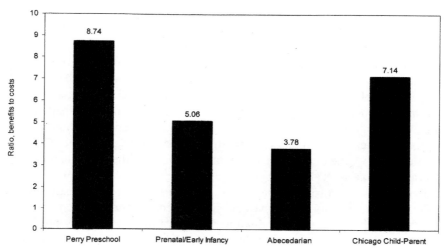

Figure 4.1.   Benefit-cost ratio for ECD programs.
Source: Barnett (1993), Karoly et. al. (1998), Masse and Barnett (2002), Reynolds et. al.
(2002).

the Chicago Child-Parent Center Program had random assignment of potentially eligible children into the intervention program or the control group. The Chicago Child-Parent Center Program did not use randomized assignment, but the control group did match the intervention group on age, eligibility for intervention, and family socioeconomic status.

All four of these studies have found that enormous payoffs result from investments in early childhood development. Specifically, as illustrated in figure 4.1, analyses of the four programs have found benefit-cost ratios that varied from a minimum of 3.78 to 1 to a high of 8.74 to 1. It should be noted that investment in a project is justified if its benefit-cost ratio exceeds 1 to 1. Moreover, in the benefit-cost analyses of all four of these programs, the costs may have been fully described, but the benefits were certainly understated. Specifically, it was not always possible to monetize the benefits that were identified (such as the monetary benefit of reduced child abuse and neglect), and not all the likely benefits were identified and monetized (such as the increased employment and earnings of parents who had children enrolled in preschool programs). Thus, the benefits of these ECD programs probably exceed the costs by margins greater than those indicated in figure 4.1.

From the perspective of public policy, it should be observed that investments in ECD programs easily pay for themselves by generating very high rates of return for participants, the nonparticipating public, and government (in the form of either reduced public service costs or higher tax payments by participants and their families). While participants and their families get part of the total benefits, it is noteworthy that the benefits to the public and government are larger and in and of themselves tend to far outweigh the costs of these programs. For example, a Federal Reserve Bank of Minneapolis study (Rolnick and Grunewald 2003) determined that annual real rates of return on public investments in the Perry Preschool program were 12 percent for the nonparticipating public and government, and 4 percent for participants, so that total returns exceeded 16 percent. Thus, it is advantageous even for nonparticipating taxpayers to pay for these programs. To comprehend how extraordinarily high these rates of return on ECD investments are, consider that according to Burtless (1999), the highly touted real rate of return on the stock market that prevailed between 1871 and 1998 was just 6.3 percent.

Even from the narrow perspective of government budgets, investments in ECD programs pay for themselves because the costs to government are outweighed by the budgetary benefits that the investments eventually produce. Figure 4.2 illustrates the benefit-cost ratio for three of the four ECD programs described in figure 4.1, assuming that all the costs are borne by government and taking into account only the benefits that generate budget savings for government. These ratios vary from a low of 2.5 to 1 for the Perry Preschool program to a high of 4.1 to 1 for the Prenatal/Early Infancy program. Unfortunately, the benefit-cost ratio to government was not calculated for the Abecedarian program.

In the next section, the benefit-cost ratios and rates of return that were calculated for the Perry Preschool Project are translated into estimates of how investments in ECD programs affect future government finances, the economy, and crime. For the purposes of this analysis, I assume that a high-quality,

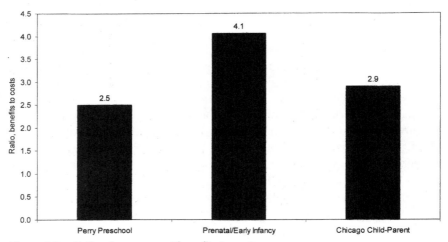

Figure 4.2.   Ratio of government benefits to costs.
Source: Barnett (1993), Karoly et al. (1998), Reynolds et. al. (2002) and author's analysis.

publicly funded ECD program is established to serve roughly all three- and four-year-old children in the United States who are living in poverty. More specifically, I assume that the program enrolls 20 percent of all three- and four-year-olds: those living in the lowest-income families and who are most at risk for poor educational performance.

BUDGET EFFECTS OF ECD INVESTMENT

Follow-up research on children who participated in high-quality ECD programs and similar nonparticipating children has found that ECD investment benefits taxpayers and generates government budget benefits in at least four ways. First, subsequent public education expenses are lower because participants spend less time in school, as they fail fewer grades and require expensive special education less often. Second, criminal justice costs come down because participants—and their families—have markedly lower crime and delinquency rates. Third, both participants and their parents have higher incomes and pay more taxes than nonparticipants. Fourth, ECD investment reduces public welfare expenditures because participants and their families have lower rates of welfare usage. Other savings to taxpayers and boons to government budgets, such as reductions in public health-care expenditures, are likely to exist, but we lack the data to quantify all these other potential savings.

Against these four types of budget benefits, we must consider two types of budget costs. These costs are the expenses of the ECD program itself and the increased expenditure on higher public education due to greater use of higher education by ECD participants.

The ECD programs do not perform miracles on poor children. Substantial numbers of ECD participants do poorly in school, commit crimes, have poor health outcomes, and receive welfare payments. The key point is that ECD participants as a group have far lower rates of these negative outcomes than do nonparticipants.

The budget effects through the year 2050 described below are a consequence of launching a government-financed, permanent, high-quality ECD program immediately in 2005 that targets 20 percent of all three- and four-year-olds— roughly all of them who live in poverty. The exact nature of the ECD program— such as whether it should be center-based or center-based with a home visiting component, full-day or half-day, year-round or nine months long, etc.—is beyond the scope of this study. Obviously, however, the precise nature of the ECD program will affect the costs and benefits. For example, the costs of a full-day preschool program are likely to be different from those for a half-day program. Likewise, the benefits of a full-day program are likely to be different from those of a half-day program because, for instance, the parents of young children are more likely to be in the labor force if their children are in a full-day program. Since it is the only ECD program for which the necessary data is available, I base the cost and benefits of this hypothetical ECD investment on the outcomes of the Perry Preschool Project.

In addition, I estimate the benefits of an ECD program that is only for poor three- and four-year-olds because of the limitations in the data. Data available from the analysis of several ECD programs make it clear, however, that benefits generated by programs that begin during the prenatal months and that continue through the third grade may be significant and perhaps even greater than those estimated here from a program for poor three- and four-year-olds only. It is worth noting that families may need two or three or more times the poverty level of income to meet basic needs and invest appropriately in the education of their children. Thus, it is possible that a larger ECD investment—one that covered children living in families up to 200 percent or more of poverty—may also yield excellent returns. Indeed, there is evidence that all children may benefit from enrollment in ECD programs.

The analysis described below considers budget effects on all levels of government—federal, state, and local—as a unified whole. As a practical matter, the source estimates have not made such a distinction, nor should they. All levels of government share in the costs of education, criminal justice, and income support. Responsibilities have shifted in the last half-century and will continue to do so over the nearly half-century time frame used in this analysis. Although a case can be made that ECD investments should be the responsibility of the federal government to address educational inequalities before children enter the school system, these investments could be made at any or all levels of government. This analysis focuses on capturing national effects of ECD investments.

Offsetting budget benefits take a while to outstrip the costs, but the gap becomes substantially favorable over time. For the first 16 years, additional costs exceed offsetting budget benefits, but by a declining margin. Thereafter, offsetting budget benefits exceed costs by a growing margin each year. This pattern is illustrated in figures 4.3 and 4.4. Annual revenue impacts and costs are portrayed in nominal terms in figure 4.3 and again as a percentage of GDP in figure 4.4. Figure 4.5 shows the annual net budget impact in nominal terms.

In the second year of the program, 2006, when the program is fully phased in, government outlays would exceed offsetting budget benefits by $19.4 billion. The annual deficit due to the ECD program would shrink for the next 14 years. By the seventeenth year of the program, in 2021, the deficit would turn into a surplus that would grow every year thereafter, culminating in a net budgetary surplus of some 0.25 percent of GDP in 2050 (the last year estimated), as illustrated in figure 4.6. Thus, by 2050, the offsetting budget benefits of ECD investments would total 0.44 percent of GDP, and the costs to

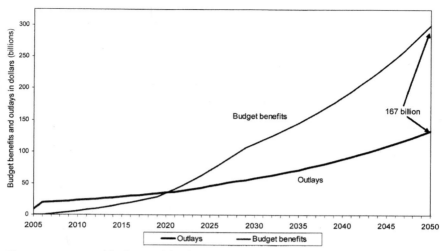

Figure 4.3.   Annual budgetary benefits and outlays.
Source: **Author's analysis.**

government of ECD investments would amount to almost 0.2 percent of GDP. In dollar amounts, by 2050 the net budget savings would total $167 billion (or $61 billion in 2004 dollars).

The reason for this fiscal pattern is fairly obvious. The costs of the program will grow fairly steadily for the first decade and a half, in tandem with modest

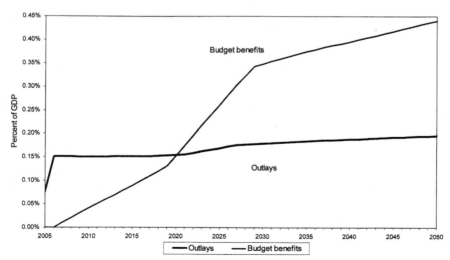

Figure 4.4.   Annual budgetary benefits and outlays as percent of gross domestic product.
Source: **Author's analysis.**

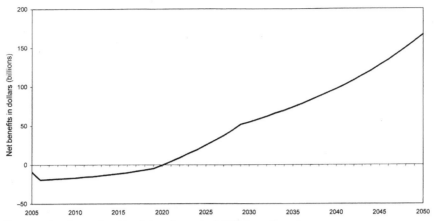

Figure 4.5.   Annual net budetary impact of ECD investments.
Source: **Author's analysis.**

growth in the population of three- and four-year-old participants. Thereafter, costs will grow at a somewhat faster pace for a few years as, in addition to the costs of educating three- and four-year-olds, the first and subsequent cohorts of participant children begin to use higher public education services. After the first two years, when the first cohort of children start entering the public school system, public education expenditures will begin to diminish, due to less grade retention and remedial education. After a decade and a half, the first cohort of children will be entering the workforce, resulting in increased earnings and thus

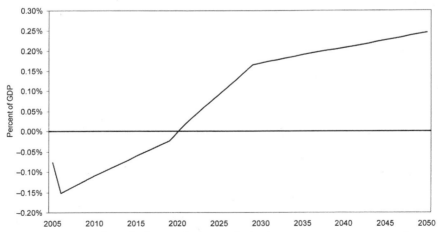

Figure 4.6.   Annual net budgetary impacts of ECD investments as a percent of gross domestic product.
Source: **Author's analysis.**

higher tax revenues and lower welfare expenditures. In addition, governments will experience lower judicial system costs.

ECONOMIC EFFECTS OF ECD INVESTMENTS

It is important to keep in mind that savings to government are not the only benefits from ECD investments. For example, benefits that did not accrue to government finances represented a sizeable portion of the total benefits found in the studies of high-quality ECD programs. In fact, 19.8 percent of the estimated total benefits found for the Prenatal/Early Infancy program, 59 percent for the Chicago Child-Parent Centers program, and 81.4 percent for the Perry Preschool program went to groups aside from government. These other benefits come in many forms.

For example, ECD investment has a significant impact on the future earnings of participants, productivity, and GDP. The guardians of participants are also likely to experience increases in earnings, since they will have more time for employment as a consequence of the day care provided to their children by the ECD program. But due to limitations in the data, I am not able to calculate the earnings increases of the guardians. In the long run, the higher future earnings of the ECD participants, who will comprise as much as a fifth of the future workforce, will translate into productivity gains and higher GDP levels.

Figure 4.7 illustrates the impact of ECD investments on GDP, showing the annual increase in earnings due to ECD investment as a percentage of GDP. The

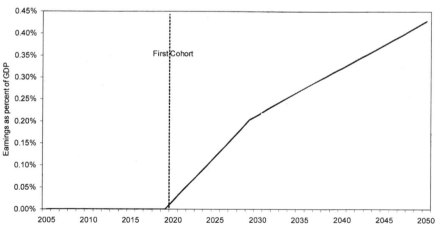

Figure 4.7. Annual earnings effects of ECD investments as a percentage of gross domestic product.
Source: Author's analysis.

initial increase in earnings occurs in 2020 when the first cohort of participating children turns 18 and enters the labor market. By 2050, the increase in earnings due to ECD investments is estimated to amount to 0.43 percent of GDP, or some $107 billion in 2004 dollars.

The increased earnings of children who participate in an ECD program not only allow the United States to compete more effectively in a global economy, but they also have positive implications for both earlier and future generations of children. These increased earnings will benefit earlier generations who reach retirement age by contributing to the solvency of Social Security and other public retirement benefit programs. Future generations will benefit because they will be less likely to grow up in families living in poverty.

CRIME EFFECTS OF ECD INVESTMENTS

Investments in ECD programs are likely to substantially reduce crime rates and the extraordinary costs to society of criminality. Some of these reduced costs are savings to government in the form of lower criminal justice system costs. These savings to government would total nearly $77 billion (or $28 billion in 2004 dollars) in 2050, and were included in the earlier discussion of the fiscal effects of ECD investments.

But there are other savings to society from reduced crime. The material losses and the pain and suffering experienced by the victims of crime would be reduced, as fewer people would be raped, murdered, and assaulted. Of course, the potential perpetrators of crime may benefit from less crime as well. For example, fewer people would experience the burdens of incarceration. However, I was not able to quantify the value of the avoidance of incarceration.

By 2050, savings to individuals from less crime would amount to $345 billion ($127 billion in 2004 dollars). Including the savings to government, the savings to society from reductions in criminality due to investments in ECD programs would total $422 billion ($155 billion in 2004 dollars). Figure 4.8 illustrates the annual benefits to individuals and to society from ECD-induced reductions in crime.

EXTRAPOLATING FROM THE PERRY PRESCHOOL PROJECT AND INCREASING THE SCALE OF ECD INVESTMENT

Making extrapolations from the Perry Preschool Project to a nationwide ECD program raises several questions. Do results from a program that operated in a small-town setting carry over to large urban, often inner-city environments

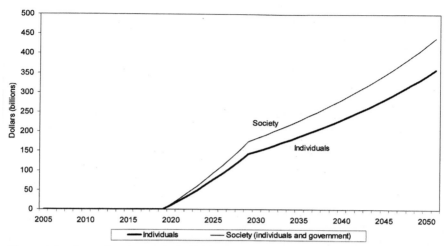

Figure 4.8. Annual savings to individuals and society from reduced crime due to ECD investment.
Source: Author's anaylsis.

where many poor children today live? Have the problems faced by poor children changed so much since the Perry Preschool Project operated in the 1960s that it is unlikely that the success of that program can be replicated? Have the dramatic changes in the U.S. welfare system over the past decade reduced the welfare savings that could be generated by an ECD program like the Perry Preschool Project? Does the fact that the Perry Preschool Project had the highest benefit-cost ratio of all the ECD programs analyzed (see figure 4.1) imply that the results for that project may overstate the net benefits of a nationwide ECD program? Finally, how confident can one be that the benefits found for the Perry Preschool Project, which was a relatively small pilot program, would apply when replicating the program, or a similar high-quality program, on a large, nationwide scale?

I believe that the results for the Perry Preschool Project would apply to a large-scale, nationwide ECD program today. The results for the Perry Preschool Project are similar to those of the Chicago Child-Parent Centers program. The Chicago Child-Parent Centers program is not a small-scale pilot program: it serves about 5,000 children annually and has served over 100,000 children to date (Reynolds et al. 2001). The Chicago program operates in a large urban, inner-city environment. The program started in 1967 but continues to serve thousands of children annually, with all their modern-day problems. Its net benefits, moreover, may actually exceed those of the Perry Preschool Project.

In fact, in terms of government finances alone, the net benefits of the Chicago Child-Parent Centers (and of the Prenatal/Early Infancy program) are higher than they are for the Perry Preschool Project (see figure 4.2). This is true even though the government savings from the Chicago Child-Parent Centers program are understated relative to those of the Perry Preschool Project because they do not include the government savings from reduced adult welfare usage on the part of the Chicago program participants.

Likewise, in terms of economic impacts alone, the benefit-cost ratio for the Chicago program exceeds that of the Perry Preschool Project. Furthermore, the total net benefits of the Chicago Child-Parent Centers program are probably greater than they are for the Perry Preschool Project. The total benefits of the Chicago program are underestimated relative to the Perry Preschool Project because they do not include the substantial savings that derive from reductions in the intangible losses due to crime.

It is not clear whether the dramatic changes in the welfare system would result in lower savings to government today than was generated decades ago by ECD investments. But even if the changes in the welfare system did mean that there would be relatively less government savings from reduced welfare usage, the results of this extrapolation would not change substantially. After all, for the Perry Preschool Project, the savings to government from reductions in welfare usage amounted to only about 9 percent of the total savings to government, and it amounted to less than 3 percent of the total benefits of the program.

This analysis did not extrapolate from the Perry Preschool Project because it is the ideal program, or even better than the three other model programs described. Instead, the Perry Preschool Project was used to calculate the budgetary, economic, and crime effects of investments in ECD programs because it is the only program for which the data exist on rates of return necessary to do these extrapolations.

The ultimate benefit-cost ratio for a large-scale, nationwide ECD program enrolling roughly 1.6 million children a year could turn out to be higher or lower than in smaller pilot programs. A large program would have the potential, not possible in small programs, to improve the school atmosphere for everyone, not just ECD participants. Raising academic performance while reducing disruptive classroom behaviors and drug or criminal activity of 20 percent of children and teenagers should benefit the other 80 percent of students who attend school with them. In addition, there may be some multiplier effects on the economy from the higher-skilled, more productive, and higher-earning ECD participants.

Indeed, it is important to note that the estimates of the benefits of the nationwide ECD program presented here do not take into consideration the positive feedback effects on future generations of children and therefore the possible savings in the future costs of the ECD investment. The program invests in the parents of the future who, as a consequence of the ECD investment, will be able to provide better educational opportunities to their children than they would without the ECD program. As a result, it may not be necessary to spend as much on ECD in the future to achieve the same educational, crime, and income effects on the children of the next generation as is estimated here. Alternatively, not scaling back the future level of ECD investment may result in much greater benefits than estimated in this study, once the generational effects are taken into account.

On the other hand, a larger-scale ECD program might draw in more kids who are less at risk than those in the pilot programs. Such kids might (or might not) have lower benefit-cost ratios than those in the pilot programs—experts are divided on this issue. See, for example, the lively debate in Heckman and Krueger (2003). Likewise, the quality of teachers and other staff may not be as good, or the teachers and staff may not be as highly motivated as those in the pilot programs.

For illustration purposes, this analysis assumes the launch of an ECD program on a national scale immediately in 2005, with full phase-in by 2006. But for practical purposes, such as the recruitment and training of teachers and staff and finding appropriate locations, a large-scale ECD program would have to be phased in over a longer period. There may be start-up costs associated with the training and recruitment of teachers and staff (and the establishment of appropriate sites) that are not accounted for in these estimates of the net benefits of ECD investment. And, of course, there may be other costs associated with the scaling up of ECD investment that have not been considered. On the other hand, the total benefits of ECD investment are understated in these estimates. Thus, although the benefit-cost ratio of a national ECD program could be somewhat higher or lower than found in the pilot programs, it is implausible that the ratio would be less than the one to one ratio necessary to justify launching the program.

THE POTENTIAL IMPACT OF ECD INVESTMENT ON THE SOLVENCY OF THE SOCIAL SECURITY SYSTEM

The fiscal pattern for investment in high-quality early childhood development has almost the mirror image of the pattern projected for Social Security by the Congressional Budget Office. Compare the fiscal pattern for ECD investments in figure 4.6 to the fiscal pattern for the Social Security system in figure 4.9 (thin line). Although as discussed in detail earlier, the risk of insolvency is a matter of considerable dispute, according to a recent CBO analysis, the Social Security system will continue to receive more in tax revenues than it pays out in benefits until 2018 (Congressional Budget Office 2004). After that, as illustrated by the thin line in figure 4.9, it runs a growing gap between benefits

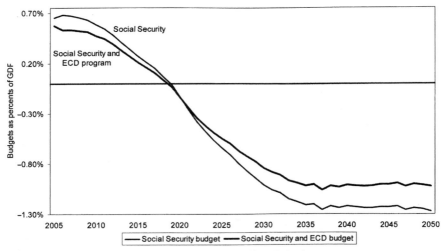

Figure 4.9.   Annual Social Security and ECD budget outlook.
Source: **CBO (2004) and author's analysis.**

paid out and tax revenues received. Between 2018 and 2052, the gap between benefits paid and tax revenues received will be filled by the interest on, and the redemption of, the bonds held in the Social Security trust fund. Hence, the fiscal pattern for Social Security depicted in figure 4.9 does not include the revenues derived from the use of the trust fund.

The thick line in figure 4.9 depicts the combined effect of the projected budget impact of ECD investment and the CBO's budget projections for the Social Security system (again, excluding the trust fund). The net savings to government from investment in an ECD program are smaller than the CBO's projected deficits for the Social Security system, but they are significant. The projected government-wide budget gain from ECD would be 0.25 percent of GDP in 2050, about one-fifth of the projected 1.27 percent of GDP deficit projected by CBO in Social Security for that year. Thus, if government savings due to ECD investment were earmarked for Social Security, such ECD investment could make a substantial contribution to the solvency of the system. This contribution toward fiscal balance would start in less than two decades and would be achieved without raising taxes or cutting benefits.

CONCLUSION

A high-quality, nationwide commitment to early childhood development would cost a significant amount of money up front, but it would have a substantial payoff in the future. The U.S. political system, with its two- and four-year cycles, tends to underinvest in programs with such long lags between when investment costs are incurred and the benefits are enjoyed. The fact that lower levels of government cannot capture all the benefits of ECD investment may also discourage them from assuming all the costs of ECD programs. Yet the economic case for ECD investment is compelling.

I estimate that providing poor three- and four-year-old children—20 percent of all children in this age range—with a high-quality program would initially cost about $19 billion a year. Such a program would ultimately reduce costs for remedial and special education, for criminal justice, and for welfare benefits, and it would increase income earned and taxes paid. Within about 17 years, the net effect on the budget would turn positive (for all levels of government combined). Within 30 years, the offsetting budget benefits would be more than double the costs of the ECD program (and the cost of the additional youth going to college).

The economic and social benefits from ECD investment amount to much more than just improvements in public balance sheets. By improving the skills of a large fraction of the U.S. workforce, these programs for poor children would increase earnings, enhance productivity, raise the GDP, reduce poverty, and strengthen U.S. global competitiveness. Crime rates and the heavy costs of criminality to society are likely to be substantially reduced as well. If we invest in young children, we could also enhance the solvency of public retirement benefits systems such as Social Security.

Investing in young children has positive implications for the current generation of children, for future generations of children, and for earlier generations. The current generation of children will benefit from higher earnings, higher material standards of living, and an enhanced quality of life. Future generations will benefit because they will be less likely to grow up in families living in poverty. And earlier generations, those who are now in retirement or nearing retirement, will benefit by being supported by higher-earning workers who will be better able to financially sustain our public retirement benefit programs such as Social Security. In other words, solving the economic and social problems of our youth will simultaneously help provide lasting economic security to future generations and to our elderly.

Thus, we should be investing in high-quality early childhood development programs to improve the quality of life of millions of our children, to reduce crime, to make the workforce of the future more productive, and to strengthen our economy. Because the retirement of the Baby Boom generation will put pressure on government budgets in coming decades, particularly in the areas of health care, we should also be investing in ECD programs to provide future budget relief and to help fund some of the nation's most important programs, such as Social Security, Medicare, and Medicaid.

APPENDIX 4.1: EXPLANATION OF THE METHODOLOGY FOR ESTIMATING THE BUDGET, ECONOMIC, AND CRIME EFFECTS OF INVESTMENTS IN ECD

I assumed that an ECD program would begin in 2005 and would serve roughly all three- and four-year-old children who live in poverty, or 20 percent of all children this age living in the lowest income families. The numbers of three- and four-year-olds entered in the estimating model were taken from recent population projections made by the U.S. Census Bureau (2004).

I assumed that the ECD program would be of high quality, and its costs and benefits were modeled on those calculated for the Perry Preschool Project. The annual average impact for various types of costs and benefits per Perry Preschool program participant that was estimated by Rolnick and Grunewald (2003) of the Federal Reserve Bank of Minneapolis was used as the baseline for the analysis. The annual costs and benefits per program participant of the preschool program were adjusted for inflation and/or wage increases every year through 2050, in line with projections made by the Congressional Budget Office (2004).

The total costs and benefits of the preschool program were determined by multiplying the number of participants of a particular age by the average value of the cost or benefit for each year the cost or benefit was produced by participants of that age, as determined by Rolnick and Grunewald (2003). Thus, for example, the reductions in the cost of providing public education per participant were assumed to kick in when that participant entered the public school system at age five and were assumed to cease when that participant turned 18 and left the school system.

5

Latino Immigrants, National Identity, and the National Interest

Rodolfo O. de la Garza

Immigration has been a contentious issue on the national political agenda for over a century, and the contours of the debate that it has raised have remained virtually unchanged. Surprisingly, although occasionally this has included protests over the number of immigrants the nation can absorb, as was the case in recent decades when groups such as Zero Population Growth and the Sierra Club opposed immigration, the core issues of the debate have centered on whether the new immigrants could be absorbed into the nation. Would they abandon the "old ways" in favor of core American values?

These questions were first raised when the initial wave of non-Western, non-Nordic Protestant immigrants, such as those from Italy and Ireland, began outnumbering those from Northern Europe and England. This concern expanded to include Asians, denying them the right to immigrate, as well as those already in the United States, denying them many of the rights and privileges that native-born citizens and legal immigrants normally enjoy.

While these same concerns now target the "new immigrants"—that is, Asians, Africans, and Hispanics—they focus on Hispanics because Hispanics are so numerous, making up approximately 50 percent of contemporary immigration, and because Hispanics share significant cultural traits (religion and language) that enhance their ability to remain outside mainstream society. Additionally, as Samuel Huntington has recently argued (Huntington 2004), given that Mexicans make up approximately half of this group and that a significant proportion of them are undocumented, the contemporary debate specifically asks how Mexican immigration will affect the nation.

The objective of this chapter is to address this issue. Specifically, it will examine the impact Latino immigrants in general and Mexican immigrants in particular are having on the nation. While the chapter addresses the cultural and economic aspects of the role of Mexicans, it will particularly emphasize the political dimensions of the subject, because the relationship immigrants develop with the polity shape their overall impact on the nation. Also, because Huntington's recent argument places Mexicans at the center of the current controversy, this chapter focuses on key elements of his argument. I would note, however, that while Huntington is a forceful advocate of anti-Mexican views, his perspective is not unique, but rather represents the views of other critics of immigration such as Patrick Buchanan and Arthur Schlesinger (see, for example, Schlesinger 1992).

IMMIGRANTS AND U.S. POPULAR CULTURE

Huntington is critical of Latino immigration because he argues that Latinos refuse to incorporate into mainstream culture and therefore threaten the nation's historical identity that is reflective of a unifying cultural experience rooted in Protestantism and the English language. Ironically, Latinos are twice as likely as all Americans to agree with that statement (see table 5.1). Nonetheless, two-thirds of Latinos agree that it is very or somewhat important to "change so that they blend into the larger society," but two-thirds also agree that it is very important "for Latinos to maintain their cultures" (Pew Hispanic Center 2004). Together, these attitudes suggest that Hispanics see no incompatibility between having a combined cultural identity, one that is located within mainstream America but built on home-country sentiments and practices.

At the societal level, the impact that Latino immigration has had on the nation's popular culture is ubiquitous and multifaceted. Indeed, the changes such immigration brings to our daily lives have so altered the cultural landscape that they are key to explaining the current rise in anti-Latino immigrant sentiment. Among the most significant of these changes is that, since the 1980s, Latinos have become a national minority. That is, rather than being regionally isolated, they now constitute substantial communities in virtually every state (see table 5.2).

Further illustrating this U.S. societal change is the number and distribution of states in which Latinos are the largest minority (see figure 5.1). This increasing national presence is particularly noteworthy among Mexicans, who historically

Table 5.1. National Perspectives of American Cultural Make-Up

	All Latinos	All Americans
U.S. is made up of many cultures	83%	92%
U.S. has a single core Anglo-Protestant culture	10%	5%

Source: Pew Hispanic Center (2004).

Table 5.2. States with Largest Latino Populations, 2000

State	State Population	Latino Population	% of U.S. Latino Population	Cumulative %
California	32,666,550	10,112,986	28.6%	28.6%
Texas	19,759,614	5,862,835	16.6%	45.3%
New York	18,175,301	2,624,928	7.4%	52.7%
Florida	14,915,980	2,243,441	6.4%	59.0%
Illinois	12,045,326	1,224,309	3.5%	62.5%
New Jersey	8,115,011	1,004,011	2.8%	65.4%
Arizona	4,668,631	1,033,822	2.9%	68.3%
New Mexico	1,736,931	700,289	2.0%	70.3%
Colorado	3,970,971	577,516	1.6%	71.9%
Massachusetts	6,147,132	377,016	1.1%	73.0%
Totals	122,201,447	35,300,000		

were concentrated in the Southwest but now have substantial and growing settlements across the country.

Latino immigrants have also established major settlements in the South, Midwest, and Northwest (see table 5.3). In New York, 32 percent of the city's immigrants came from Latin America in 2000 (New York City Department of City Planning Population Division 2005), easily outnumbering Europeans, who historically were the most numerous. New York Mexicans total 122,600, outnumbered only by Dominicans, with 369,200. Given that Mexico is much more distant than many other Latin American nations and has no historical relationship with the region, the size of this New York Mexican immigrant population is especially noteworthy.

The impact of these immigrants on the nation's popular culture is obvious and powerful. The most widely accepted and universal consequence is culinary. For almost a decade, Latino marketers have boasted that salsa outsells catsup. A drive across the country attests to the validity of this claim: tacos, fajitas,

Table 5.3. Top 10 Counties of Latino Population Growth

County	State	2000 Latino	Numeric Change	% Change	% Latino
Benton	AR	13,469	12,100	891.1%	8.8%
Forsyth	NC	19,577	17,475	831.4%	6.4%
Washington	AR	12,932	11,406	747.4%	8.2%
Durham	NC	17,039	14,986	729.6%	7.6%
Whitfield	GA	18,419	16,098	693.6%	22.1%
Gwinnett	GA	64,137	55,667	657.2%	10.9%
Mecklenburg	NC	44,871	38,178	570.4%	6.5%
Wake	NC	33,985	28,589	529.8%	5.4%
Hall	GA	27,242	22,684	529.8%	19.6%
Elkhart	IN	16,300	13,368	529.8%	8.9%

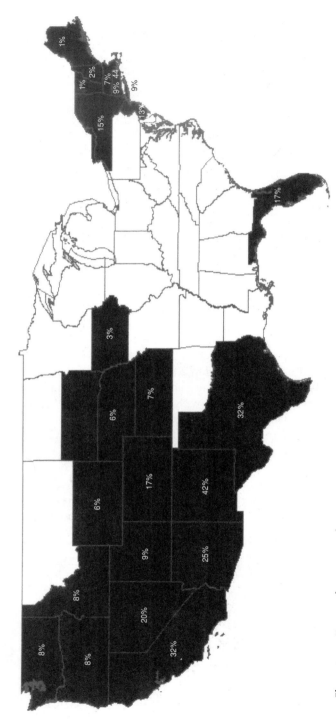

Figure 5.1.   Twenty-three states where Latinos are the largest minority group (2000 Census).

and jalapeños are available in every town and city in the nation. Like pasta and pizzas, Mexican food has become an integral part of the American diet, and its addition to the nation's menu has improved the nation's table, just as Italian food did previously. More headline grabbing has been the rise to preeminence of Latinos in the national pastime, baseball: Pedro Martinez, Alex Rodriguez, and Sammy Sosa, for example. And there is no doubt Latinos have raised the level at which American baseball is played.

Latinos have similarly impacted the nation's entertainment industries. Hispanics have their own situation comedy on a major network: *The George Lopez Show*. Performers such as John Leguizamo have their own Broadway shows. And Latinos have substantial roles in TV shows such as *CSI Miami*. Jimmy Smits and Jennifer Lopez are in the ranks of the nation's most popular contemporary film and television stars, and prominent musical artists include Gloria Estefan and Ricky Martin.

Even though Latino cultural impact is altering the face and style of the nation, these changes have been welcomed by mainstream society. There are at least three possible explanations for why even the most vitriolic anti-immigrant nativists are quiet in the face of these developments. First, no one associates these changes in popular culture with any threat (other than heartburn). Second, mainstream society so welcomes these contributions that they are beyond criticism, even though there can be little doubt that the cultural practices Hispanics are introducing into the nation are changing the very core of mainstream culture. Third, immigration critics save their energies for specific cultural practices or influences that they claim undermine core American values.

IMMIGRANTS, CORE AMERICAN VALUES, AND POLITICAL INCORPORATION

Contemporary anti-Hispanic immigration sentiments nonetheless also include cultural arguments. The most important of these objections is linguistic: Latino immigrants, it is charged, insist on maintaining Spanish to the exclusion of English. This argument leads to the allegation that because they remain linguistically separate, they are never socialized into mainstream culture, but rather retain home-country values. Consequently, Mexicans and Hispanics in general, whether they are immigrants or native-born, not only will not integrate into the polity, it is argued, but will, instead, remain politically faithful to their countries of origin to the detriment of the U.S. "national interest."

In fact, numerous sources conclusively vitiate charges that Latinos are linguistically isolated from mainstream America. The Latino National Political Survey reported that of those who do not describe themselves as equally competent in both languages, 67 percent of native-born Mexican Americans, 68 percent of Puerto Ricans, and 68 percent of Cuban Americans rate themselves as better in *English* than Spanish, whereas 8 percent, 5 percent, and 4 percent of Mexican Americans, Puerto Ricans, and Cuban Americans, respectively, rate their Spanish as better than their English. The foreign born, predictably, rate their Spanish much higher, but even that group includes few Spanish monolinguals. Indeed, 81 percent of Mexican immigrants report some English competence, as do 88 percent of island-born Puerto Ricans and 75 percent of Cubans (de la Garza et al., 1992, 42). The 2002 Pew Hispanic Center survey reports similar findings. While it is not surprising that 94 percent of the native born reported they could carry on a conversation in English very or pretty well, the fact that 44 percent of the foreign born reported this level of competence is unexpected (Pew Hispanic Center 2002). In 2004, Pew found 96 percent of the native-born indicated that they could carry on a conversation in English very or pretty well, while 38 percent of immigrants ranked themselves similarly (Pew Hispanic Center 2004). Buttressing this finding is the importance Latinos, especially the foreign-born, attach to learning English. While 86 percent of non-Hispanic whites and native-born Latinos agree that individuals need to learn English to succeed, 91 percent of the foreign-born voice this view (Pew Hispanic Center 2002).

These patterns illustrate that English is the dominant language of native-born Mexican Americans and other Latinos, and that Hispanic immigrants of all nationalities learn English. Indeed, Latin American immigrants "become proficient in English at a more rapid pace than immigrants from other non-English-language countries (Stevens 1994).

Even more noteworthy is how immigrants evaluate the importance of English. In 1990, approximately 40 percent of Mexican American, Cuban American, and Puerto Rican citizens agreed that English should be the nation's official language, and over 90 percent of each group also agreed that citizens and residents should learn English (de la Garza et al. 1992, 97 and 98). Similar survey results are evident from the Pew 2002 survey that found that 91 percent of Latino immigrants agreed that immigrants need to learn English to succeed, whereas 86 percent of native-born Latinos and non-Hispanic whites shared this perspective (Pew Hispanic Center 2002). Also, over 50 percent of U.S. Hispanics believe that immigrants must learn English to say they are part of American society (Pew Hispanic Center 2004). Their commitment to English notwithstanding, Latinos also support knowing and maintaining Spanish. Almost 95 percent say future generations of Hispanics should speak Spanish.

Clearly, allegations regarding anti-English attitudes and behavior among U.S. Hispanics in general, and the Mexican-origin native-born and immigrant population in particular, are not empirically grounded. Rather than threaten a core American value, Hispanic linguistic patterns are more easily seen as supporting the centrality of English to American life. The knowledge of and commitment to Spanish by Hispanics thus should be seen as a resource that could serve the nation's security and foreign policy goals, as well as its economic well-being. As economic and political relations with Latin America expand, the presence of Latino bilinguals here will insure that the U.S. government will never confront in Latin America the problem of the absence of linguistically competent officials that it faces with Arabic, for example. Also, Hispanic bilinguals constitute a pool of linguistically and culturally competent individuals who are uniquely situated to advance private and public U.S. interests. In other words, Latino bilinguals seem more likely to enhance rather than undermine the national interest.

Claims that Latino social values undercut other aspects of today's U.S. sociopolitical mainstream are equally unsupported. Latinos, especially immigrants, voice stronger support than Anglos for so-called "family values," such as opposition to divorce, homosexuality, illegitimate children, and abortion (Pew Hispanic Center 2002). They are also committed to economic individualism (de la Garza et al. 1992). Indicative of this latter attitude is that in California, less than 2 percent of native-born and naturalized Hispanic citizens, most of whom are Mexican, receive any public assistance, even though all of them are eligible to receive such benefits (Cortina et al. 2004).

Hispanics generally also are more religious than Anglos. Compared to 61 percent of Anglos who indicate that religion is very important to their lives, 64 percent of native-born Latinos and 71 percent of Latino immigrants describe themselves this way (Pew Hispanic Center 2002). Moreover, 30 percent of all U.S. Hispanics identify as "born-again Christians" although almost three-quarters (74.3 percent) are Catholic and only 16.7 percent are Protestant (Washington Post/Univision/TRPI 2004). Clearly, these patterns challenge claims that Latinos threaten the nation's core linguistic and religious culture.

Also refuting such claims is the extent to which Latinos support the nation's core political values. There is, for example, no statistical evidence that ethnic attachments alienate Latinos from mainstream society (Dowley and Silver 2000). More noteworthy is that, regardless of whether they are native or foreign born, speak English, or have an intense ethnic consciousness, Mexican American citizens, including the naturalized, have been found to be at least as patriotic and supportive of core political values, such as political tolerance and economic individualism, as U.S. Anglos (de la Garza et al. 1996).

An additional measure of the linkage between Latino values and the "national interest" is the difference between Latino perspectives of Latin America versus the United States. A test of two hypotheses, one explaining Hispanic perspectives as a function of cultural ties, and the other arguing that Latino perspectives are shaped by socialization in the United States, found strong support for the latter and no support for the former (de la Garza et al. 1997). The study's most noteworthy finding was that, regardless of national origin, those of Mexican, Cuban, and Puerto Rican origin all were much more positively oriented toward the United States than to the region in its entirety or to any specific other nation, including their country of origin.

This pro-American perspective notwithstanding, there are notable differences between U.S. Latino and Anglo foreign policy views. For example, Latino elites have voiced more concern about the environment and world hunger than about military power and the security of our allies (Pachon et al. 2000). More noteworthy is that Hispanics were more likely than Anglos, by 56 percent to 49 percent, to agree that the United States was responsible for the hatred that motivated the 9/11 attacks (Davis and Silver 2003). This particular attitude may reflect the historical Latin American view of U.S. foreign policy as arrogant and unsupportive of Latin American well-being. Despite this perspective, given that 75 percent of Latin American immigrants agree there was no justification for the attack (Tomás Rivera Policy Institute 2002), it cannot be argued that immigrants support anti-American terrorism.

There are fewer differences regarding Latin America. Latinos support the government's goals of strengthening democracy and promoting international trade and investment. It is also noteworthy that the foreign policy preferences of Latino elites run counter to the preferences of Latin American states. A majority support unilateral U.S. responses to problems related to drug trafficking and massive immigration resulting from political turmoil in Mexico, and more than 40 percent support similar responses to human rights violations in the hemisphere (Pachon et al. 2000). Such American initiatives are anathema to Latin American states.

What is perhaps most noteworthy about Hispanic foreign policy involvement is how little there is (Dominguez 2004). Except for the Cuban American National Foundation, no Latino organization has targeted foreign policy issues (Hakim and Rosales 2000). Although this is slowly changing, as is evident in the institutionalization of the Hispanic Council on International Relations, Latinos are unlikely to engage with foreign policy as home-country advocates in the foreseeable future. To the contrary, these patterns suggest Latinos "may not form a political community with the people of their homeland. They have limited political interest in their homelands. They often think badly of those who govern the countries that they or their ancestors left. They hold different political values from the people in the homeland and do not even favor easier immigration rules for Latin Americans seeking to enter the United States. They typically lack the resources to influence U.S. foreign policy" (Dominguez 2004).

Critics like Huntington also argue that transnationalism encourages immigrants to retain home-country ties rather than incorporate into American society. By slowing the acquisition of English and the learning of mainstream social and political values, it is said, maintaining home-country ties stimulates the willingness of Latino immigrants to become home-country lobbyists.

Central to this process are home-town associations (HTAs) that immigrants initially established to create social spaces where those from the same community of origin could come together to reinforce old country ties. This quickly led to HTA-sponsored projects, such as improving local water systems or building sports arenas, that were intended to improve conditions in communities of origin. Home-country governments quickly moved to assist in the establishment of HTAs and, by creating matching funds programs, to help HTAs finance more and bigger projects (de la Garza and Hazan 2003). Perhaps the major reason officials promote these ties is that they expect stronger relations will insure that emigrants continue to remit funds to the families they left behind (Leiken 2000, 16). Such a flow of dollars is essential to the economic stability of Mexico, El Salvador, and other countries (Cortina and de la Garza 2004).

Mexican officials, and to a lesser degree officials from Central American and Caribbean countries, are also pursuing similar relationships because of the strongly held view that HTAs may be used to mobilize emigrants into being lobbyists for their country of origin. Mexican officials are circumspect about articulating this goal, but they have voiced it clearly in meetings with me, personally, and at meetings with Mexican American leaders (de la Garza et al. 1997, 74). Such origin-country outreach, according to one analyst, should be seen as part of the broader *acercamiento* characterizing contemporary U.S.-Mexico relations that includes NAFTA, increased trade and investment, and expanded intergovernmental cooperation on a wide variety of issues (Leiken 2000).

To date, however, HTAs have not developed into home-country lobbyists, and there is no sign they will. To the contrary, HTAs and other types of immigrant associations "are primarily concerned with facilitating immigrants' incorporation into the United States political system" (de la Garza and Hazan 2003, iii). Thus, HTAs promote naturalization, offer English courses and seminars on topics such as small business development, and provide college counseling. The president of an HTA federation (a state- or national-level association of HTAs) explained:

> As an association we have to say to people, "become citizens, you're not betraying your nation, you keep your roots inside of yourselves and nobody can take your roots away, no one can change our love for where we were born. But think about your kin and your grandchildren, they are the ones who need you to pave the way so that they don't have so many problems in the future, especially the ones who were born here, they're not going to live in Mexico." (Leiken 2000, 22)

**Table 5.4.   Hispanic Immigrant Participation in Home-Country-Focused Social and
Cultural Activities since Immigration**

	Mexicans	Salvadorans	Dominicans
Attended cultural or educational event related to home country	26.60%	23.10%	43.90%
Been a member of organization promoting cultural ties between U.S. and home country	6.70%	5.60%	12.80%
Been a member of organization of people from community of origin	8.50%	7.80%	22.60%
Sought assistance from country of origin embassy or consulate	6%	5%	3%

Source: DeSipio et al. (2003).

Illustrative of the pattern of HTA activities is the extent to which Latino immigrants in general are linked to the home country. Despite highly publicized celebrations on Mexican Independence Day (September 15) and the festivities associated with Cinco de Mayo, and New York City's October 12 Dia de la Raza parade in which Latino communities of all nationalities participate, few Latino immigrants regularly participate in social or cultural activities linking them to the home country (see table 5.4).

Additionally, immigrants are not remitting in accord with home-country governmental objectives. Specifically, they have essentially rejected governmental efforts to remit in support of economic development projects. Instead, approximately 80 percent remit exclusively to support their families. Another 31 percent send money for familial purposes and community projects, such as improving local parks, athletic fields, and water systems (Cortina and de la Garza 2004). Virtually none send money explicitly to support government-sponsored economic development projects.

While money sent for familial purposes is an example of transnational ties, these payments are not indicative of the kinds of linkages with home-country governments that trouble Huntington or that those governments are pursuing. Family remittances do not directly target or contribute to the benefit of society per se. Their societal impact is indirect in that these monies alleviate extreme poverty among remitters' family members. Society benefits when remittance recipients use these funds to acquire private medical attention, for example. Valuable as they are to specific families, however, these funds do not qualify as indicators of immigrant political ties to the home country.

Immigrants are also disdainful of involvement with home-country political issues (see table 5.5). Further illustrating low levels of involvement with home country politics is that immigrants are substantially more likely to be concerned about U.S. issues than about issues in their country of origin (see table 5.6).

Table 5.5. Hispanic Immigrant Participation in Home-Country-Focused Political Activities since Immigration

	Mexicans	Salvadorans	Dominicans
Followed home-country politics in Spanish media	63.60%	48.00%	67.10%
Voted in home country	9.50%	8.50%	15.00%
Contributed money to a political candidate	2.00%	2.80%	6.30%
Attended rally in U.S. for home-country candidate or political party	2.70%	2.30%	17.30%
Contacted by home country to participate in home-country affairs	3%	1.80%	11.60%

Source: DeSipio et al. (2003).

The type of activities that HTAs emphasize, combined with the limited extent to which immigrants involve themselves with home-country affairs, suggests that accusations claiming Latinos remain apart from U.S. society because they remain committed to their countries of origin are groundless. It is true, however, that few immigrants actively engage with U.S. society (see figure 5.2). This could be explained by factors such as low socioeconomic status, being undocumented, and a general fear of discrimination, all of which could be ameliorated by changes in U.S. governmental policies. Thus, there is no basis for viewing immigrants as political threats because of their home-country ties. Instead, it is more useful to view them as potential citizens who, under improved circumstances, would be an asset to society and the polity.

Another charge implicitly leveled by Huntington and others is that U.S. Hispanics will unite into a cohesive voting bloc that will advance its own interests at the expense of the nation's. As was true in 1990 (de la Garza et. al. 1992), in 2004 Latinos do not behave as a political group united by ethnicity. Latinos do not see themselves as united politically (Pew Hispanic Center 2004), and they report that they will not vote for a candidate because of shared ethnicity unless the Latino and non-Latino candidate are similarly qualified (Pew Hispanic Center 2004; de la Garza et al. 1992). Analyses of Hispanic voting behavior confirm these claims (Michelson 2002).

Table 5.6. Focus of Political Concern: U.S. or Home Country

	Registered Citizens	Not Registered Citizens	Non-Citizens
More concerned with U.S.	79.00%	76.00%	57.00%
Equally concerned with both	11.00%	8.00%	20.00%
More concerned with home country	6.00%	6.00%	14.00%

Source: Pew Hispanic Center, 2004.

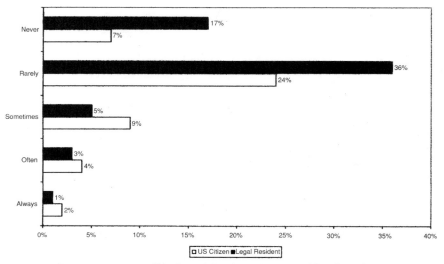

Figure 5.2.   U.S. political participation, citizens and legal residents.

IMMIGRANTS AND THE ECONOMY

The positive economic impact of immigration is well established. Public perceptions to the contrary notwithstanding, the National Research Council reports that immigrants do not displace American workers, nor do they lower wages, and overall they contribute $1–10 billion to the U.S. economy annually (Smith and Edmonston 1997). From an economic perspective, therefore, if the nation accepted more immigrants, it would enjoy even greater benefits (Chang 2005).

Immigration provides workers for low-level jobs that the native born are unwilling to take, at wages that fall well below what native workers demand. They are such a vital part of the service sector that the activity in the nation's major cities would screech to a halt, as native-born parents would have to rearrange work schedules to care for their children, for example. Restaurants could not open because of the absence of waiters, cooks, and dishwashers, and cities would have to stop garbage collection. The general disruption that the absence of immigrants would cause is well illustrated in the recently released satirical film *A Day without Mexicans.*

So much attention is given to lower-end workers that the economic value Latino immigrants contribute through their roles in high-end professions, such as medicine, is usually overlooked. Indeed, personal experience and observations suggest that the quality, cost, and availability of medical services in Houston, Miami, and New York would change substantially but for the presence of Latin American doctors. Furthermore, many of these professionals enrich the nation's medical services at extremely low cost because they come here already with medical degrees.

Latino immigrants also contribute to the U.S. economy in conventional ways. Unless employers keep them off the books, they pay taxes and contribute to Social Security, and there is widespread agreement that their contributions are essential to the maintenance of the Social Security system (Rosenbaum and Toner 2005; Greenspan 2004).

Thanks to their cultural knowledge, immigrants also benefit the nation by providing an advantage in gaining access to foreign financial and commercial markets. A key segment of this arena is the fees generated by the multi-billion-dollar remittance industry. In California alone, fees generated by remittances to Mexico total $338 million (Cortina et al. 2004). These fees generate jobs and provide profits to stockholders that could be used for additional investments. Along the same line, in addition to the role they play as domestic consumers, Hispanic immigrants enhance the nation's commercial sector by developing export markets for U.S. retailers with outlets in immigrants' countries of origin. The appliances purchased from these firms are paid for in the United States and picked up by relatives from outlets in the home country. Cultural knowledge also contributes to the development of ubiquitous ethnic markets here that provide jobs as well as group-specific products for ethnic and non-ethnic clients.

It is argued, nonetheless, that immigrants drain resources because they consume more in social services than they pay in taxes. This claim is based on the cost of educating immigrant children or the U.S.-born children of immigrants. Even if the latter are included in the analysis, which is not normally the case, this claim is static rather than dynamic. That is, it does not consider the long-term U.S. tax benefits that result from educating these children. As National Research Council reports show, when these benefits are considered, immigrant contributions to the economy exceed the value of services they utilize.

CONCLUSION

Latino immigrants have inserted themselves into the fabric of the nation. They are influencing every facet of popular culture—from music to food and art to sports. These influences are so ubiquitous and so established that it is no exaggeration to suggest that they have Latinized American culture in the same way that Italians and Irish, to name but two groups, did historically. Like those immigrants, Latinos are enriching the nation as they embrace and alter its cultural core.

Latinos, however, have the potential to shape the cultural future more profoundly than did the Italians and Irish. Unlike either of those immigrant groups, large and growing Latino communities are nationally dispersed in the United States. This means that, while St. Patrick's Day celebrations have long been concentrated in the Northeast, Cinco de Mayo is celebrated from Seattle to New York. Also, because of continuous immigration, Spanish will become the nation's second language. This will influence how we speak, our literature, and the legitimacy of being bilingual, a beneficial attribute the nation has historically shunned. No other immigrant group has so expanded the nation's cultural horizon.

There is also a consensus regarding Hispanic immigration's positive impact on the economy. Not only do Hispanic immigrants fill the service jobs that keep the nation running, but they do so at rates that make our economy relatively competitive. Additionally, they are taxpayers, real estate investors, and consumers. Less recognized is their substantial contribution to the financial world via the fees they pay for remittances. Their development of ethnic enclaves enables them to contribute significantly to job creation. Finally, as highly trained professionals in medicine and other fields, they add valuable resources to the economy at bargain prices. In short, Latino immigrants are an essential part of the nation's economy.

Politically, the Latino contribution is less tangible. As with previous immigrants, the values they bring with them are not transformative of the polity. Nonetheless, they so believe in the core U.S. political values that they invigorate our faith in the American dream. Nothing about their values or attitudes supports claims that they undermine the polity's foundation. To the contrary, they believe in political tolerance, democracy, and the common good at levels at least as high as those of Anglos. While they differ regarding aspects of foreign policies, their disagreements are no more noteworthy than those of numerous interest groups, including non-Hispanic ethnic lobbies.

Regrettably, as recent elections have shown, not all Americans cherish democratic values. To the extent that Latinos help renew the nation's faith in itself and the values on which the nation was founded, Latinos will improve the polity.

(*Note*: I would like to thank Jerónimo Cortina, Research Associate, Tomás Rivera Policy Institute, for his assistance in preparing this paper.)

6

Ending America's Waste of Its Most Precious Resource—Its People

Peter Edelman

H. L. Mencken once wrote: "For every problem there is a solution that is neat and simple, and wrong." A profound problem in the United States is the continuing waste of the talent and potential of millions of people—especially as we head into an era when we are likely to face shortages of people to do all of the work that needs doing in our nation.

It is tempting to say, and some people do, that if only we did x or y or z the problem would be solved. Fix our public schools. Provide proper job training. Pay every worker a living wage. End racism. Elect a Democratic president. But, like many challenges confronting our nation, this ongoing tragedy reflects multiple failures and requires multiple changes in both public policy and private action for significant change to occur. Those multiple changes are the subject of this chapter.

The first half of the chapter deals with the demand side of the question—how to get enough people working, earning a living income, receiving appropriate benefits, and protected by a decent safety net. The second half is about investing in people, especially children and youth, so they are ready to participate fully and fairly in the labor market when they reach an appropriate age.

THE CONTEXT

Even with the recent recession, we have been fortunate for about a decade to have had a national economy with relatively low unemployment. The unemployment rate in early 2005 was still much lower than it was when President Bill Clinton took office. For 20 years before that, the United States routinely had an unemployment rate of around 7 percent and often higher. Nonetheless, it

189

is appropriate to begin by saying that if we want not to waste human resources in the United States, we should always run a full employment economy. We should have fiscal and monetary policies designed to maximize employment at the same time that they serve other legitimate purposes.

Similarly, it is impossible in 2005 to discuss full utilization of America's human resources without placing the issue in a global context. This subject could fill a shelf of books, but at the very least, we should insist that trade arrangements with other nations or groups of nations be premised on fair labor standards and reasonable environmental protections. We should resist and repeal tax provisions that reward sending jobs out of the country. Globalization is very real, but many jobs that disappeared overseas could have been kept at home by better public policy.

Yet, talking about our economy on a national scale obscures the employment disparities among groups and across locales. Unemployment (and underemployment) among many minorities runs far higher than the national rate, as does unemployment in particular places, especially inner cities and various rural areas. These groups and locales need special attention. To be even more explicit, we cannot discuss the waste of our precious human resources without having race and all the issues associated with it squarely before us.

We are wasting our human resources for a long list of reasons: inadequate schooling and other poor preparation; racial, ethnic, and other discrimination; geographic isolation and lack of transportation; gaps in physical accessibility for the disabled; lack of mental health services; weak protection for victims of domestic violence; unavailability of treatment for drug and alcohol abuse; and more. I will speak to many of these issues, and others, in the course of this chapter. It should be evident by now that making full use of our human resources is a complex challenge (although it is also true that, for some of our people, one intervention will make all the difference).

Finally, the context includes a bedrock point that liberals too often do not say out loud. That is the simple idea (simple to say, anyway) that everyone has a personal responsibility to work toward success in school and in the workplace, and to fulfill family and civic obligations. Concomitantly, all the various communities (some place-based and some not) to which we belong have a mirror-image responsibility to provide supports that enhance our ability to succeed in fulfilling our individual and personal responsibilities. This community responsibility includes both public policy and private action in various organizational and individual forms.

A LIVING INCOME

If we were permitted only one solution to the waste of our American human resources, I believe it would be to assure that everyone in the United States has a living income, based primarily on work. In 2003, about 31 percent of American families had incomes below twice the poverty line of $14,680 for a family of three. Multiple studies and analyses suggest that twice the so-called poverty line is the point at which people generally become able to meet their usual costs of living. So, with regional variations, we should define the living income at approximately twice the poverty line. In some parts of the country, the appropriate figure for a living income will be considerably higher, and in others somewhat lower.

The wages of the entire lower half of the workforce have been virtually stagnant for about three decades. The median wage for all jobs has been stuck at about $13 an hour (in inflation-adjusted terms) since the early 1970s, with the little increase that did occur coming only in the last half of the 1990s. This means that half of all American workers have jobs that pay less than about $27,000 annually, assuming they work 40 hours a week all year. Maybe some have overtime, but many more have only part-time or seasonal work, or both. On the other hand, many families have more than one wage earner and therefore earn more. Even so, there has been a massive failure in the labor market that has gotten worse and worse since about 1973. (And all of this says nothing about the 35.9 million people with incomes below the poverty line, and the 15.25 million people with incomes below half the poverty line, or below $7,500 for a family of three—a total that has grown by more than 3 million people since President George W. Bush took office.)

Of course, the American economy did not stay still for 30 years. The income of the country as a whole approximately doubled, but nearly all of the return went to people in the top half, and mainly to the top 1 percent. I believe the vast majority of the American people have no idea how grossly skewed the distribution of our growth has been.

Is this a racial story? No, in the sense that low-wage work is, shall we say, an equal-opportunity scourge. But emphatically yes, as well, because the median household income of non-Hispanic whites is $48,000 and the median family income of African Americans is $30,000. Whereas 31 percent of Americans have incomes below twice the poverty line, about half of all African Americans have incomes that low. The same is true for Hispanics.

Achieving an income floor (including income equivalents) at twice the poverty line is not at all simple, so describing it as "one solution" is misleading. But an income base at that level would be a phenomenally constructive step. Workers would have less financial stress, which would radiate to their family lives as well as pay off in the workplace. Many would be able to save more. Some could move to more desirable neighborhoods. Some could pursue further education and training. Since one element of a living income would be health coverage, workers would be healthier, live longer, and on those accounts as well be more productive on the job.

What are the elements of a strategy to achieve a living income? I suggest six: raising the minimum wage; improving the Earned Income Tax Credit; creating living wage campaigns; strengthening the ability of labor unions to organize, devising asset development policies, and investing in job creation for people unable to find work. In this first half of the chapter, I will also discuss important policies that have an income-equivalent value—health coverage, child care, affordable housing, and college tuition assistance—and therefore are part of a living-income strategy (in addition to their intrinsic importance for other purposes). Finally, also to be discussed below, it is imperative that we have an adequate safety net for people who have lost their jobs or are for one reason or another not in a position to work.

Raising the Minimum Wage

Raising the minimum wage is a necessary component of a living-income strategy, although far from a full strategy in itself. The current federal minimum wage of $5.15 an hour is more than $2 an hour below the level of the minimum wage in the late 1960s, measured in current dollars. A $7 federal minimum wage would amount to a pay raise of about 36 percent, and would bring a worker with two children almost to the poverty line as of the moment, and leave a family of four about $4,000 short of getting out of poverty. This is very much worth doing, but clearly not sufficient. Some economists argue that even such a modest increase will destroy jobs. However, the current weight of economic opinion and research is that a $7 minimum wage will have relatively little negative effect.

Of all national steps that would benefit low-wage workers, a modest increase in the federal minimum wage is the most politically feasible at the present time. But increasing the minimum wage should be pursued at the state level, too. In two "red" states, Nevada and Florida, successful ballot measures in 2004 raised their state minimum wages to a dollar above the current federal minimum, and the legislature in New York overrode Republican Governor Pataki's veto of an increase to $7.15. Such state increases, helpful in themselves, tend to create pressure for an increase at the federal level. Businesses in states with minimum wages higher than the federal minimum should want to alleviate the disadvantage of having to pay low-wage workers more than competitors in other states are required to do. Additional state ballot measures and legislative campaigns would be useful, especially until the federal minimum is increased.

Improving the Earned Income Tax Credit

The Earned Income Tax Credit is a vital but tricky piece of public policy. In 2005, it added $4,290 to the income of a full-time minimum-wage worker with two children, and $2,604 to the income of such a worker who has one child. Many believe the large EITC increase of 1993 (along with the fortuitous availability of low-wage work) helped draw welfare recipients into the labor market following enactment of the welfare reform legislation of 1996. Adding about 40 percent to the return from a minimum-wage job brought a single-parent family with two children to an income level that exceeded the poverty line in the late 1990s.The tricky issue is that the EITC has to be kept in delicate balance with the minimum wage. In short, the EITC shouldn't let employers off the hook. One reason the credit has had bipartisan support is that low-wage employers think it is an attractive policy. That is politically useful, but employers have a responsibility to pay workers a decent wage. I have no doubt that some undetermined number of employers are getting a free ride from the EITC, saving wages they would otherwise have to pay their workers themselves.

But wages are something else again. It deeply troubles me that we have allowed wages to stagnate, and the EITC is a necessary wage equivalent for millions of workers (although we are not the only country that finds it necessary to have a wage supplement). To be sure, some of this reflects the change in the nature of work. Good-paying jobs have disappeared offshore and to technology. The service-sector jobs that have come in their stead (at least replacement jobs have come) pay far less. Labor unions have fallen prey to weakened legal protections and weak regulatory enforcement, changes in public attitudes, and in some areas, the unions' own lethargy.

All of that said, the EITC needs improvement. There should be a category for families with three or more children. We must ameliorate the penalties that effectively accrue when two low-wage single parents with children marry. The phase-out of benefits as income increases also needs reexamination in light of the real costs of maintaining a household.

Another idea worthy of consideration is a substantial EITC payment to a noncustodial parent who has a low-wage job and is meeting his or her child-support obligations. Too many low-income noncustodial parents (mainly men) with child-support obligations face a set of issues that borders on absurdity. They are often subject to child-support orders that far exceed their ability to pay, and typically, any money they do pay is kept wholly or almost wholly by the state to offset welfare payments to the custodial parent and the children. If they get an "on the books" job, they take home nothing or almost nothing for themselves, and their children receive no benefit either. Quite logically, they often take "off the books" work for which they are paid in cash, and then they pay a portion of their earnings, under the table, to support their children. Changing child-support rules to get money passed through to support the children is one step that needs to be taken on a national basis. This proposition has been received favorably in Congress but never enacted by both houses in the same biennium. At the state level, Governor Pataki of New York proposed in January 2005 to expand his state's Earned Income Tax Credit for low-income noncustodial fathers who have fulfilled their child-support obligations.

Mentioning Governor Pataki reminds me to say that continued work to get state EITCs enacted more widely is very important. Although the precise amount varies by state and individual income level, a state EITC can add several hundred or even a thousand dollars to the income of a low-wage working family with two children. Also important to mention is that, at the federal level, Congress in 2001 added a refundable feature to the child tax credit, which can also add about $1,000 to the income of families earning between $10,000 and $16,000. Somewhat oddly, or perhaps meanly is the better word, Congress refused to extend the refundable credit to families earning less than $10,000. This remains an agenda item for people who work on these policies.

Living Wage Campaigns

Over a hundred local jurisdictions have now enacted living wage laws or ordinances. These laws usually cover employees of the governmental unit and of companies that contract with that government. Some also cover employees of companies that receive specific tax abatements from the jurisdiction. Three universities—Harvard, Stanford, and Wesleyan—also have living wage floors. Currently, in most jurisdictions, the wage floor established is in the $9 to $10 range. Some of the schemes have a duplex schedule, with a lower wage permitted for companies that offer health coverage to their employees and a higher figure required for those that do not. Typically, the percentage of the total number of employees in the local labor market who are covered by the living wage law is quite small, in the single digits.

All or nearly all of the living wage laws have come as a result of organizing and lobbying led by groups like ACORN (2005), often in partnership with local affiliates of unions like the Service Employees International Union. They are quite valuable as yardsticks to set exemplary standards in local labor markets, and they sometimes have an effect in tightening wages locally for work that is not specifically covered by the living wage law itself. If the county government's office cleaners are covered by the living wage law, for example, the employees of other office cleaning companies may find themselves the beneficiaries of the law even though it does not apply to them directly. The living wage campaigns also give the people who participate in the advocacy a sense of efficacy—no small thing in a world where so many decisions that affect our lives are made by people whose deliberations seem far away and unreachable by the advocacy of "ordinary" citizens.

We should be starting a campaign for a national living wage. Every contractor with the federal government and every company that gets special tax breaks from the federal government should have to pay all of its employees a living wage. Why not?

Labor Law Reform

Union members earn more than their nonunion counterparts and are far more likely to have health coverage through their employer and a pension plan to which their employer contributes. Yet union membership is steadily declining. One reason is the sophisticated intimidation tactics that employers can utilize to oppose representation elections in the workplace, in some instances legally or at least because they have no fear of an effective sanction. Polls show nearly three times the number of employees actually unionized would like to have union representation, but they fear employer reprisal if they participate in a unionization drive.

The biggest problems are the employers' ability, de jure or de facto, to campaign against organizing drives by anti-union pressure exerted on the workers as a captive audience on the job, and the meager sanctions available against employers (which employers can resist by prolonged legal moves going all the way to the appellate courts if need be). A sophisticated consultant industry has developed to advise employers on how to resist unionization efforts.

Senator Edward Kennedy (D-MA) and Representative George Miller (D-CA), with 30 Senate and 168 House co-sponsors, have introduced the Employee Free Choice Act, which would level the playing field. The legislation would toughen the definitions of impermissible employer interference in representation elections and increase substantially the sanctions for employer violation of the law. Enactment of the legislation is hardly promising in the current Congress, but pursuing it is a vital plank in a platform of constructive steps toward increasing wages to a living level for more workers.

Asset Development

Many people are one paycheck away from poverty, and part of their problem is that they have no cushion of savings to fall back on. We have had one asset development policy for a long time, of course—the mortgage interest deduction—and it has been a resounding success. The percentage of Americans who own their own home has shot up since World War II, and the act of purchasing a home has been a phenomenally smart (or fortuitous) investment decision for millions of Americans. Numerous asset development ideas targeted particularly to lower-income people have been put forward in recent years—individual development accounts (IDAs) are the most prominent example.

The interest of the public in these ideas is indicated by the fact that President George W. Bush makes a major point of talking about an "ownership society" (although the substance of his ideas does not live up to the force of his rhetoric). An important challenge in the coming years is for public officials and outside advocates to put forward ideas with substance.

The basic idea of IDAs is to encourage savings among lower-income families through an incentive structure, such that some source, public or private, would match at some level investments in savings deposits. During the Clinton presidency, federal legislation financed some modest IDA demonstrations, with encouraging results. States and private foundations have financed such initiatives as well, usually for narrowly defined populations or purposes, such as encouraging recent welfare recipients to pursue education and training, or adding to the effective income of child-care workers. Most IDA programs limit use of the savings to identified purposes like home ownership, micro-enterprise, college education, or job training. About half the states have or have had IDA initiatives of one kind or another.

Two other major categories of asset development proposals relate to retirement and to savings from birth. President Clinton proposed Universal Savings Accounts (USAs), an idea for a refundable federal tax credit to match individual contributions to retirement accounts for the purpose of supplementing Social Security. Vice President Al Gore proposed something similar, called Retirement Savings Plus, in his 2000 presidential campaign. His proposal also partook of the IDA idea, in that it permitted withdrawals after five years for specific purposes like purchasing a home, paying for college, or paying unexpected medical bills. Both the Clinton and the Gore proposals were means tested, and both were completely independent of Social Security, thus raising none of the problems that attend President Bush's proposals for partial privatization of Social Security.

Many policy analysts in various countries have offered proposals for accounts to be established from the public treasury for every child at birth and added to for the first five years of life, so that by the time a child reaches retirement (or adulthood, depending on the proposal), the initial investment has automatically become quite substantial, just through the accrual of interest. Again, uses would be limited to retirement, or to specified purposes similar to those mentioned above in connection with IDAs.

Job Creation

Occasionally, I hear people advocate recreating the Civilian Conservation Corps and the Works Progress Administration—the legendary job creation programs of the New Deal. These, of course, were programs mainly for people thrown out of work because of the Great Depression. Our most acute problem in 2005 is that people, especially young people, are having difficulty finding their way into the labor market. I include this issue here because if we are talking about wasting human resources, we surely waste human resources when a person who could add value to the economy through work does not do so for lack of an available job for which he or she is qualified.

What policies might we pursue? One appropriate use of job creation is as a transitional policy—part of a training and placement strategy—to help young people, welfare recipients, perhaps ex-offenders, and maybe displaced workers find their way to stable employment. Such initiatives exist already in a number of incarnations. The various service and conservation corps around the country, for example, regard themselves as direct descendants of the New Deal, and they play exactly the kind of transitional role I am suggesting, as do others.

I want to put another idea on the table here. That is the creation of jobs on public payrolls (or on nonprofit payrolls, but financed with public funds) to do things that we want done. This might include child care, park maintenance, highway building, taking care of the elderly and disabled, building homes, and any number of other things. Obviously no one should have such a job without being qualified, trained, and otherwise suitable for the task.

That said, however, we seldom think in terms of a priority for the unemployed or the underemployed in hiring for new or expanded job opportunities. Outreach for such hiring, and even the location for the work, could be tied to places, whether urban or rural, where disproportionate numbers of people have no work. Jobs for people who don't have them are certainly part of a strategy to get a living income to more people.

SOCIAL INCOME

One reason so many millions of Americans struggle to pay their bills each month, or are just plain poor, is that they have costs that the public has a moral responsibility to defray, at least for people at their income levels or below. I am talking, obviously, about health coverage, child care, the huge escalation in rental costs in large portions of the country, and the cost of postsecondary education.

It is one thing to argue, as I would and do, that certain measures that have income value should be totally or at least partially government responsibilities and not fall solely on the shoulders of employers. There are important design questions about sharing responsibility among employers, employees, and government (and not just the federal government), but health care and child care are part of a "social" wage for which the government bears at least a means-tested responsibility, and the same is true for housing and the cost of college attendance (but without the employer in the equation in those instances).

Health Coverage

The constellation of health issues that contributes to our waste of human resources is more complex and profound than the fact that 45 million people in the United States now have no health coverage, an increase of more than 6 million since 2000. Americans are suffering from an epidemic of preventable disease that is costing the economy tens of billions of dollars in lost hours from work and reduced productivity. We need national leadership on nutrition, exercise, tobacco, alcohol, and drugs. The wave of obesity and diabetes engulfing the country goes much beyond the fact that 45 million people have no health coverage, as serious as that is.

Nonetheless, it is past time to enact a system of universal health coverage. Senator Edward Kennedy recently proposed a thoughtful and workable idea that he called, simply, Medicare for All (and in this area as in others, simple is definitely good). Besides the effect that an equitable health financing structure coupled with public health measures would have on preventing the waste of human resources, it would, if properly structured, serve as a key component in delivering a livable income to the 30 percent of Americans without such an income at present.

At the same time, a clear and present danger looms over the future of Medicaid, the federal health program that serves more than 50 million people and, as the number served strongly implies, covers many people whose income exceeds the poverty line. In a number of states, Medicaid effectively increases the income of families living below double the poverty line—the people who do earn a living income. President Bush, having seemed to discover fiscal responsibility in his second term, is proposing deep cuts in the Medicaid program, both in the income levels of those afforded eligibility and in the benefits covered by the program. Success with any of his proposals would take income away from people already receiving less, often far less, than a living income.

Child Care

I will revisit the issue of child care when I come to discussing investment in children. Here I want to raise it from an income (and work) perspective. One of the major subplots of the implementation of the 1996 welfare law is the number of women who have lost jobs because they had to care for a child who became ill and had to stay home from school or child care, lost out on jobs because of the difficulty of getting their children to child care and then getting to and from work themselves, or had to place their child with an unreliable caregiver because they couldn't afford anything of higher quality. And so on.

We have had a fairly substantial increase in the federal investment in child care over the past 15 years. The bad news is that, even with that increase, federal child-care assistance reaches only about one in seven children whose family income qualifies them for a subsidy. A major reason working families, especially families with preschool children, have such a difficult time financially is the cost of child care (and the cost is high even though the average wage of child-care workers is only about $15,000 annually). The need for increased child-care funding includes after-school arrangements for school-age children, as well. A decent national investment in child-care assistance for every family that needs it would make a great difference in helping us move toward a goal of a living income for every family.

Housing

The crisis in the cost of rental housing is not ubiquitous, being mainly coincident with urban areas that have hot economies. But in no state can a worker with a minimum-wage job afford the HUD-determined Fair Market Rent for a two-bedroom apartment. In city after city, homeless families with children, who now constitute about 40 percent of the homeless population, report that the level of their income—often from work—forced them to choose between paying the rent and eating.

We have been on a net downward trend in the supply of affordable housing essentially since Ronald Reagan became president. His most enduring contribution to domestic social policy was the destruction of any substantial policy to build or rehabilitate lower-income housing. The Low-Income Housing Tax Credit, enacted in 1986, was a modest step toward subsidizing increases in supply, but its contribution has been overwhelmed by the continuing and inexorable trend of supply decreases that goes on from year to year. Now, Section 8 vouchers, a staple income supplement since the Nixon presidency, are under substantial attack from the Bush administration. Section 8 vouchers add income to 2 million households. They have never come close to providing assistance to all whose income speaks to their need for help. And now, even the relatively minimal number of people they do reach is at risk of being substantially reduced.

A partial solution has been at hand for some years. A bipartisan coalition in Congress backs enactment of a National Housing Trust Fund. Fully financed, it could add 1.5 million units of affordable housing annually to the nation's housing supply. Instead, President Bush's budget for fiscal 2006 proposes to take federal support for low-income housing in a sharply different direction.

Help for all whose income speaks to a need for assistance with the cost of housing would be a key element in developing a living income strategy for those whose incomes are below twice the poverty line.

Postsecondary Education

One of the worst side effects of President Bush's fiscal policies has been the very large increase in state public college tuition almost everywhere in the country.

Hit hard by revenue reductions caused by a combination of the recession and the linking of state tax systems to the federal tax structure, states responded by promulgating steep rises in their fees for public colleges.

Pell Grants have not kept up with these rising tuition costs. The maximum grant for 2004–2005 was $4,050, far less than the total cost of attendance at most public institutions. It rankles many people to see President Bush now proposing a $500 increase in the maximum Pell Grant over a period of five years. This is less than the president promised in his 2000 election campaign. The proposed increase is also far less than is needed to keep pace with the large state tuition increases and to close the several-billion-dollar shortfall in Pell funding expected over the next few years. Adequate federal assistance for community college attendance and for relatively low-tuition public four-year colleges is a key element in a living income strategy.

THE SAFETY NET

The previous discussion covers much of the safety net that adds to the income of lower-income workers, and protects people who have no work or occasional or part-time work. The American safety net, unlike that of every other industrialized country, is a patchwork, full of holes. Some populations within the United States receive no help at all. Others are covered, but limited appropriations mean that only a fraction of those eligible receive aid. If one looks, not too closely, at a list of the various programs that exist to help the poor and in some cases the near poor, it seems extensive and not unimpressive. But when one looks at the less than adequate appropriations and income and other eligibility limits, the reality is quite different.

In particular, cash assistance for families with children ("welfare") was radically redesigned in 1996, with results that have been injurious to large numbers of people, especially in states that chose to run punitive programs, as the law fully permitted. We can only hope that the time will come when we can have a thoughtful public discussion about welfare. The goal would be to transform what worked well in some states under the 1996 law into federal policy that continues to encourage work (but in more positive ways), provides some basic protections for recipients, and yet preserves state flexibility where appropriate.

In contrast with what has happened with welfare, the food stamp program, which was transformed into a modest minimum income guarantee in the 1970s at about 30 percent of the poverty line, constitutes a major social policy success. While the program is still not fully adequate to end hunger in America, it has been effective in ending the severe malnutrition extant in some areas in the late 1960s. It is important to protect the food stamp program from erosion or retrogressive structural change.

Perhaps the one safety-net program that deserves special mention here is the unemployment insurance (UI) system, which is desperately in need of reform and redesign. Currently, only about 40 percent of people who have lost their jobs get UI benefits, and benefits in many states are extremely limited in amount and duration. People who had part-time work or low-wage jobs, or have not had work experience over a long enough period of time, do not qualify for benefits. And benefits often run out before a person has found another job. All of this causes the number of beneficiaries at any one time to be surprisingly low. The case for reform has been well and repeatedly made. There is insufficient interest in the current administration and in Congress to get action on the problem.

WHO GETS THE JOBS THAT ARE AVAILABLE?

We have talked thus far about how many jobs there will be and how much they will pay, directly or indirectly, with particular emphasis on issues relating to the lower half or third of the income spectrum. A further and vitally important issue is the discrimination that is a continuing source of wasting human resources. This must be confronted, front and center.

The victims of illegal (or morally unacceptable) discrimination make up a long list. Practically anyone can be the object of discrimination for some reason. Historically, African Americans and Native Americans are surely our most long-standing minority targets of discrimination, and women were relegated to second-class status from the beginning. Now things are somewhat more complicated. We have laws that ban most employment discrimination. The only area in which there is no legal protection in most parts of the country is sexual orientation. Yet even with protection on paper, individuals continue to face discrimination because of race, ethnicity, gender, religion, disability, and other protected categories, and many suffer from the consequences of discrimination from an earlier time.

It is easy to say (easier to say than to accomplish fully) that we must vigorously enforce all laws that prohibit discrimination and not leave enforcement only to individual litigation. There is slippage and evasion, but no one would disagree with the principle. The harder issues that arise can be grouped in a category that might be loosely summarized as steps—sometimes costly steps—to get beyond discrimination. Some of these are controversial; others are merely expensive. Grouping them is definitely to list apples and oranges, so I hope I will not offend anyone who thinks I have joined his or her cause to others in an inappropriate way.

Affirmative Action

Affirmative action is a hot-button issue in our country. Numerically based remedies remain legal when there is a judicial finding of egregious discrimination against a class that has been systemically excluded from an entire category of jobs. The Supreme Court recently gave its blessing to taking race into account in university admissions, as long as it is done with extreme care, and apparently on a time-limited basis as well, of 25 years from the date of the Court's decision.

Yet women and many minorities remain underrepresented in many professions and fields. Continuing effort is needed from the cradle onward, to attract the interest of members of underrepresented groups and see that they have the preparation and support they need to qualify for admission and selection for the various steps along the way to acceptance in the area of their interest.

Paid Family and Medical Leave

The United States remains an outlier among industrialized nations in its grudging attitude toward workers who need time off for reasons other than their own illness, especially during the weeks before and months following the birth of a child. This affects both women and men, but it is especially a barrier to the achievement by women of their full professional or career potential. The enactment of unpaid family and medical leave in 1993 was a great step forward, and all of those associated with that achievement deserve great credit. It is time now to require the investment of the necessary resources to improve this important policy and extend financial support to workers who have difficulty using unpaid leave for important family and medical obligations and needs. Flexible or "family friendly" workplaces are important for family stability and to end the underutilization of women in the workplace.

Accommodations for the Disabled

We have made enormous strides in including the disabled in the workplace, but we have a long way to go. Many workplaces have made major accommodations of both physical environments and hiring policies. Nor is there a bright line between what is appropriate and what is too costly, either financially or in human terms. But the level of unemployment in the disabled community, among people who could succeed in the world of work if they had the chance, is still unacceptably high. We are definitely wasting human resources in this area.

The Intersection of Poverty with Race, Ethnicity, and Immigration Status

Poverty is a racial issue. Poverty among African Americans, Hispanics, and Native Americans is actually much reduced from what it had routinely been in earlier years, hovering at about 23 percent, but poverty among whites is under 10 percent.

The problem is not merely that employers are encountering people of color and refusing to hire them, although surely some of that occurs. The issue is bound up in what people call structural racism or institutional racism. Lower-income minorities, disproportionately poor to begin with, tend to cluster around other poor people of their same race or ethnicity, and the concentration of so many of the poor all living in the same area has a number of multiplier effects. One result is disproportionate attendance at inferior schools. Another is that children grow up in families where, too often, no father is present, the children are not read to or encouraged to read, drugs or alcohol may be consumed in excess, and violence is endemic. Even good schools would have difficulty making up for these deficits. Neighborhood influences are not constructive, either, with violence spilling out into the street and a peer culture that derides achievement as being "white."

In these circumstances, constructive opportunities for enrichment and association with caring adults during off-school hours are crucial, and too often not present. In their teens, youth—especially young men—routinely get entangled in the juvenile justice system, followed almost inexorably by incarceration in the adult correctional system. Young women have children while far too young to be able to raise them in a responsible way. By the time these young people should be in college or in the labor force, they are out of school without a high school diploma and offer little to a prospective employer.

Is this a story of race discrimination? Not in the sense of segregation mandated by law and pervasive discrimination based solely on race or ethnicity. At the same time, it is indeed about race and the racially disparate ways in which a series of systems and agencies operate, even if they deal neutrally with the racially skewed picture that confronts them. We are wasting America's human resources in a disproportionately racial and ethnic way. Our solutions must take this into account.

Ex-offenders

A special category, largely coincident with the intersection of race and poverty, is that of ex-offenders. The reluctance of employers to hire ex-offenders is not shocking, but that does not make it right in the frequency with which it occurs.

With 600,000 people pouring out of our nation's prisons and jails annually—disproportionately people of color and disproportionately from backgrounds of poverty—the waste of human resources associated with unjustified refusals to hire ex-offenders is immense.

A modest awakening is occurring in this area. The Bush administration has developed some small initiatives for the training and placement of ex-offenders. More programs are springing up in localities around the country. But the most important remedy is to prevent so many people from going to jail in the first place. This involves everything from improving schools and job opportunities to reducing discrimination and changing criminal sentencing structures, especially with regard to possession and small-time selling of illegal drugs.

More attention is needed to the situation of people recently released from prison or jail and, more broadly, to (in many states) the continuing consequences for those merely arrested and never charged with anything. Start with the latter. In many states, arrest records become an unalterable part of a person's biography, and they induce refusals to hire even though that person has not violated the law. A finding of innocence after being tried has the same effect in many places. Having successfully completed probation where there was no jail sentence remains on the permanent record and effectively blocks people from jobs. Convictions for certain kinds of crimes become legal blocks to be hired for some jobs—sometimes rightly, to be sure. In some states, released felons are not allowed to get drivers licenses. All of this needs to be examined. It is a state by state endeavor, although federal incentives and model laws could make a substantial difference in bringing about more rapid change.

One can hope that the tight labor markets of the future will force change, just as the tight labor market of the 1990s was a boon to welfare recipients seeking work. But special efforts are needed to reform misguided laws and change overly judgmental public attitudes.

INVESTING IN OUR FUTURE

Thus far, we have discussed raising incomes, adding jobs and distributing available work equitably, and improving the quality of work in the here and now. I want to turn to the complex of issues that adds up to investing in our future.

Early Childhood Development

The conversation begins with prenatal care, and with expectant mothers taking proper care of themselves. The themes of personal and public or community responsibility that should be symbiotic and intertwined appear as political poles from the very beginning—from before conception, actually. A material percentage of the human resources we waste is made up of people who were doomed from the start by their mother's behavior while they were in the womb, or by the inaccessibility of prenatal care, or both combined. Liberals who want to talk only about universal prenatal care are as seriously misguided as conservatives who want only to stress personal responsibility.

Public policy and accompanying public attitudes are hypocritical. Stay home with your child and bond, we say to mothers of means. Go out and work right away, we say to any mother who receives cash assistance from the state to help support her child. Our labor market is in essence no more forgiving than the state. A mother in a two-parent family where the husband has a full-time low-wage job may be just as pressured to go right back to work as a single mother under our current welfare policy. Research shows that high-quality, center-based child care creates no special risk of harm to an infant or toddler, but how many lower-income parents can afford child care like that?

So the disparities begin early, and they tend to perpetuate themselves from generation to generation. But if we recognize that disparities are caused by both a failure of responsibility within the home and a failure to provide adequate early childhood development programs outside the home, what does that suggest for our public and community policy? Are there ways we can reach parents and get them to see the importance of reading to their children, the damage done by allowing violence to be the normative way of dealing with conflict, and the importance of exposing children to enriching experience in the outside community?

The answer, obviously, is yes. There are successful programs, evaluated programs, that have made a difference in breaking into the cycle, in changing mores, in helping parents see a different way of relating to their children. If we say we want all children to be ready for school by age five, and we know that so many are not because of the deep deficits they already have, compared with other children who were parented differently, why don't we invest in trying to reach more parents in these proven ways?

Good developmental child care, Head Start, and pre-kindergarten will make up for the deficits from home in many cases, and complement good parenting in many others. Compared to where we were as a country, and state by state, we are much better off in this area than we were 40 years ago. The problem is that we also have millions more mothers in the labor market, so it is not at all clear that the child-care situation has improved on a net basis.

One way or another, we are now spending over $7 billion annually in federal funds on child care, plus $6.7 billion on Head Start. We are still reaching only about half of those eligible for Head Start, and as I said before, our federal child-care investment covers about one in seven of those children whose families are eligible for federal child-care assistance based on their level of income.

So the first item on the early childhood agenda is clear: increase the federal investment. But that is not enough. States and localities have to get into the act in a much bigger way. We will never get to where we want to be without a major state and local commitment. The goal should be child care provided in a seamless, systematic way, with a sliding scale payment schedule, to all children whose parents want them to participate. A significant proportion of that care, especially for four-year-olds, should be developmental in nature, not simply custodial.

A few states have moved in this direction. Georgia was the leader in introducing universal pre-K. Florida recently enacted three hours a day of substantive preschool for four-year-olds. The Florida story is particularly instructive. The former publisher of the *Miami Herald*, backed by visionary philanthropists, began a planning process and then a lobby to get the state to act. In 2002, Florida voters passed a ballot measure changing the state's constitution to require that all four-year-olds receive pre-K by 2005. It received 59 percent of the vote. The people of a conservative state responded because they were bombarded with a lobbying process that included powerful and influential people, broad media coverage, and wide grassroots participation. A textbook case. Easy to prescribe, hard to pull off in practice.

The overall agenda is one of breadth and depth: universality for four-year-olds, adequate services down to the infant and toddler level for working parents (and care gets more expensive the younger the child), sufficient hours of truly developmental care, merging child care and Head Start into one seamless system, raising pay for Head Start teachers and child-care workers, and investing in proper training for all teachers and care providers.

Our reach is beginning to approach an appropriate level of ambition. Our grasp is improving, too, but we have a way to go.

Schooling

The bottom line: there are no magic bullets. Amazing how Americans reach for the panacea. "Vouchers," they say. "If only we had vouchers." But there is no substitute for fixing our public schools so they offer a good education to every child. Just no substitute.

I don't mean to say that I find vouchers an easy issue. How do you argue with the African American parents in Cleveland and Milwaukee who embraced vouchers to escape the horrible public schools in which their children were trapped? I'm still against vouchers, but in a much more nuanced way. We never should have come to a time when vouchers could be taken seriously as a public policy proposal. The demand for vouchers arose because we allowed our central-city public schools to deteriorate so badly. The public schools are our agent of the common good. The public schools are the place where children should be socialized to be part of the larger community, part of civil society. That so many of our schools are failing in their mission is a tragedy. The answer is not to compound the offense by blowing up the public school system. It is to fix the schools for all of the children.

Let me say it in a different way. We have had school options for children throughout American history. The Boston Latin School, founded in 1635, was our country's first public school. Over time, our public school system became universal and diverse in its educational offerings. Bronx High School of Science came along in 1938. Then came magnets. And now charters. And, of course, if people wanted to pay, they have always been able to attend nonpublic schools. The one thing we never did was to use public money to pay tuition for private K–12 education. Vouchers involve crossing that line. But given that we always accepted the idea of alternatives to one's neighborhood school, the voucher can also be seen as part of a continuum, especially if sufficient funding of the public schools is maintained. So the line between vouchers and other alternatives is not as bright as some would say. But it is a line, and I still believe we should not cross it.

Okay. So what do we do? A lot of things. Attract additional talented people into teaching, with pay, public recognition, and better training, especially in-service training. Pay more attention to developing talented and trained principals to lead schools. Create smaller classes, more homework, longer school days, and longer school years. (We are still following a ridiculous school calendar that was established to respond to the needs of nineteenth-century farmers!) Enact high school reform, especially smaller schools within schools. (How did we ever invent these massive 3,000-student high schools? How did we ever come to believe that bigger is always better?) Establish career academies geared to going to work in a particular industry, such as computers, or travel and entertainment, or health care (an innovation that has been carefully evaluated). Provide more connection to the world of work for young people who are not college bound or just need some practical experience to remain engaged. Encourage greater parent participation and engagement.

How about doing what I call affirmative action for five-year-olds? Especially in neighborhoods of concentrated poverty, we have so many children coming to school who need not just good teachers, but our very best teachers. Why not arrange incentives and policies so that exceptionally talented teachers will be drawn to teach the children who need them the most? And not just when they are five years old.

What are we doing instead? No Child Left Behind. NCLB. The idea isn't wrong. Every child can learn, so every child can be held to reasonable standards. But then you have to teach every child. You can't blame the child for not learning when the child hasn't been taught. And you haven't got a prayer of living up to the promise of the statute if you don't appropriate the funds that were authorized in the legislation (putting aside the question of whether the authorization was enough to begin with). And you have to put the requisite effort and funding into it at the local level as well. The idea of NCLB was at least more complex than some of the simplistic fixes that get thrown around by some people, but as implemented, it's closer to being a slogan than a solution.

Off-School Hours

With so many mothers in the workforce, with the awful performance of so many schools, and with negative neighborhood influences, we have become much more concerned with what children and youth are doing when they are not in school. America has certainly paid attention to what we now call the off-school hours, and it has done so from the time people began to flock to the cities from the farms and the number of new immigrants shot up. The settlement houses of the early twentieth century were in part places for young people to go in the off-school hours. The YMCAs, the Scouts, Boys and Girls Clubs, Little Leagues, youth orchestras, and so forth have been around for a long time, and they provide activities and enrichment in the off-school hours.

But the phenomena mentioned above have revived and intensified interest, especially concerning young people who need something extra that their parents can't afford. With all the talk, though, and even with the enactment in the late 1990s of a billion-dollar federal program to support after-school initiatives, we still don't have it right. However, some excellent individual programs and citywide initiatives are quite encouraging.

The federal program—Twenty-first Century Learning Centers—turned out to be less than optimal in three major ways. First, the applicants had to be schools or schools in partnership with nonprofits, so the nonprofits of the after-school world were largely excluded from the program. Second, the money went mostly to elementary school programs, with a little to middle schools, and almost none for high school age youth. Third, the program is heavily academic in most places, which tends to leave out the developmental aspects that are in fact a major aim, explicitly or implicitly, of most after-school activities.

Then, when President Bush came into office, Congress turned the program into a block grant at his request. Now the money is dribbled out by the states to local school systems so that everyone gets a sliver. It is now impossible to do anything worthwhile without putting together a package of funding from multiple sources, which is fine in some places, and not possible in others.

Consequently, the federal money no longer stimulates much in the way of new initiatives. The interesting work that is going on—and there is quite a lot— is locally driven. Two especially interesting efforts are the Harlem Children's

Zone in New York and After School Matters in Chicago. They are polar opposites in origin. HCZ is bottom up, growing gradually in Central Harlem for the past 20 years under the charismatic leadership of Geoffrey Canada, to the point where it is a complex, multifaceted $24 million program virtually saturating a 24-square-block chunk of the city. ASM, much more recent in origin, was founded primarily by Maggie Daley, the wife of the mayor of Chicago, and is a top-down initiative that is gradually reaching out to cover more and more areas of the city and more and more young people.

Communities Taking Responsibility for All of Their Children and Young People

If we are going to stop the waste of human resources in our country, we need in every community to make a civic commitment to all of our young people, to see that they finish high school and go to college or find a job. This will take money, to be sure, and much of that money will need to be tax dollars, but this is a commitment that requires more than money. It means civic leadership to make sure that systems and agencies do what they are supposed to do, and it means individual involvement to see that children and youth who need something extra have caring adults in their lives on a continuing basis. We need voluntary involvement in many areas, but none is more important than mentoring and tutoring children and youth who need extra help and support and the sense that adults whom they respect care deeply about them and about what happens to them.

This means creating a continuum in the community from the cradle to adulthood, a continuum to replace the cradle-to-prison pipeline, as the Children's Defense Fund is now denominating it. We tend to talk about programs and about money. We can have huge government funding for this or that or whatever, but without the leadership and the commitment and the competence in communities, that money will be wasted.

It is local leadership and community involvement, along with adequate resources, that will produce better schools. It is employer partnerships with schools and colleges, especially community colleges, and nonprofits that will produce a clearer pathway into the labor force for youth at risk. The faith community has a role to play, especially in mentoring and tutoring and adopting struggling families. So do people in each neighborhood. Every part of the community has a role to play in helping youth successfully transition into adulthood. Starting in adolescence, the continuum includes the schools and positive youth development activities in the off-school hours, and it has to include connection to the world of work as soon as young people are of an age where getting some information and exposure will start to acculturate them and familiarize them with what work is all about.

It is vitally important to increase the number of young people who graduate from high school—not with GEDs, but with regular high school diplomas. That is the single best step to increase someone's chances of successfully gaining access to the labor market. And, if more young people graduate from high school, many more could be going to college. For some, going to community college where they might take specific job-focused programs is another enormously useful step, although it is also the case that many of the jobs projected to appear in the next two decades will require only a high school diploma.

Some youth will fall by the wayside. The community has a moral responsibility to minimize that number. If youth see a promise of opportunity, fewer will get in trouble with the law, and fewer will have children at young ages. But some will drop out and possibly get into more lasting trouble. The community needs to have ways of picking up the pieces. I already talked about the need for special attention to ex-offenders. But whether or not a person has gotten into difficulty with the law, there should be opportunities like Job Corps, service and conservation corps, YouthBuild, Americorps, and special pathways back by way of community colleges—all geared to people who dropped out of high school for whatever reason and now want to get back on track.

A promising recent initiative to prepare at-risk youth for the labor market was the Youth Opportunity Grant (YOG) program, scrapped by the Bush administration last year. This initiative was begun in 36 sites around the country, both urban and rural, by the Clinton administration. It received $250 million annually in federal funds, and even a bit more for a couple of years. YOG sites were saturation models in particular neighborhoods or rural areas, designed to reach large numbers of the youth in those places. The typical grant was on the order of $5 million annually for five years. The idea was a combination of job training, including the "soft skills" of attitude and punctuality, and work experience. The model is mainly for youth who had dropped out, although some participants were still in school. Early evaluation showed some sites to be producing promising outcomes, but the Bush administration zeroed the program out. A number of communities have been pleased enough at the performance of the program that they have used part of their regular federal Workforce Investment Act job training funds, as well as local funds, to keep the program going. It is an important program, and it should be brought back nationally, with increased funding at the earliest possible time.

Other Federal Legislation Relating to the Continuum from Adolescence to Adulthood

I've mentioned Americorps and the Workforce Investment Act. I want to say a few more words about each of those, as well as suggest a new national apprenticeship program.

Americorps gives Americans of every background a chance to serve and help others in our country. One important set of Americorps participants is made up of people from lower-income communities. With a greater investment, which the program deserves—it ought to take in at least 100,000 new participants a year—it can be a bridge to the labor market for a significant number of lower-income youth, and a bridge that develops their civic awareness and commitment to participate in our democracy at the same time.

The Workforce Investment Act, despite being renamed in recent years (as seems to happen every 10 to 15 years), is no more satisfactory than it ever was. Both its youth and adult portions should be redesigned into two distinct parts. One would be a national formula grant program that builds on the current structure, but with clear outcome targets, and rigorous measurement criteria and reporting requirements to assure accountability. The second would be a national demonstration component, again with clear design criteria and evaluation requirements. It should not be so difficult to find ways to define with greater clarity what we want employment and training legislation to accomplish and to be able to find out whether the funds have in fact brought about the results we were seeking.

Finally, and extremely important, it is time to design and implement a new national apprenticeship program. The school-to-work legislation of the Clinton era has disappeared from the national conversation. There is a kind of implicit agreement that it was not very successful. In fact, that is not the case. Some of the same ideas, but this time far more targeted to young people in the greatest need of assistance and much more involving of employers for design of the training and development of the apprenticeship component, constitute the basis for a promising initiative. Discussion of the details of such an apprenticeship program should be on the table and part of the agenda for the next progressive administration.

NATIONAL POLICY FOR THE NEXT HALF-CENTURY—PUSHING BACK AGAINST THE BABY BUST

National policy is really just the tip of the iceberg, in my view. I hope I've made that clear. What goes on in communities is at the heart of whether we make real progress in ending the waste of human resources in the United States. Nonetheless, national policy is crucial. Indeed, in the area of achieving a living income, it's the major area for policy outside of getting employers to pay higher wages.

Even though we must pay more attention to what people should be doing in their communities, it is useful to recap some of the national policy items that we should be working on if we want to stop the waste of human resources in this great and wealthy nation:

- The elements of a living income, including continuing increases in the minimum wage, improvements in the Earned Income Tax Credit, federal living wage legislation, labor law reform, asset development measures, and job creation to meet pressing national needs. And a "social" wage, including universal health coverage, child-care assistance for all who need it, a new affordable housing production initiative and sufficient income support for low-income renters, and adequate assistance with defraying the cost of college attendance.
- Repairing the gaping holes in the safety net for people out of work, especially reforming the unemployment insurance program, improving income maintenance for families with children, and protecting the food stamp program from erosion or structural change.
- Strong civil rights enforcement, paid family and medical leave, and active policies to help the disabled get into the labor force.
- A national policy on early childhood development, fulfillment of the promise of No Child Left Behind, redesign of the Twenty-first Century Learning Centers program, a new life for Americorps, revival of the Youth Opportunity Grant program, a new national apprenticeship program, and complete reform of the Workforce Investment Act.

CONCLUSION

The coming demographic realities create a tremendous opportunity for the United States to make full use at long last of all of its human resources. The challenge is complex. Meeting it involves a multiplicity of policies and commitments—new national policies, adequate investments at all levels, and serious efforts by communities to get all shoulders pushing the vehicle of change, moving it up a hill that has been waiting to be conquered for as long as the American nation has been on the planet.

Conclusion

Fred R. Harris

Throughout the world, the total fertility rate (number of children of childbearing-age women) is dropping—rapidly and steeply in some countries. This decline in fertility rate, to levels below replacement (2.1 children per woman), is particularly noted in developed countries. Thirty-one of them have fertility rates at 1.5 or below, including nations in Europe and the western part of the former Soviet Union, Canada, Japan, South Korea, Taiwan, and Singapore. Fourteen of these report a "lowest-low" fertility rate (1.3 children or lower)—Spain, Italy, and Japan, for example. But the fertility rate decline is also seen, now, in many developing countries. While fertility is still five children per woman in some least-developed countries, it has dropped below replacement levels in about 20 developing countries.

The reasons for the decline in fertility rate are several. More women are working outside the home. Levels of education have risen. There is greater access to contraception. People are getting married at a later age. Women are having their first child at a later age, there is wider spacing between their children if more than one, and they are stopping childbearing earlier. There are more divorces.

Fertility rate decline is a very important global trend, like global warming, that policy-makers need very much to be aware of and to start planning for. But is declining fertility rate a good thing or a bad thing, overall? Certainly, as world population growth slows, there will be less stress on the environment and on natural resources. That is a good thing, of course. But just as deflation can cause a lot of problems for an economy, as inflation does, a declining fertility rate with resultant population aging and a dropping worker/nonworker ratio can cause, among other things, greater pressures on a country's social security system, greater need to improve worker productivity, and greater pressures for

213

acceptable levels of legal immigration. These are issues that the United States must confront, though it is today an example of fertility-rate exceptionalism among developed countries—America's rate being exactly at the replacement level of 2.1, at least partly because of the presence of large numbers of minority and immigrant families.

Some developed countries have begun to increase their pronatalist policies—greater provision of child care, more generous maternity leaves, and child allowances—and though such pronatalist policies are worthwhile for other reasons, they have so far had little noticeable impact on increasing fertility. No country where the fertility rate has dropped far below replacement level has ever been able to get itself back up anywhere near that level. Some countries, such as Spain, are trying to attract more immigrants (though no country can hope that immigration could ever reach the highest levels necessary to stop population aging), and other countries, notably Japan, continue to be traditionally hostile to greater immigration, leaving that as a closed avenue down which a solution to the problem of fertility rate decline cannot be pursued.

In the United States, the Baby Bust, except for the aberration of the post–World War II Baby Boom, is part of a longtime trend. The fertility rate for native-born, non-Hispanic whites is below replacement level, more like that of Europe, though the overall U.S. fertility rate is at replacement level, at least in part due to the presence of large numbers of minority and immigrant families.

The U.S. Social Security system is not in "crisis," nor is it going to go "bankrupt" or "bust." Even the Social Security trustees admit that under their most pessimistic predictions, Social Security will be able to pay full benefits out of annual revenues until the year 2017, will be able to pay full benefits thereafter from the accumulated trust fund until the year 2041, and will still thereafter be able to pay 70 percent of all benefits then due, which in real dollars will be more money for recipients then than present beneficiaries receive. But the predictions of the Social Security trustees are too gloomy. The trustees have seriously underestimated what U.S. wage levels and the rate of productivity, economic growth, population growth, and immigration will be over the next 75 years. More realistic estimates would eliminate any supposed future Social Security shortfall. But, even if the Social Security trustees' pessimistic predictions are accepted, the future actuarial soundness of the system can be assured through relatively simple adjustments—such as eliminating the wage cap of $90,000 on which Social Security taxes are paid and refusing to make permanent the Bush administration's income tax cut for persons making over $1 million a year.

An overwhelming case can be made for greater government investment in early childhood development, particularly for poor children, investment that would pay great dividends, in reduced crime and increased individual earnings, for example—and notably, too, in increased taxes collected, including increased federal tax collections with which to pay future Social Security benefits.

Levels of immigration into the United States are not going to drop precipitously in the future, as the Social Security trustees have predicted. It does not make sense that if U.S. jobs go unfilled in the future by residents, fewer immigrants will come to take them. Immigration will continue at presently relatively high levels. The U.S. Census reports that there are about 35.7 million foreign-born persons presently in the United States, about 11 million of them from Mexico. The undocumented population in the country totals nearly 11 million, with Mexicans making up more than half of them and those from other Latin American countries making up nearly another fourth (Pew Hispanic Center 2005). Even though the fertility rate in Mexico and other Latin American countries is declining, it is still above replacement levels, and the present population numbers and young average age in those countries make clear that Mexico and the rest will continue to serve as powerful engines of migration to the United States for many, many years to come.

Nativist claims by Samuel P. Huntington and others that the presence of so many Mexicans in the United States is a threat to the U.S. "Anglo Protestant" culture are false. Mexicans and their children actually assimilate remarkably well, adapting themselves relatively quickly to the English language and to U.S. values. Immigrants are needed, and will continue to be needed, to fill jobs here, and their presence is economically beneficial for the United States; they do not depress wages or take jobs away from residents. The United States should therefore accept, regularize, and legalize immigration at appropriate levels, grant amnesty and residency to those who have been working in America a long time, and increase support for the education and training—and thus increased productivity—of immigrants and their families, as well as give greater attention to their socialization to U.S. history, the political system, and the English language (National Immigration Forum 2004; Immigration Daily 2004).

We must end the present waste in the United States of so much of our human resources. Better education and training—and thus increased productivity—for presently underutilized members of the potential workforce (including poor people and minority and immigrant families) is essential. New efforts should include the encouragement of unionization, a hefty increase in the minimum wage, more money for jobs and child care, and, again, increased investment in early childhood development.

In summary, we are lucky in the United States that the fertility rate here stands at the replacement level, though the rate for native-born, non-Hispanic whites is below that level. A sound and prosperous future for America will involve acceptance, regularization, and legalization of appropriate levels of immigration and an increase in several kinds of governmental efforts to increase the productivity of all our people, including those presently underutilized, particularly poor people and minority and immigrant families.

References

ACORN (Association of Community Organizations for Reform Now). 2005. "Living Wage Victories." www.acorn.org/index.php?id=878.

Adsera, A. 2004. "Changing Fertility Rates in Developed Countries: The Impact of Labor Market Institutions." *Journal of Population Economics* 17, no. 1, 17–43.

Ahn, N., and P. Mira. 2002. "A Note on the Changing Relationship between Fertility and Female Employment Rates in Developed Countries." *Journal of Population Economics* 15, 667–682.

AIU Insurance Company. 2001. *Cost of Children.* Tokyo: AIU Insurance Company. In Japanese.

Anderton, Douglas L., and Lee L. Bean. 1985. "Birth Spacing and Fertility Limitation: A Behavioral Analysis of a Nineteenth Century Frontier Population." *Demography* 22, no. 2.

Aries, Philippe. 1980. "Two Successive Motivations for the Declining Birth Rate in the West." *Population and Development Review* 6, 645–650.

Asahi Shimbun. 2004. "Falling Academic Scores." December 10. In Japanese.

———. 2005. "METI Organizes Research Group to Explore Possibility of Government Support for Dating and Related Services That Encourage Marriage." January 25. In Japanese.

Asher, David L. 2000. "Japan's Financial Mt. Fuji." Washington, D.C.: American Enterprise Institute. (PowerPoint presentation.)

Associated Press. 2005. "Bush to Seek Cuts in Medicaid, Benefits." January 22.

Bachu, Amara. 1999. "Trends in Premarital Childbearing, 1930–1994." CPS, Special Report. October.

Baker, Al. 2004. "Over Pataki Veto, Minimum Wage to Rise to $7.15." *New York Times.* December 7.

Baker, Dean, and David Rosnick. 2004. "Basic Facts on Social Security and Proposed Benefit Cuts/Privatization." Center for Economic and Policy Research, Washington, D.C., November 16.

Barmby, T., and A. Cigno. 1990. "A Sequential Probability Model of Fertility Patterns." *Journal of Population Economics* 3, no. 1, 31–51.

Barnett, W. Steven. 1993. "Benefit-Cost Analysis of Preschool Education: Findings from a 25-Year Follow-up." *American Journal of Orthopsychiatry* 63, no. 4, 500–508.

Barnett, W. Steven. 1995. "Long-Term Effects of Early Childhood Programs on Cognitive and School Outcomes." *The Future of Children* 5, no. 3, 25–50.

Becker, Gary. 1960. "An Economic Analysis of Fertility." In A. Coale et al., *Demographic and Economic Change in Developed Countries*. Princeton, N.J.: Princeton University Press.

Becker, G. S. 1981. *A Treatise on the Family*. Cambridge, Mass.: Harvard University Press.

Belanger, A., and G. Ouellet. 2002. "A Comparative Study of Recent Trends in Canadian and American Fertility, 1980–1999." In A. Belanger, ed., *Report on the Demographic Situation in Canada, 2001*. Ottawa: Statistics Canada.

Bernstein, Jared. 2004. "Minimum Wage and Its Effects on Small Business." Testimony before the U.S. House Subcommittee on Workforce Empowerment and Government Programs, April 29.

Bettio, F., and P. Villa. 1998. "A Mediterranean Perspective on the Breakdown of the Relationship between Participation and Fertility." *Cambridge Journal of Economics* 22, no. 2, 137–171.

Billari, F. C., M. Castiglioni, T. Castro Martín, F. Michielin, and F. Ongaro. 2002. "Household and Union Formation in a Mediterranean Fashion: Italy and Spain." In United Nations Economic Commission for Europe, E. Klijzing and M. Corijn, eds., *Dynamics of Fertility and Partnership in Europe: Insights and Lessons from Comparative Research*. 2:17–42. Geneva/New York: United Nations.

Billari, F. C., and H.-P. Kohler. 2004. "Patterns of Low and Lowest-low Fertility in Europe." *Population Studies* 58, no. 2, 161–176.

Billari, F. C., P. Manfredi, and A. Valentini. 2000. "Macro-demographic Effects on the Transition to Adulthood: Multistate Stable Population Theory and Application to Italy." *Mathematical Population Studies* 9, no. 1, 33–63.

Billari, F. C., D. Philipov, and P. Baizán. 2001. "Leaving Home in Europe: The Experience of Cohorts Born around 1960." *International Journal of Population*.

Billari, F. C., and C. Wilson. 2001. "Convergence towards Diversity? Cohort Dynamics in the Transition to Aulthood in Contemporary Western Europe." Max Planck Institute for Demographic Research, Rostock, Germany, Working Paper #2001-039. www.demogr.mpg.de.

Bongaarts, John. 2001. "Fertility and Reproductive Preferences in Post-Transition Societies." *Population and Development Review* 27, 260–281.

Bongaarts, John, and G. Feeney. 1998. "On the Quantum and Tempo of Fertility." *Population and Development Review* 24, no. 22, 271–291.

Bongaarts, John, and S. C. Watkins. 1996. "Social Interactions and Contemporary Fertility Transitions." *Population and Development Review* 22, no. 44, 639–682.

Bourgeois-Pichat, Jean. 1974. "France." In Bernard Berelson, ed., *Population Policy in Developed Countries*. New York: McGraw-Hill.

Boushey, Heather, et al. 2001. *Hardships in America: The Real Story of Working Families*. Economic Policy Institute. Washington, D.C.

Brewster, K. L., and R. R. Rindfuss. 2000. "Fertility and Women's Employment in Industrialized Nations." *Annual Review of Sociology* 26, 271–296.

Burtless, Gary. 1999. "Risk and Returns of Stock Market Investments Held in Individual Retirement Accounts." Testimony before the House Budget Committee, Task Force on Social Security Reform, May 11.

Cabinet Office. 2001. *White Paper on the National Life Style*. Tokyo: Government of Japan. In Japanese.

———. 2003. *Annual Report on Japanese Economy and Public Finance/Economic Survey of Japan*. Tokyo: Government of Japan. In Japanese.

———. 2004. *Annual Report on National Accounts*. Tokyo: Government of Japan. In Japanese.

Caldwell, John C., Pat Caldwell, and Peter McDonald. 2002. "Policy Responses to Low Fertility and Its Consequences: A Global Survey." *Journal of Population Research* 19, 1–24.

Caldwell, John C., and Thomas Schindlmayr. 2003. "Explanations of the Fertility Crisis in Modern Societies: A Search for Commonalities." *Population Studies* 57, 241–263.

Campbell, Frances, Craig Ramey, Elizabeth Pungello, Joseph Sparling, and Shari Miller-Johnson. 2002. "Early Childhood Education: Young Adult Outcomes from the Abecedarian Project." *Applied Development Science* 6, no. 1, 42–57.

Carneiro, Pedro, Flavio Cunha, and James Heckman. 2003. "Interpreting the Evidence of Family Influence on Child Development." Paper presented at Economics of Early Childhood Development: Lessons for Economic Policy, conference co-hosted by the Federal Reserve Bank of Minneapolis and the McKnight Foundation, in cooperation with the University of Minnesota, October 17.

Castles, Francis G. 2003. "The World Turned Upside Down: Below Replacement Fertility, Changing Preferences and Family-friendly Public Policy in 21 OECD Countries." *Journal of European Social Policy* 13, no. 3.

Center on Budget and Policy Priorities. 2004. "The Implications of the Social Security Projections Issued by the Congressional Budget Office." Washington, D.C., June 14.

Chamie, J. 2004. "Low Fertility: Can Governments Make a Difference?" Paper presented at the annual meeting of the Population Association of America, Boston, Mass., April 1–3. http://paa2004.princeton.edu.

Chang, Howard F. 2005. "Report on International Migration." Paper presented at Columbia University Global Colloquium on International Migration and Academic Freedom, Columbia University, New York, January 18–19.

Chen, Edwin. 2005. "Bush Unveils $15-Billion Plan to Raise the Pell Grant Ceiling." *Los Angeles Times*. January 15.

Chesnais, Jean-Claude. 1992. *The Demographic Transition, 1720–1984*. Oxford: Clarendon Press.

———. 1996. "Fertility, Family, and Social Policy in Contemporary Western Europe." *Population and Development Review* 22, no. 4, 729–739.

———. 2001. "A March toward Population Recession." *Population and Development Review* 27, 255–259.

Cicirelli, Victor G. 1969. *The Impact of Head Start: An Evaluation of the Effects of Head Start on Children's Cognitive and Affective Development*. Athens: Ohio University and Westinghouse Learning Corporation.

Cigno, A. 1991. *Economics of the Family*. Oxford: Clarendon Press.

Coale, Ansley J., and Melvin Zelnik. 1963. *New Estimates of Fertility and Population in the United States*. Princeton, N.J.: Princeton University Press.

Committee for Economic Development. 2002. *Preschool for All: Investing in a Productive and Just Society*. New York: CED.

Congressional Budget Office. 2004. "The Outlook for Social Security." Washington, D.C., June.

Congressional Research Service. 2005. "Estimated Effect of Price-Indexing Social Security Benefits on the Number of Americans 65 and Older in Poverty." Memorandum to the Senate Finance Committee, Library of Congress, Washington, D.C., January 28.

Corijn, M. 1999. "Transitions to Adulthood in Europe for the 1950s and 1950s Cohorts." Brussels: CBGS-Werkdocument #4.

Cortina, Jeronimo, and Rodolfo O. de la Garza. 2004. "Immigrant Remitting Behavior and Its Developmental Consequences for Mexico and El Salvador." Edited by Andrea Gutierrez. Los Angeles: Tomás Rivera Policy Institute.

Cortina, Jeronimo, Rodolfo de la Garza, Sandra Bejarano, and Andrew Weiner. 2004. "The Economic Impact of the Mexico-California Relationship." Los Angeles: Tomás Rivera Policy Institute.

Council of Large Public Housing Authorities. 2004. "The Section 8 Funding Crisis: A Chronology." Washington, D.C. www.clpha.org/page.cfm?pageID=560.

Council of Europe. 2003. *Recent Demographic Developments in Europe*. Strasbourg: Council of Europe Publishing. www.coe.int.

Currie, Janet. 2001. "Early Childhood Education Programs." *Journal of Economic Perspectives* 15, no. 2, 213–238.

Currie, Janet, and Matthew Neidell. 2003. "Getting Inside the Black Box of Head Start Quality: What Matters and What Doesn't?" National Bureau of Economic Research, Working Paper 10091. November.

Dalla Zuanna, G. 2001. "The Banquet of Aeolus: A Familistic Interpretation of Italy's Lowest Low Fertility." *Demographic Research* 4, no. 5, 133–162. www.demographic-research.org.

Davis, Darren W., and Brian D. Silver. 2003. *Americans' Perceptions of the Causes of Terrorism: Why Do They Hate Us?* Department of Political Science, Michigan State University. www.msu.edu/user/bsilver/RootsMarch25-Final.pdf.

de la Garza, Rodolfo O., Louis DeSipio, F. Chris Garcia, John Garcia, and Angelo Falcon. 1992. *Latino Voices: Mexican, Puerto Rican, and Cuban Perspectives on American Politics*. Boulder, Colo.: Westview Press.

de la Garza, Rodolfo O., Angelo Falcon, and F. Chris Garcia. 1996. "Will the Real Americans Please Stand Up: Anglo and Mexican-American Support of Core American Political Values." *American Journal of Political Science* 40, no. 2, 335–51.

de la Garza, Rodolfo O., and Myriam Hazan. 2003. "Looking Backward, Moving Forward: Mexican Organizations in the U.S. as Agents of Incorporation and Dissociation." Claremont, Calif.: Tomás Rivera Policy Institute.

de la Garza, Rodolfo O., Jerome Hernandez, Angelo Falcon, F. Chris Garcia, and John A. Garcia. 1997. "Mexican, Puerto Rican, and Cuban Foreign Policy Perspectives: A Test of Competing Explanations." In F. Chris Garcia, ed., *Pursuing Power: Latinos and the Political System*. Notre Dame, Ind.: University of Notre Dame Press. 401–426.

Del Boca, D. 2002. "The Effect of Child Care and Part Time Opportunities on Participation and Fertility Decisions in Italy." *Journal of Population Economics* 15, no. 3, 549–573.

Delgado, M., and T. Castro Martín. 1998. *Fertility and Family Surveys in Countries of the ECE Region, Standard Country Report Spain*. Geneva: United Nations.

Demeny, P. 1987. "Re-linking Fertility Behavior and Economic Security in Old Age: A Pronatalistic Reform." *Population and Development Review* 13, no. 1, 128–132.

———. 2003. "Population Policy Dilemmas in Europe at the Dawn of the Twenty-first Century." *Population and Development Review* 29, no. 1, 1–28.

DeNavas-Walt, Carmen, et al. 2004. *Income, Poverty, and Health Insurance Coverage in the United States: 2003*. U.S. Census Bureau, Current Population Reports, P60-226. Washington, D.C. www.census.gov/prod/2004pubs/P60-226.pdf.

De Sandre, P. 2000. "Patterns of Fertility in Italy and Factors of Its Decline." *Genus* 56, nos. 1–2, 19–54.

DeSipio, Louis, Harry Pachon, Rodolfo de la Garza, and Jongho Lee. 2003. "Immigrant Politics at Home and Abroad: How Latino Immigrants Engage the Politics of Their Home Communities and the United States." Los Angeles, Calif.: Tomás Rivera Policy Institute.

Deutsch, Martin. 1967. *The Disadvantaged Child: Selected Papers of Martin Deutsch and Associates*. New York: BasicBooks.

Diprete, T. A., S. P. Morgan, H. Engelhardt, and H. Pacalova. 2003. "Do Cross-national Differences in the Costs of Children Generate Cross-national Differences in Fertility Rates?" *Population Research and Policy Review* 22, nos. 5–6, 439–477.

Dolado, J. J., F. Felgueroso, and J. F. Jimeno. 2000. "Youth Labour Markets in Spain: Education, Training and Crowding-out." *European Economic Review* 44, 943–956.

Dominguez, Jorge. 2004. "Latinos and U.S. Foreign Policy." Paper commissioned by Tomás Rivera Policy Institute.

Doteuchi, Akio. 2004. "Toward a Prosperous Society with a Declining Birthrate: Enhancing the Social Environment for Childcare Support." NLI Research. Manuscript located on the Internet.

Dowley, Kathleen M., and Brian D. Silver. 2000. "Subnational and National Loyalty: Cross-National Comparisons." *International Journal of Public Opinion Research* 12, 357–71.

Duce Tello, R. M. 1995. "Un modelo de Elección de Tenencia de Vivienda para España." *Moneda y Crédito* 201, 127–152.

Easterlin, Richard A. 1980. *Birth and Fortune: The Impact of Numbers on Personal Welfare.* Chicago: University of Chicago Press.

———. 1961. "The American Baby Boom in Historical Perspective." *American Economic Review* 51, no. 5, 869–911.

Economic Policy Institute. 2004. "Characteristics of State UI Benefits, 2003." Table B. *EPI Issue Guide: Employment Insurance.* Washington, D.C. www.epinet.org/issueguides/unemployment/table_b.pdf.

———. 2004. "Historical Values of the U.S. Minimum Wage, 1960–2003." Table 4. *EPI Issue Guide: Minimum Wage.* Washington, D.C. www.epinet.org/issueguides/minwage/table4.gif.

Economist. 2002a. "Special Report: Half a Billion Americans? Demography and the West." *Economist* 364, no. 8287, 22. August 24.

———. 2002b. "A Tale of Two Bellies: The Remarkable Demographic Difference between America and Europe." *Economist* 363, no. 8287, 11. November 3.

Employee Free Choice Act. 2003. S 1925, HR 3619. 108th Congress.

Engelhardt, H., T. Kögel, and A. Prskawetz. 2004. "Fertility and Women's Employment Reconsidered: A Macro-level Time Series Analysis 1960–2000." *Population Studies* 58, no. 1, 109–120.

Ermisch, J. F. 1988. "The Econometric Analysis of Birth Rate Dynamics in Britain." *Journal of Human Resources* 23, no. 4.

Esping-Andersen, G. 1999. *Social Foundations of Postindustrial Economies.* Oxford: Oxford University Press.

European Commission. 1998. "Dual-earner Families. New Ways to Work." Informational Bulletin no. 4. Brussels: European Union Network "Family and Work" and New Ways to Work Survey.

Feeney, Griffith. 1986. *Period Parity Progression Measures of Fertility in Japan.* NUPRI Research Paper series no. 35. Tokyo: Nihon University Population Research Institute.

Feeney, Griffith, and Yasuhiko Saito. 1985. *Progression to First Marriage in Japan: 1870–1980.* NUPRI Reseach Paper series no. 24. Tokyo: Nihon University Population Research Institute.

Fernández Cordón, J. A. 1997. "Youth Residential Independence and Autonomy: A Comparative Study." *Journal of Family Issues* 16, no. 6, 567–607.

Foster, C. 2000. "The Limits to Low Fertility: A Biosocial Approach." *Population and Development Review* 26, no. 2, 209–234.

Forster, M. F., and I. G. Toth. 1997. "Poverty, Inequalities and Social Policies in the Visegrad Countries." *Economics of Transition* 5, no. 2, 505–510.

Frejka, T. 1980. "Fertility Trends and Policies: Czechoslovakia in the 1970s." *Population and Development Review* 6, no. 1, 65–93.

Fukutake, Tadashi. 1989. *The Japanese Social Structure.* Tokyo: University of Tokyo Press.

Garces, Eliana, Duncan Thomas, and Janet Currie. 2000. "Longer Term Effects of Head Start." Working Paper series 00-20. Rand Corporation. December.

Gauthier, A. H., and J. Hatzius. 1997. "Family Benefits and Fertility: An Econometric Analysis." *Population Studies* 51, no. 3, 295–306.

Gauthier, Anne H. 1991. "Family Policies in Comparative Perspective." *Discussion Paper No. 5.* Oxford: Centre for European Studies, Nuffield College.

―――. 1993. "Family Policies in Comparative Perspective." *Discussion Paper No. 5.* Oxford: Centre for European Studies, Nuffield College.

―――. 1996. *The State and the Family: A Comparative Analysis of Family Policies in Industrialized Countries.* New York: Oxford University Press.

―――. 2002. "Family Policies in Industrialized Countries: Is There Convergence?" *Population* 57, no. 3, 447–474.

Goldin, Claudia. 1990. *Understanding the Gender Gap: An Economic History of American Women.* New York: Oxford University Press.

Goldin, Claudia, and L. F. Katz. 2002. "The Power of the Pill: Oral Contraceptives and Women's Career and Marriage Decisions." *Journal of Political Economy* 110, no. 4, 730–770.

Goldman, N., C. F. Westoff, and C. Hammerslough. 1984. "Demography of the Marriage Market in the United States." *Population Index* 50, no. 1, 5–25.

González, M. J., T. Jurado, and M. Naldini. 2000. "Introduction: Interpreting the Transformation of Gender Inequalities in Southern Europe." In M. J. González, T. Jurado, and M. Naldini, eds., *Gender Inequalities in Southern Europe: Women, Work and Welfare in the 1990s.* London: Frank Cass.

Gordon, Robert. 2003. "Exploding Productivity Growth: Context, Causes, and Implications," *Brookings Papers on Economic Activity* 2, 207–298.

Granovetter, M. S. 1973. "The Strength of Weak Ties." *American Journal of Sociology* 78, no. 6, 1360–1380.

―――. 1985. "Economic Action and the Social Structure: The Problem of Embeddedness." *American Journal of Sociology* 91, no. 3, 481–510.

Grant, J., S. Hoorens, S. Sivadasan, M. van het Loo, J. DaVanzo, L. Hale, S. Gibson, and W. Butz. 2004. *Low Fertility in Population Aging: Causes, Consequences and Policy Options.* Santa Monica, Calif.: Rand Corporation. www.rand.org.

Greenspan, Alan. 2004. "Remarks by Chairman Alan Greenspan." Paper presented at the symposium sponsored by the Federal Reserve Bank of Kansas City, Jackson Hole, Wyo., August 27.

Greenstein, Robert. 2001. "The Changes the New Tax Law Makes in Refundable Tax Credits for Low-Income Working Families." Center on Budget and Policy Priorities, Washington, D.C.

Grootaert, C., and J. Braithwaite. 1998. "Poverty Correlates and Indicator-based Targeting in Eastern Europe and the Former Soviet Union." World Bank, Policy Research Working Paper no. 1942.

Grossbard-Shechtman, A. 1985. "Marriage Squeezes and the Marriage Market." In K. Davis, ed., *Contemporary Marriage: Comparative Perspective on a Changing Institution.* New York: Russell Sage Foundation. 375–395.

Haines, Michael R. 1996. "Long-Term Marriage Patterns in the United States from Colonial Times to the Present." NBER Working Paper Series, Historical Paper 80. March.

―――. 2000. "The White Population of the United States, 1790–1920." In Michael R. Haines and Richard H. Steckel, *A Population History of North America.* Cambridge: Cambridge University Press. 305–370.

Hajnal, J. 1965. "European Marriage Pattern in Perspective." In D. V. Glass and D. E. Eversley, eds., *Population in History: Essays in Historical Demography.* Chicago: Aldine Publishing. 101–143.

Hakim, Peter, and Carlos A. Rosales. 2000. "The Latino Foreign Policy Lobby." In Rodolfo O. de la Garza and Harry Pachon, eds., *Latinos and U.S. Foreign Policy: Representing the "Homeland"?* Lanham, Md.: Rowman and Littlefield. 133–136.

Hank, K., and M. Kreyenfeld. 2000. "Does the Availability of Childcare Influence the Employment of Mothers? Findings from Western Germany." *Population Research and Policy Review* 19, no. 4, 317–337.

Heckman, James. 1999. "Policies to Foster Human Development." Working Paper 7288, National Bureau of Economic Research, Cambridge, Mass.

Heckman, James, and Alan Krueger. 2003. *Inequality in America: What Role for Human Capital Policies?* Cambridge, Mass.: MIT Press.

Heitlinger, Alena. 1976. "Pro-natalist Population Policies in Czechoslovakia." *Population Studies* 30, 123–135.

Henry J. Kaiser Family Foundation. 2005. "The Medicaid Program at a Glance." Kaiser Commission on Medicaid and the Uninsured, Washington, D.C. www.kff.org/medicaid/loader.cfm?url=/commonspot/security/getfile.cfm&PageID=50450.

Heuveline, P., J. Timberlake, and F. Furstenberg. 2003. "Shifting Childrearing to Single Mothers: Results from 17 Western Countries." *Population and Development Review* 29, no. 1, 47–71.

Hobbs, Frank, and Nicole Stoops. 2002. "Demographic Trends in the 20th Century." U.S. Census Bureau, Census 2000, Special Reports, Series CENSR-4. Washington, D.C.: U.S. Government Printing Office.

Hobcraft, John. 2004. "Method, Theory, and Substance in Understanding Choices about Becoming a Parent: Progress or Regress?" *Population Studies* 58, 81–84.

Hobcraft, John N., and K. E. Kiernan. 1995. "Becoming a Parent in Europe." In European Association for Population Studies/International Union for the Scientific Study of Population, *Evolution or Revolution in European Population, Vol. 1, Plenary Sessions, European Population Conference Milan.* Milan: Franco Angeli.

Hohn, Charlotte. 1988. "Population Policies in Advanced Countries: Pronatalist and Migration Strategies." *European Journal of Population* 3, 453–481.

Hollmann, Frederick W., Tammany J. Mulder, and Jeffrey E. Kallan. 2000. "Methodology and Assumptions for the Population Projections of the United States: 1999 to 2100." U.S. Census Bureau, Population Division Working Paper no. 38. January 13.

Huntington, Samuel P. 2004. *Who Are We? The Challenges to America's National Identity.* New York: Simon and Schuster.

Hyatt, D. E., and W. J. Milne. 1991. "Can Public Policy Affect Fertility?" *Canadian Public Policy* 17, no. 1, 77–85.

Immigration Daily. 2004. "Mexican Immigrant Workers and the U.S. Economy: Increasingly Vital Role." American Immigration Law Foundation. August 18. www.ilw.com/lawyers/articles2002,0906-ailf.shtm.

Japan Times. 2005a. "'Freeters': Free by Name, Nature; Exploitative Corporate Culture Breeds Nomadic Workers." January 29.

———. 2005b. "Workforce Grows 0.4%; Monthly Wages Fall 0.7%. February 2.

Japanese Association for Sex Education. 2001. *Sexual Behavior of Youth.* Tokyo: Shogakukan. In Japanese.

Japan Institute of Life Insurance. Various years. *Survey on Life Security.* Tokyo: Japan Institute of Life Insurance. In Japanese.

Joshi, H. 1998. "The Opportunity Costs of Childbearing: More than Mothers' Business." *Journal of Population Economics* 11, 161–183.

Karoly, Lynn. 2001. "Investing in the Future: Reducing Poverty through Human Capital Investments." In S. Danziger and Robert Haveman, eds., *Understanding Poverty.* Cambridge, Mass.: Harvard University Press.

Karoly, Lynn, Peter Greenwood, Susan Everingham, Jill Hoube, Rebecca Kilburn, C. Peter Rydell, Matthew Sanders, and James Chiesa. 1998. "Investing in Our Children: What We know and Don't Know about the Costs and Benefits of Early Childhood Interventions." Washington, D.C.: Rand Corporation.

Karoly, Lynn, M. Rebecca Kilburn, James H. Bigelow, Jonathan P. Caulkins, and Jill S. Cannon. 2001. "Assessing Costs and Benefits of Early Childhood Intervention Programs: Overview and Application to the Starting Early Starting Smart Program." Rand Corporation.

Kaufman, Leslie. 2005. "Unmarried Fathers Gain Tax Incentives in Pataki Proposal." *New York Times*. January 17.

Kent, M. M., and M. Mather. 2002. "What Drives U.S. Population Growth?" *Population Bulletin* 57, no. 4, 3–39.

Kiernan, K. 1986. "Leaving Home: Living Arrangements of Young People in Six West-European Countries." *European Journal of Population* 1, no. 2, 177–184.

Kinsella, Kevin, and Victoria A. Velkoff. 2001. *An Aging World: 2001*. U.S. Census Bureau, series P95/01-1. Washington, D.C.: U.S. Government Printing Office.

Kitagawa, Evelyn M. 1953. "Differential Fertility in Chicago, 1920–40." *Population Studies* 58, no. 5.

Klein, Herbert S. 2004. *A Population History of the United States*. Cambridge: Cambridge University Press.

Klijzing, E., and M. Corijn, eds. 2002. *Fertility and Partnership in Europe: Findings and Lessons from Comparative Research*. Vols. 1–2. Geneva/New York: United Nations.

Kögel, T. 2004. "Did the Association between Fertility and Female Employment in OECD Countries Really Change Its Sign?" *Journal of Population Economics* 17, no. 1, 45–65.

Kohler, Hans-Peter. 2001. *Fertility and Social Interactions: An Economic Perspective*. Oxford: Oxford University Press.

Kohler, Hans-Peter, and J. R. Behrman. 2003. "Partner + Children = Happiness? An Assessment of the Effect of Fertility and Partnerships on Subjective Well-being in Danish Twins." Philadelphia: University of Pennsylvania. (Mimeo.)

Kohler, Hans-Peter, J. R. Behrman, and S. C. Watkins. 2000. "Empirical Assessments of Social Networks, Fertility and Family Planning Programs: Nonlinearities and Their Implications." *Demographic Research* 3, no. 7, 79–126. www.demographic-research.org.

Kohler, Hans-Peter, F. C. Billari, and J. A. Ortega. 2002. "The Emergence of Lowest-low Fertility in Europe during the 1990s." *Population and Development Review* 28, no. 4, 641–681.

Kohler, Hans-Peter, and I. Kohler. 2002. "Fertility Decline in Russia: Social versus Economic Factors." *European Journal of Population* 18, no. 3, 233–262.

Kohler, Hans-Peter, and J. A. Ortega. 2002. "Tempo-adjusted Period Parity Progression Measures, Fertility Postponement and Completed Cohort Fertility." *Demographic Research* 6, no. 6, 91–144. www.demographic-research.org.

Kohlmann, A., and S. Zuev. 2001. Patterns of Childbearing in Russia 1994–1998." Max Planck Institute for Demographic Research, Rostock, Germany, Working Paper #2001-018. www.demogr.mpg.de.

Lassibille, G., L. N. Gómez, I. A. Ramos, and C. D. Sánchez. 2001. "Youth Transition from School to Work in Spain." *Economics of Education Review* 20, no. 2, 139–149.

Lee, Sangheon. 2004. "Working-hour Gaps: Trends and Issues." In Jon C. Messenger, ed., *Working Time and Workers' Preferences in Industrialized Countries*. London: Routledge.

Leibenstein, Harvey. 1957. *Economic Backwardness and Economic Growth*. New Haven, Conn.: Yale University Press.

Leiken, Robert S. 2000. "The Melting Border: Mexico and Mexican Communities in the United States." Washington, D.C.: Center for Equal Opportunity.

Lesthaeghe, Ron. 1995. "The Second Demographic Transition in Western Countries: An Interpretation." In Karen O. Mason and An-Magritt Jensen, eds., *Gender and Family Change in Industrialized Countries*. Oxford: Clarendon Press.

Lesthaeghe, Ron, and D. van de Kaa. 1986. "Twee Demografische Transities?" In R. Lesthaeghe and D. van de Kaa, eds., *Bevolking: Groei en Krimp*. Deventer: Van Loghum Slaterus. 9–24.

Livi Bacci, Massimo. 1961. *L'immigrazione e l'assimilazione degli italiani negli Stati Uniti secondo le statistiche demografiche americane*. Milano: Giuffrè.

————. 2001. "Desired Family Size and the Future Course of Fertility." *Population and Development Review* 27, 282–289.

————. 2004. "A Fund for the Newborn: A Proposal for Italy." Paper presented at the annual meeting of the Population Association of America, Boston, Mass., April 1–3. http://paa2004.princeton.edu/abstractViewer.asp?submissionId=40323.

Llobrera, Joseph, and Bob Zahradnik. 2004. "A Hand Up: How State Earned Income Tax Credits Help Working Families Escape Poverty in 2004." Center on Budget and Policy Priorities, Washington, D.C. www.cbpp.org/5-14-04sfp.htm.

Lokshin, M., and M. Ravallion. 2000. "Short-lived Shocks with Long-lived Impacts? Household Income Dynamics in a Transition Economy." World Bank, Policy Research Working Paper no. 2459.

Love, John, Jeanne Brooks-Gunn, Diane Paulsell, and Allison Fuligni. 2002. *Making a Difference in the Lives of Infants and Toddlers and Their Families: The Impacts of Early Head Start*. Princeton, N.J.: Mathematica Policy Research, Inc.

Lutz, Wolfgang. 2005. "Low Fertility and Public Policy in Europe." PowerPoint presentation and summary presented at the Forum on Emerging Population Challenges in China and East Asia, East-West Center, Honolulu, April 13–14.

Lutz, Wolfgang, B. C. O'Neil, and S. Sherbov. 2003. "Europe's Population at a Turning Point." *Science* 299, no. 5616, 1991–1992.

Lutz, Wolfgang, and V. Skirbekk. 2004. "How Would 'Tempo Policies' Work? Exploring the Effect of School Reforms on Period Fertility in Europe." Unpublished working paper. http://paa2004.princeton.edu/abstractViewer.asp?submissionId=40611.

Lynch, Robert G. 2004. *Exceptional Returns: Economic, Fiscal, and Social Benefits of Investment in Early Childhood Development*. Washington, D.C.: Economic Policy Institute.

Macura, M. 2000. "Fertility Decline in the Transition Economies, 1989–1998: Economic and Social Factors Revisited." In UN Economic Commission for Europe, *Economic Survey in Europe, 2000/1*. Geneva: United Nations. 189–207.

Martin, J. A., B. E. Hamilton, P. D. Sutton, S. J. Ventura, F. Menacker, and M. L. Munson. 2003. "Births: Final Data for 2002." *National Vital Statistics Reports* 52, no. 10. www.cdc.gov/nchs/births.htm.

Masse, Leonard, and W. Steven Barnett. 2002. "A Benefit Cost Analysis of the Abecedarian Early Childhood Intervention." National Institute for Early Education Research, Rutgers University, New Brunswick, N.J.

Mathews, T. J., and M. E. Hamilton. 2002. "Mean Age of Mother, 1970–2000." *National Vital Statistics Report*, www.cdc.gov/nchs/births.htm.

Mayer, K. U. 2001. "The Paradox of Global Social Change and National Path Dependencies: Life Course Patterns in Advanced Societies." In A. E. Woodward and M. Kohli, eds., *Inclusions and Exclusions in European Societies*. London: Routledge. 89–110.

May, Elaine Tyler. 1988. *Homeward Bound: American Families in the Cold War Era*. New York: Basic Books.

Mayer, Albert, and Carol Klapprodt. 1955. "Fertility Differentials in Detroit, 1920–1950" *Population Studies* 9, no. 2, 154.

McDonald, P. 2000a. "Gender Equity in Theories of Fertility Transition." *Population and Development Review* 26, no. 3, 427–440.

————. 2000b. "The 'Toolbox' of Public Policies to Impact on Fertility: A Global View." Paper presented at the annual seminar of the European Observatory on Family Matters, Low Fertility, Families and Public Policies, Sevilla, Spain.

McIntosh, C. Alison. 1981. "Low Fertility and Liberal Democracy in Western Europe." *Population and Development Review* 7, 181–207.

Medicare Trustees. 2004. "Annual Report of the Board of Trustees of the Federal Hospital Insurance and Federal Supplementary Medical Trust Funds." Washington, D.C.

Michelson, Melissa R. 2002. "Competing Vote Cues and the Authenticity of Representation: Latino Support for Anglo Democrats and Latino Republicans." Paper presented at the Annual Conference of Midwest Political Science Association, Chicago, Ill., April 25–28.

Milanovic, B. 1998. *Income, Inequality, and Poverty during the Transition to Market Economy.* Washington, D.C.: World Bank.

Ministry of Education. Various years. *School Basic Survey.* Tokyo: Government of Japan. In Japanese.

Ministry of Health and Welfare. Various years. *Vital statistics.* Tokyo: Government of Japan. In Japanese.

Ministry of Health, Labour, and Welfare. 2004. *Handbook of Labour Statistics.* Tokyo: Government of Japan.

————. 2005. News release relating to vital statistics, posted on Internet website. In Japanese.

————. Various years. *Survey on Employment Management.* Tokyo: Government of Japan. In Japanese.

Mishel, Lawrence, et al. 2004. *The State of Working America 2004–2005.* Ithaca, N.Y.: Cornell University Press.

Monnier, A., and J. Rychtarikova. 1992. "The Division of Europe into East and West." *Population: An English Selection* 4, 129–159.

Montgomery, M. R., and J. B. Casterline. 1996. "Social Learning, Social Influence, and New models of Fertility." *Population and Development Review* 22 (Suppl.), 151–175.

Morgan, S. P. 2003. "Is Low Fertility a 21st Century Demographic Crisis?" *Demography* 40, no. 4, 589–603.

Morgan, S. P., and R. B. King. 2001. "Why Have Children in the 21st Century? Biological Predispositions, Social Coercion, Rational Choice." *European Journal of Population* 17, no. 1, 3–20.

Munich, D., J. Svejnar, and K. Terrell. 1999. "Return to Human Capital under the Communist Wage Grid and during the Transition to a Market Economy." *Journal of Comparative Economics* 27, 33–60.

National Immigration Forum. 2004. Press Release, "There They Go Again." August 25.

Newell, A., and B. Reilly. 2000. "Rates of Return to Educational Qualifications in the Transitional Economies." *Education Economics* 7, no. 1, 67–83.

New York City Department of City Planning Population Division. 2005. "The Newest New Yorkers." New York: New York City Government.

Neyer, G. 2003. "Family Policies and Low Fertility in Western Europe." MPDID Working Paper WP 2003-021.

NIPSSR (National Institute of Population and Social Security Research). 2003. *Child Related Policies in Japan.* Tokyo: NIPSSR.

Oden, S., L. J. Schweinhart, and D. P. Weikart. 2000. "Into Adulthood: A Study of the Effects of Head Start." Ypsilanti, Mich.: High/Scope Press.

OECD (Organization for Economic Cooperation and Development). 2005. *First Results from PISA 2003.* Paris: OECD. www.pisa.oecd.org.

Ogawa, Naohiro. 2000. "Women's Career Development and the Timing of Births: The Emergence of a New Fertility Mechanism?" In Population Problems Research Council, *The Population of Japan: An Overview of the 50 Postwar Years.* Tokyo: Mainichi Newspapers of Japan.

———. 2003. "Japan's Changing Fertility Mechanisms and Its Policy Responses." *Journal of Population Research* 20, 89–106.

———. 2004. "Effects of the Childcare Leave Scheme and Day-care Services upon the Participation of Married Women in Japan's Labor Force." In *Changing Family Norms among Japanese Women in an Era of Low Fertility.* Tokyo: Mainichi Newspapers of Japan.

Ogawa, Naohiro, and Robert L. Clark. 1995. "Earnings Patterns of Japanese Women: 1976–1988." *Economic Development and Cultural Change* 43, 293–313.

Ogawa, Naohiro, and John F. Ermisch. 1994. "Women's Career Development and Divorce Risk in Japan." *Labour* 8, 193–219.

———. 1996. "Family Structure, Home Time Demands, and the Employment Patterns of Japanese Married Women." *Journal of Labor Economics* 14, 677–702.

Ogawa, Naohiro, and Robert D. Retherford. 1993. "The Resumption of Fertility Decline in Japan, 1973–92." *Population and Development Review* 19, 703–741.

———. 1997. "Shifting Costs of Caring for the Elderly Back to Families in Japan: Will It Work?" *Population and Development Review* 23, 59–94.

Orazem, P. F., and M. Vodopivec. 1995. "Winners and Losers in Transition: Returns to Education, Experience and Gender in Slovenia." *World Bank Economic Review* 9, no. 2, 201–230.

Pachon, Harry, Rodolfo O. de la Garza, and Adrian Pantoja. 2000. "Foreign Policy Perspectives of Hispanic Elites." In Rodolfo O. de la Garza and Harry Pachon, eds., *Latinos and U.S. Foreign Policy: Representing the "Homeland"?* Lanham, Md.: Rowman and Littlefield. 21–42.

Palomba, R., and L. L. Sabbadini. 1993. "Female Life Strategies: The Way of Compromise." *Proceedings of the 23rd IUSSP General Conference, Montreal.* 2:219–231.

Pampel, F. C. 2001. *The Institutional Context of Population Change: Patterns of Fertility and Mortality across High-Income Nations.* Chicago: University of Chicago Press.

Pew Hispanic Center. 2002. "2002 National Survey of Latinos." Pew Hispanic Center/Kaiser Family Foundation.

———. 2004. "2004 National Survey of Latinos: Politics and Civic Participation." Pew Hispanic Center/Kaiser Family Foundation.

———. 2005. "Estimates of the Size and Characteristics of the Undocumented Population." March 21.

Plusquellic, Donald L. 2004. "Keeping America Strong: Mayors '04 Metro Agenda for America's Cities." United States Conference of Mayors, Washington, D.C.

Presser, H. B. 1999. "Toward a 24-hour Economy." *Science* 284, 1778–1779.

Prime Minister's Office. 1997. *Survey on Gender Equality.* Tokyo: Prime Minister's Office, Office for Gender Equality. In Japanese.

Reher, D. S. 1997. *Perspectives on the Family in Spain, Past and Present.* Oxford: Oxford University Press.

———. 1998. "Family Ties in Western Europe: Persistent Contrasts." *Population and Development Review* 24, no. 2, 203–234.

Reid, T. R., and Evelyn Nieves. 2004. "Voters Show Willingness to Increase Taxes." *Washington Post.* November 4.

Retherford, Robert D., Naohiro Ogawa, and Rikiya Matsukura. 2001. "Late Marriage and Less Marriage in Japan." *Population and Development Review* 27, 65–102.

Retherford, Robert D., Naohiro Ogawa, Rikiya Matsukura, and Hajime Ihara. 2004. *Trends in Fertility by Education in Japan: 1966–2000.* Tokyo: Nihon University Population Research

Institute. Honolulu: East-West Center. Tokyo: Statistical Research and Training Institute, Ministry of Public Management, Home Affairs, Posts and Telecommunications.

Retherford, Robert D., Naohiro Ogawa, and Satomi Sakamoto. 1996. "Values and Fertility Change in Japan." *Population Studies* 50, 5–25.

Reynolds, Arthur, Judy Temple, Dylan Robertson, and Emily Mann. 2001. "Age 21 Cost-Benefit Analysis of the Title 1 Chicago Child-Parent Center Program: Executive Summary." Institute for Research on Poverty. www.waisman.wisc.edu/cls/cbaexecsum4.html.

———2002. "Age 21 Cost-Benefit Analysis of the Title 1 Chicago Child-Parent Centers." Institute for Research on Poverty, Discussion Paper no. 1245-02. www.ssc.wisc.edu/irp/.

Rindfuss, R. R., K. L. Brewster, and A. L. Kavee. 1996. "Women, Work, and Children: Behavioral and Attitudinal Change in the United States." *Population and Development Review* 22, no. 3, 457–482.

Rindfuss, R. R., D. Guilkey, P. S. Morgan, O. Kravdal, and K. B. Guzzo. 2004. "Child Care Availability and Fertility in Norway: Pro-natalist Effects." Paper presented at the annual meeting of the Population Association of America, Boston, Mass., April 1–3. http://paa2004.princeton.edu.

Rindfuss, R. R., K. B. Guzzo, and S. P. Morgan. 2003. "The Changing Institutional Context of Low Fertility." *Population Research and Policy Review* 22, no. 5–6, 411–438.

Rolnick, Art, and Robert Grunewald. 2003. "Early Childhood Development: Economic Development with a High Public Return." *Fedgazette*. Federal Reserve Bank of Minneapolis. March.

Rosenbaum, David E., and Robin Toner. 2005. "To Social Security Debate, Add Variable: Immigration." *New York Times*. February 16, A18.

Rothstein, Richard. 2004. *Class and Schools: Using Social, Economic, and Educational Reform to Close the Black-White Achievement Gap.* Washington, D.C.: Economic Policy Institute.

Rutkowski, J. 1996. "High Skill Pay Off: The Changing Wage Structure during Economic Transition in Poland." *Economics of Transition* 4, no. 1, 89–111.

Sá, C., and M. Portela. 1999. "Working and Studying: What Explains Youngsters' Decisions." Luxembourg Employment Study, Working Paper no. 15.

Sánchez-Mangas, R., and V. Sánchez-Marcos. 2004. *Reconciling Female Labor Participation and Motherhood: The Effect of Benefits for Working Mothers.* FEDEA Studies on the Spanish Economy.

Sanderson, Warren C. 1979. "Quantitative Aspects of Marriage, Fertility and Family Limitation in Nineteenth Century America: Another Application of the Coale Specifications." *Demography* 16, no. 3, 339–358.

Schlesinger, Arthur Meier. 1992. *The Disuniting of America.* New York: Norton.

Schweke, William. 2004. *Smart Money: Education and Economic Development.* Washington, D.C.: Economic Policy Institute.

Schweinhart, Lawrence. 1993. "Significant Benefits: The High/Scope Perry Preschool Study through Age 27." Ypsilanti, Mich.: High/Scope Press. 15:55.

———. 2003. "Benefits, Costs, and Explanation of the High/Scope Perry Preschool Program." Paper presented at the meeting of the Society for Research in Child Development, Tampa, Fla., April 26.

Scrivner, Scott, and Barbara Wolfe. 2003. "Universal Preschool: Much to Gain but Who Will Pay." Institute for Research on Poverty, Discussion Paper no. 1271-03.

Shellenbarger, Sue. 2004. "How Working Parents Cope with Rising Child-Care Costs." *Wall Street Journal.* Oct. 21.

Shimada, Haruo, and Yoshio Higuchi. 1985. "An Analysis of Trends in Female Labor Force Participation in Japan." *Journal of Labor Economics* 3, 355–374.

Shoemaker, Nancy. 1999. *American Indian Population Recovery in the Twenteith Century*. Albuquerque: University of New Mexico Press.

Shryock, Henry S., and Jacob S. Siegel. 1971. *The Methods and Materials of Demography*. Washington, D.C.: U.S. Bureau of the Census.

Sleebos, J. 2003. "Low Fertility Rates in OECD Countries: Facts and Policy Responses. OECD Social, Employment, and Migration Working Papers no. 15.

Smith, James P., and Barry Edmonston, eds. 1997. *The New Americans: Economic, Demographic, and Fiscal Effects of Immigration*. Panel on the Demographic and Economic Impacts of Immigration. Washington, D.C.: National Research Council.

Sobotka, T. 2004a. "Is Lowest-low Fertility in Europe Explained by the Postponement of Childbearing?" *Population and Development Review* 30, no. 2, 195–220.

———. 2004b. *Postponement of Childbearing in Europe*. Population Studies Series. Amsterdam: Dutch University Press.

Social Security Administration. 2005. "The 2005Annual Report of the Board of Trustees of the Federal Old-Age and Survivors Insurance and Disability Insurance Trust Funds." Board of Trustees, Washington, D.C., March 23.

Stark, L., and H.-P. Kohler. 2002. "The Debate over Low Fertility in the Popular Press: A Cross-national Comparison, 1998–1999." *Population Research and Policy Review* 21, no. 6, 535–574.

———. 2004. "The Popular Debate about Low Fertility: An Analysis of the German Press, 1993–2001." *European Journal of Population* 20, no. 4, 293–321.

Statistics Bureau. 2001. *Annual Report of the Labour Force Survey*. Tokyo: Statistics Bureau, Government of Japan.

Stevens, Gillian. 1994. "Immigration, Emigration, Language Acquisition, and the English Language Proficiency of Immigrants in the U.S." In Barry Edmonston and Jeffrey Passel, eds., *Immigration and Ethnicity: The Integration of America's Newest Arrivals*. Washington, D.C.: Urban Institute Press. 163–186.

Stier, H., N. Lewin-Epstein, and M. Braun. 2001. "Welfare Regimes, Family-supportive Policies, and Women's Employment along the Life-course." *American Journal of Sociology* 106, no. 6, 1731–1760.

Suzuki, T. 2003. "Lowest-low Fertility in Korea and Japan." *Journal of Population Problems* 59, no. 3, 1–16.

Technical Panel on Assumptions and Methods. 2003. *Report to the Social Security Advisory Board*. Washington, D.C.: Social Security Advisory Board.

Thompson, Warren S., and P. K. Whelpton. 1933. *Population Trends in the United States*. New York: McGraw-Hill.

Tokyo Metropolitan Government. 1992. *Public Opinion Survey Regarding Equality of the Sexes*. Tokyo: Tokyo Metropolitan Government, Bureau of Life and Culture. In Japanese.

Tomás Rivera Policy Institute. 2002. "Survey of Immigrant Political and Civic Activities."

Tsuya, Noriko O., and Larry L. Bumpass. 2004. *Marriage, Work and Family Life in Comparative Perspective: Japan, South Korea and the United States*. Honolulu: University of Hawaii Press.

United Nations. 2000. *Replacement Migration: Is It a Solution to Declining and Ageing Populations?* New York: United Nations.

———. 2003a. *World Fertility Report 2003*. New York: United Nations.

———. 2003b. *World Population Prospects: The 2002 Revision*. New York: United Nations.

———. 2004. *World Population Policies 2003*. New York: United Nations.

U.S. Census Bureau. 2001. *Population Change and Distribution, 1990–2000*. Census 2000 Brief. April. www.census.gov.

———. 2004. "Projected Population of the United States, by Age and Sex: 2000 to 2050." Population Division, Population Projections Branch, Washington, D.C., May 18.

———. 2004. *Statistical Abstract of the United States, 2004*, 63. Washington, D.C.

U.S. Conference of Mayors. 2004. *Hunger and Homelessness Survey*. Washington, D.C.

U.S. Department of Health and Human Services. 2003. *State Spending under the FY 2002 Appropriation for the Child Care and Development Fund*. Child Care Bureau, Washington, D.C. www.acf.dhhs.gov/programs/ccb/research/02acf696/overview.htm.

———. 2004. "Head Start Program Fact Sheet." Head Start Bureau, Administration for Children and Families, Washington, D.C. www.acf.hhs.gov/programs/hsb/research/2004.htm.

U.S. Department of Labor. 2004. *Child Daycare Services*. Bureau of Labor Statistics, Washington, D.C. www.bls.gov/oco/cg/cgs032.htm#earnings.

———. 2005. *Labor Force Statistics from the Current Population Survey*. Bureau of Labor Statistics, Washington, D.C. http://data.bls.gov/cgi-bin/surveymost?bls.

U.S. Department of the Treasury. 2004. Earned Income Credit Table. Internal Revenue Service, Washington, D.C.

U.S. Joint Project of the Bureau of Labor Statistics and the Bureau of the Census. 2004. *Current Population Survey: 2004 Annual Social and Economic Supplement*. Washington, D.C.

van de Kaa, Dirk J. 1987. "Europe's Second Demographic Transition." *Population Bulletin* 42, no. 1, 1–59.

———. 1997. "Options and Sequences: Europe's Demographic Patterns. *Journal of the Australian Population Association* 14, no. 1, 1–30.

———. 2001. "Postmodern Fertility Preferences: From Changing Value Orientation to New Behavior." In R. Bulatao and J. B. Casterline, eds., *Global Fertility Transition*. Supplement to *Population and Development Review* 27. New York: Population Council.

Washington Post/Univision/TRPI. 2004. "Pre-Election Survey of Latino Registered Voters, October 2004."

Watkins, S. C. 1990. "From Local to National Communities: The Transformation of Demographic Regimes in Western Europe, 1870–1960." *Population and Development Review* 16, no. 2, 241–272.

Willis, R. J. 1973. "A New Approach to the Economic Theory of Fertility Behavior." *Journal of Political Economy* 81, no. 2 (pt. 2), 14–64.

Wilson, C. 2001. "On the Scale of Global Demographic Convergence 1950–2000." *Population and Development Review* 27, no. 1, 155–172.

———. 2004. "Fertility below Replacement Level." *Science* 304, no. 5668, 207–209.

Wolfe, Barbara, and Scott Scrivner. 2003. "Providing Universal Preschool for Four Year-Olds." In Isabel Sawhill, ed.,*One Percent for the Kids*. Washington, D.C.: Brookings Institution Press.

Zakharov, S. V., and E. I. Ivanova. 1996. "Fertility Decline and Recent Changes in Russia: On the Threshold of the Second Demographic Transition." In J. Da Vanzo and G. Farnsworth, eds., *Russia's Demographic Crisis*. Santa Monica, Calif.: Rand Conference Proceeding. 36–83.

Zhao, Z. 2001. "Low Fertility in Urban China." Paper presented at the IUSSP Seminar on International Perspectives on Low Fertility, Tokyo, March 21–23.

Index

Note: Page numbers in italic type indicate figures or tables.

Abecedarian Early Childhood Intervention, 157, 160, 162
abortions: in Japan, 6, 20; in United States, 143, *144*
ACORN (Association of Community Organizations for Reform Now), 194
Adsera, A., 104
affirmative action, 202
African Americans: abortions for, 143; dual-parent households among, 135; fertility rate of, 90, 91, *120*, 123, 144; median family income of, 191
After School Matters, Chicago, 209
after-school programs, 208–9
age at marriage: fertility in relation to, 66–67; in Japan, 7, *8*, 13–20, *14*; in United States, 119, 122–23, 127, *133*
age-specific fertility rate (ASFR), 5
aging. *See* population aging
Ahn, N., 73
American Indians. *See* Native Americans
Americorps, 211
Angel Plan, 34. *See also* New Angel Plan
apprenticeship programs, 211
arranged marriage, in Japan, *17*, 17–18
ASFR (age-specific fertility rate), 5
asset development, 195–96
assimilation of immigrants, 175, 176
at-risk youth, 210

Baby Boom, 113, 115, 126–29; behavior changes in, 127, 129; factors in, 126–27
Baker, Dean, 156
Billari, Francesco C., 66
birth control. *See* contraception
Blacks. *See* African Americans
bonuses, for childbearing, 98, 102
Boston Latin School, 207
Brewster, K. L., 73
Bronx High School of Science, 207
Buchanan, Patrick, 176
Burtless, Gary, 162
Bush, George W., and administration, 150, 191, 195, 196, 198–200, 204, 208, 210, 214

Caldwell, John C., 42
Canada, 90
Canada, Geoffrey, 209
Castles, Francis G., 104
celibacy, in Japan, 7–8, *8*, *14*, 14
Center on Budget and Policy Priorities, 156
Cheney, Dick, 150
Chicago Child-Parent Centers Program, 157, 160–61, 167, 169–70
child allowances, 32–33, 102
child bonuses, 98, 102

231

About the Contributors

Francesco C. Billari is associate professor of demography at Bocconi University, Milan, Italy. He is also chair of the European Association for Population Studies and associate editor of *Demographic Research*.

Alan Curtis is president of the Milton S. Eisenhower Foundation. He served as an urban policy adviser to the U.S. Secretary of Housing and Urban Development, was director of President Carter's Urban and Regional Policy Group, and is the author or editor of ten books, including, as editor, *Patriotism, Democracy, and Common Sense: Restoring America's Promise at Home and Abroad*.

Rodolfo O. de la Garza is Eaton Professor of Administrative Law and Municipal Science and director of the Master of Public Administration Program at Columbia University. He formerly served as vice president of the American Political Science Association and is presently vice president of the Tomás Rivera Policy Institute. He is the editor, co-editor, or co-author of numerous books and articles on Hispanic politics, foreign policy, and immigration, including *Muted Voices: Latinos and the 2000 Election*.

Peter Edelman is a professor of law at Georgetown University, teaching courses in constitutional law and American poverty. He served as legislative assistant to U.S. Senator Robert Kennedy and was later assistant secretary for planning and evaluation in the U.S. Department of Health and Human Services. He is the author of *Searching for America's Heart: RFK and the Renewal of Hope*.

Fred R. Harris is a former U.S. senator from Oklahoma. He served on the Kerner Commission. He is professor of political science at the University of New Mexico, author or editor of twenty books, including, as co-editor, *Locked in the Poorhouse: Cities, Race, and Poverty in the United States*. He is co-chair of the board of trustees of the Milton S. Eisenhower Foundation.

Herbert S. Klein is Governeur Morris Professor of History at Columbia University and a research fellow at the Hoover Institution, Stanford University. He has published 145 scholarly articles (in six different languages) and is the author or co-author of seventeen books, including *A Population History of the United States*.

Hans-Peter Kohler is associate professor of sociology and research associate, Population Studies Center, University of Pennsylvania. He has been widely published in leading journals, including *Demography, Population Development Review*, and *Journal of Development Economics*. He is the author of *Fertility and Social Interaction: An Economic Perspective* and the co-editor of *The Biodemography of Human Reproduction and Fertility*.

Robert G. Lynch is associate professor and chair of the Department of Economics at Washington College, where he has taught since 1998. He is the author of numerous works analyzing the effectiveness of state and local government economic policies in promoting economic development and creating jobs.

Naohiro Ogawa is deputy director of the Nihon University Population Research Institute and professor of economics at Nihon University, Japan. He previously worked in the Population Division of the United Nations Economic and Social Commission for Asia and the Pacific.

José Antonio Ortega is associate professor of economics at the University of Salamanca, in Spain. He has developed demographic methods for low and lowest-low fertility and investigated the determinants of lowest-low fertility from a theoretical and empirical perspective.

Robert D. Retherford is coordinator of Population and Health Studies at the East-West Center in Honolulu and is a member of the affiliate graduate faculty in sociology at the University of Hawaii. He is past president of the Society for the Study of Social Biology, which is the publisher of the journal *Social Biology*.